The CRISIS of CANADIAN DEMOCRACY

The Government of Canada

The government of Canada is a constitutional monarchy and parliamentary democracy, consisting of three main branches:

Legislative branch (Parliament)

- **The King/Crown**: Head of state/symbol and repository of state authority. Represented in Canada by the **governor general**, who grants royal assent to bills and performs ceremonial duties.
- **The House of Commons**: Elected **members of Parliament (MPs)**, who represent constituencies, debate policies, and vote on legislation.
- **The Senate**: Appointed by the prime minister, senators represent regions and review, refine, and propose legislation.

Executive branch

- **The prime minister**: Head of government. Leader of the governing party, the cabinet, and the executive. Sets government direction and priorities.
- **The Cabinet**: Group of ministers appointed by the prime minister to advise him. Oversee government departments and help develop policies.
- **The Privy Council Office (PCO)**: Body of civil servants providing nonpartisan support to the prime minister and cabinet.
- **The Prime Minister's Office (PMO)**: Provides political support and advice to the prime minister, focusing on the government's agenda and priorities.

Judicial branch

- **The Supreme Court of Canada**: The highest court and final court of appeal. Ensures laws align with the Constitution.
- **Federal courts**: Including the **Federal Court, Federal Court of Appeal, and Tax Court**. Handle cases involving federal laws.

The CRISIS of CANADIAN DEMOCRACY

sh.
SUTHERLAND HOUSE

TORONTO, 2025

Sutherland House
416 Moore Ave., Suite 304
Toronto, ON M4G 1C9

Copyright © 2025 by Andrew Coyne

All rights reserved, including the right to reproduce this book or portions thereof in any form whatsoever. For information on rights and permissions or to request a special discount for bulk purchases, please contact Sutherland House at sutherlandhousebooks@gmail.com.

Sutherland House and logo are registered trademarks of The Sutherland House Inc.

First edition, May 2025

If you are interested in inviting one of our authors to a live event or media appearance, please contact sranasinghe@sutherlandhousebooks.com and visit our website at sutherlandhousebooks.com for more information.

We acknowledge the support of the Government of Canada.

Manufactured in Canada
Cover designed by Leah Ciani and Jordan Lunn
Book composed by Karl Hunt

Library and Archives Canada Cataloguing in Publication
Title: The crisis of Canadian democracy / Andrew Coyne.
Names: Coyne, Andrew, (Columnist), author.
Description: Includes bibliographical references.
Identifiers: Canadiana (print) 20250129841 | Canadiana (ebook) 20250129884 | ISBN 9781990823916 (hardcover) | ISBN 9781998365937 (softcover) | ISBN 9781998365272 (EPUB)
Subjects: LCSH: Canada—Politics and government—21st century. | LCSH: Democracy—Canada. | LCSH: Political corruption—Canada.
Classification: LCC JL65 .C73 2025 | DDC 320.971—dc23

ISBN 978-1-990823-91-6 (hbk)
ISBN: 978-1-998365-93-7 (pbk)
eBook 978-1-998365-27-2

Contents

1	Democracy in Canada	1
2	Government vs. Parliament	17
3	Leader vs. Caucus	50
4	Prime Minister vs. Cabinet	73
5	Unelected vs. Elected	109
6	Campaigns	143
7	Elections	176
8	The Crisis	237
	Notes	249
	Acknowledgements	262
	Index	263

For Shannon

1
Democracy in Canada

ONE OF THE THINGS Canadians think they know about Canada is that it is a democracy: among the greatest democracies on earth, in fact. Democracy may be in decline or in retreat elsewhere, notably in the United States, but in Canada it remains, as we perceive it, in relatively good health, a model for others to follow.

It is the ambition of this book to deprive Canadians of this comfort. Far from a democratic example to the world, our parliamentary system is in a state of advanced disrepair—so advanced it is debatable whether it should still be called a democracy.

Put simply, we do not live in the system we think we do. We have the form of a democracy but not the substance; the rituals but not the reality. Because we preserve the forms and rituals, people find it hard to accept how far the substance has been eaten away. We are so heavily invested in our self-image as one of the world's great democracies that evidence to the contrary tends not to penetrate: it cannot be true because it must not be true, because "we are a democracy." But at some point the facts become unanswerable.

The plain truth is that none of the institutions of our democracy work as intended, or as we imagine they do, or as they used to, or as they do elsewhere. Some are best described as having ceased to work at all. The rot has set in at every level, from the corrupt and chaotic process by which the parties choose their candidates and leaders, to the sordid fraternity hazings that are modern election campaigns, to the random distortions in representation imposed by our electoral system, to the many dysfunctions of our increasingly irrelevant House of Commons, to the almost total concentration of power in the office of the prime minister. While any one of these on its own might not trouble us unduly, their accumulated weight should.

The effect has been to invert all of the institutional relationships characteristic of a properly functioning parliamentary democracy. The government does not answer to the Commons so much as the Commons answers to the government; party leaders are not accountable to the members of Parliament* (MPs) in their caucus, but rather caucus is accountable to the leader; the prime minister is no longer a member of Cabinet so much as Cabinet has become an extension of the prime minister. And so on.

How can this be? We have our faults, but is it not true that we rank among the world's healthiest democracies? Didn't the Economist Intelligence Unit, in its latest (2023) annual Democracy Index,[1] rank us thirteenth among the world's democracies, one of only twenty-four "full democracies" around the world? Didn't Freedom House rank us fifth (tied with Uruguay and the Netherlands) in its annual *Freedom in the World* report,[2] with a score of thirty-nine out of forty for "political rights"?

This is true, and worth celebrating, especially at a time when so many democracies have been backsliding. By many of the usual measures Canada is indeed an exemplary democracy. Our elections are free, in the sense that no adult citizen is prevented from voting

---

* Strictly speaking, Parliament is made up of three parts: the elected House of Commons, the unelected Senate, and the King, represented by the governor general. But it is conventional shorthand to refer to the House of Commons as "Parliament," and to its members as members of Parliament.

or standing for office, and fair, in the sense that all ballots cast are counted accurately. Elections take place without significant voter intimidation or fraud. Power transfers peacefully. Corruption, if not unknown, is at least contained.

We are, what is more, a liberal democracy, with strong guarantees of civil liberties and safeguards for judicial independence. We are not a dictatorship; we do not fear the midnight knock upon the door. Most important of all, perhaps, we enjoy the benefits of a healthy democratic culture. We do not regard those across the partisan divide as enemies. Polarization is relatively mild. The losers in an election accept the outcome as legitimate; the winners do not take this as the opportunity for revenge.

But we are not a *fully functioning* democracy. The types of metrics that go into the EIU or Freedom House indices ought to be regarded as a bare minimum; that our elections are not actually fixed is hardly something to brag about. Observing the basic procedural formalities of democracy is one thing, but elections that are truly fair for all, or a Parliament that genuinely holds government to account, are quite another.

It is by these more substantive yardsticks that we fall short. Government may not be our master, as in Churchill's epigram,[3] but neither is it quite our servant. Government in a parliamentary democracy is supposed to be answerable to the people through their elected representatives in Parliament. But the parliaments we elect do not represent us in any meaningful way; the governments they are supposed to instruct and watch and check do not really answer to them. Our representative democracy is not quite representative. Our parliamentary democracy has a large hole where Parliament used to be.

No democracy is perfect; people in every country complain about the faults in theirs. But ours compares unfavourably in many respects, from the strictness of our system of party discipline, to the deviations we permit from the principle of one person, one vote, to the powers and prerogatives of our prime ministers and beyond. If democracy is not thought to be in the same peril here as elsewhere it may be because there is less of it to lose; having lost so much already we have less and less reason to care as each new piece is washed away.

That, rather than our system's matchless splendour, may explain our collective complacency. Our democracy has been in decline for so long that few can remember what it was like before, or why it should matter that it is no longer. Complain about the state of Canadian democracy and the response is as often as not a world-weary "but this is nothing new" or "the same complaint was heard decades ago," as if this were a comment on the seriousness of the concern, rather than the cynicism of the respondent. We should beware, of course, of falsely idealizing how politics used to be in this country, but we should equally steer clear of the lazy assumption that "it's always been this way." It hasn't. It's worse now; clearly, markedly worse.

This is not a commentary on recent political controversies, or an indictment of any one party: the dismantling of Canadian democracy is a glittering bipartisan achievement. Each prime minister comes to power vowing to clean up the mess left by the one before; each then proceeds, not only to repeat the sins of his predecessor,* but to invent new ones to add to the pile. And each justifies his own assaults on democracy in light of those of the others.

* * *

I suppose the best way to answer the question "is Canada's democracy in crisis?" is to ask: what would a democracy that was *not* in crisis look like?

What does a democracy look like? What, in particular, does a *parliamentary* democracy look like? Without idealizing, we could probably get some consensus for the following:

---

* Warning: For the sake of readability I am going to use "he" and "his" throughout: because it is too excruciating to say "he or she" every time, and because our prime ministers and party leaders to date have overwhelmingly been men. Readers who wish to substitute "she" and "her" are invited to do so.

- At regular intervals the people choose from among their number individuals to represent them in Parliament.
- Elections are contested by candidates selected by their fellow party members in competitive local nomination races.
- The candidates compete for voters' approval, in part on the basis of their party identification and differing programs of government, in part on their individual qualities.
- Everyone gets a vote and every vote counts equally.
- Voters are free to mark their ballot for the party and candidate of their choice.
- The majority rules.
- Members of Parliament, once elected, propose, debate, scrutinize, and vote on bills, mind the public's money, and generally hold the government to account.
- The prime minister makes decisions and runs the government with the help and advice of cabinet. Ministers are individually responsible for their departments and collectively responsible for the direction of the government.
- The government must at all times hold the "confidence," or support, of the House. If at any time it loses that confidence it must either resign or cause Parliament to be dissolved and a new election called.

That is how our system is supposed to work. But that is not how our system actually works. If our democracy were only deficient in one or another item on that list—fair votes, meaningful elections, accountability to Parliament—you might say it was unsatisfactory, but not "in crisis." What makes the situation critical is that none of them apply.

Let's follow the process from start to finish.

Candidates, as a rule, are not nominated by a vote of the existing party members in a given riding. Rather, candidates stage little putsches, stacking meetings with busloads of new recruits whose memberships may well have been purchased for them. Alternatively they are simply appointed, de facto or de jure, by the party leader. However the nomination may be obtained, as a practical or even legal matter it is impossible for any candidate to run without the leader's endorsement—so all candidates are essentially the leader's appointees. In the classic Westminster model—the British parliamentary tradition we inherited at our birth—members of a party caucus choose the leader. Only in Canada does the leader choose the caucus.

So no, candidates in our elections are not typically selected by local party members in competitive nomination races.

How is the leader chosen? By the same mad process of mass membership sales to people with no history of involvement in the party and no intention of participating in it further—an electoral college that, as the historian Christopher Moore has written, "dissolves the moment it picks a leader."[4] Which leaves the leader, by happy coincidence, accountable to no one.

The candidates, once chosen, are exposed to those wretched spasms of malevolence we call elections. Aspiring MPs may have thoughts on the issues of the day, but it doesn't really matter what they think because all policy is set by the parties, which is to say by the party leaders. And it doesn't matter where the parties or the leaders stand because at any given time they tend to stand for the same thing, and because whatever they stand for today, they will stand for the reverse tomorrow.

Recent Canadian elections have set new standards for dishonesty: not just the usual calculated ambiguity, but flat-out lies. Parties routinely campaign on one thing and do the precise opposite once in power; they flip-flop not only on minor details but on the central planks of their platforms. But then at least the lies are about something substantive. If it weren't for them the campaigns would be barely worth discussing: a blur of attack ads, photo ops, more attack ads, and news coverage heavily focused on polls, gaffes, and inside-baseball discussions of strategy, mostly about attack ads.

So no, elections are not contests between candidates on the basis of their differing philosophies of government.

At length the votes are counted and we find we have elected a Parliament that looks nothing like what we voted for, with a distribution of seats, thanks to the fun-house distortions of our first-past-the-post electoral system, that bears no resemblance to the actual division of opinion in the country.

It is a system in which the winning candidate in a riding will often be the choice of less than one-third of the voters; in which a party may win a majority of the seats in the House with less than 40 percent of the vote—less, sometimes, than their nearest rival; in which voters are routinely told that, for fear of splitting the vote, they cannot vote for the party they prefer, but must vote for some other party they dislike in order to keep yet another party they detest from being elected; and in which the results in many ridings or even whole regions are such foregone conclusions that the parties hardly bother to campaign there, leaving the entire election to be decided by a few "battleground" ridings. It is also a system in which the parties that concentrate their support regionally are massively favoured over those that take a national view, electing many more members with many fewer votes. Liberals in the West; Conservatives in Vancouver, Toronto, and Montreal; and federalists in Quebec are all greatly underrepresented, distorting our perception of the country and needlessly aggravating regional tensions.

Results are further distorted by the vast disparities in the numbers of voters per riding, such that it takes as many votes to elect one Tory MP in some Alberta ridings as it takes to elect six Liberal MPs in PEI and Labrador. In effect, the votes of some citizens are worth five times, or ten times, or twenty times as much as another's, depending on which party they were cast for and in which riding.

So no, ours is not a system in which every vote counts equally. Neither is it one in which voters are free to support the party of their choice. And certainly it is not a system of majority rule. It might better be described, rather, as "institutionalized minority rule."

At any rate, a "majority" of what? Turnout in federal elections has fallen to near 60 percent; at the provincial level it is now common to see turnouts of less than 50 percent; municipally, you're lucky to get 40 percent. Combine that with the dwindling share of the vote going to the winning party as the number of parties multiplies, and governments are routinely elected with the support of as little as 20 percent of the voting-age population.

So no, the people of Canada do not choose who will govern them. A small and unrepresentative fraction of the people do.

* * *

Nevertheless, the election over with, we send our representatives off to Parliament ... though they might as well have stayed home, for all the difference most of them are able to make. The consensus on this is depressingly broad: members of Parliament have little role or responsibility left to them but to stand up and sit down when they are told.

What do we elect MPs to do? Debate? The arguments are rote; attendance is sparse; no one's mind is changed. That's when debate is permitted, and not, as happens dozens of times every session, curtailed by "time allocation."

Propose legislation? In a typical year, only a handful of private members' bills pass into law.

Examine legislation? Not when dozens of laws of vastly differing purpose can be bundled together into huge omnibus bills, hundreds of pages long—the whole of the government's spring or fall agenda, in one bill—leaving scant hours to study any individual initiative. In particular, the "business of supply," the fundamental prerogative of parliaments going back to Simon de Montfort*—the process by which the government asks the House of Commons to "supply" it with funds to meet its obligations—has broken down almost entirely. Some years governments do not even bother to present a budget.

---

* The English noble credited with convening the first parliament, in 1265.

Vote on legislation? Canada has among the strictest systems of party discipline in the democratic world, affording individual MPs the least leeway to vote as their conscience or their constituents dictate. Not for nothing are MPs sometimes referred to as "$200,000 voting machines."* Indeed, MPs cannot ask questions in the House, or make members' statements, without the permission of party officials—and when they do, are as often as not confined to reading out lines written for them by party communications staff.

That is what is left to MPs: to do as they are told, speak as they are told, vote as they are told. Perhaps one or another MP might be of a mind to rebel against this fate. Very well—good luck getting those nomination papers signed. For most, the thought does not occur to them. They are products of the system and have absorbed its values. If they were unwilling to put up with this sort of humiliation, they would not have put themselves forward as candidates. And if nothing else succeeded in securing MPs' cooperation, there is always the prospect of advancement. No one who steps out of line will wind up in Cabinet, or in a parliamentary leadership role, or on a high-profile committee, or with speaking time in the House. Ambition is the real party whip[†], commanding obedience where mere threats might not.

The reality is that MPs no longer have any real power, individually or collectively, to hold governments to account. Government backbenchers long ago gave up trying, although once it was expected of them. Rather than ask tough questions about how the government is spending our money, more and more government MPs take a direct hand in spreading it about. They prefer to show up at announcement ceremonies, giant novelty cheques in hand, to take the credit.

---

* An MP's annual salary as of April 2024 was $203,100.
† Members of Caucus appointed by the leader to enforce party discipline, organize votes, and communicate between party leadership and backbencher. Also a verb: to "whip" a vote means to insist MPs vote with the party. From "whipper-in," referring to someone who keeps hounds from straying during a hunt.

Opposition MPs, meanwhile, find their daily existence is a constant exercise in futility. They can't get their questions answered, can't get the documents they demand, can't trust the figures in them if they do. Committees, whose purpose is supposedly to facilitate detailed examination of issues and legislation and to put government operations under more intense scrutiny than would otherwise be possible, have become farces: stonewalled by government members, unable to compel witnesses to appear, often meeting behind closed doors.

And on those rare, rare occasions when a government is finally being held to account, when it really starts to feel the heat, usually in a minority Parliament, it prorogues—suspends sittings, shuts down, closes doors, sometimes for months at a time.

So no, MPs do not, in any meaningful sense, perform any of the responsibilities commonly ascribed to them. Parliament is no longer the place where important matters are debated, decided or announced. It has become a largely ceremonial body, a glorified electoral college, its role confined to manufacturing a majority out of the increasingly fragmented results of our elections.

Even the confidence convention, the bedrock requirement that a government must command the confidence of the House at all times, is under assault. Heading for certain defeat in a confidence vote in 2008, Stephen Harper simply prorogued. Having arguably lost a confidence vote in 2005, Paul Martin stalled for nine days, until, with the help of a timely floor-crosser, he was able to win a do-over. More recently, Justin Trudeau also prorogued to avoid a confidence vote, emulating in 2025 what he had denounced in 2008.

There is worse to come, possibly. Recent Canadian elections have yielded a procession of minority parliaments; more are likely. Each such Parliament carries within it the seeds of a constitutional crisis. Suppose the government were to be defeated on a vote of confidence, and suppose that happened a short time—say, less than a year—after an election. Now suppose the defeated prime minister were to recommend to the governor general that the House be dissolved and an election called. Convention dictates the governor general would be within her rights instead to call upon another party or parties to form a government, assuming they had the support of a majority of the House. But successive Conservative leaders have made clear they would not accept this. What if, the governor general having refused his advice, the prime minister refused to resign?

It's only a convention, after all. Like ministerial responsibility, Cabinet solidarity, and others, it binds prime ministers for as long as they feel like being bound by it. When they no longer do, it doesn't.

* * *

This is the critical dilemma facing us. In other countries, executive power is subject to various checks and balances, whether in the formalized separation of powers that an American president must negotiate, or the multiparty coalitions that are the norm in Europe. Our system has no such checks and balances; the few that were in place, the conventional constraints of parliamentary democracy and cabinet government, have withered on the vine.

Prime ministers in any Westminster system have always been powerful, but ours have amassed powers that are quite without parallel—because of the powers themselves, but also because so many of them are entirely the prime minister's personal prerogative, without supervision or constraint of any kind. As it has been said, we have a presidential system without the Congress.[5]

These include the vast array of appointments at the prime minister's command, from the governor general to the Senate to the Supreme Court to every senior post in the bureaucracy. And, of course, the Cabinet: at thirty-nine ministers, the largest in the democratic world, by far. Throw in the many parliamentary secretaries and committee chairs—the prime minister appoints all of them, too—and just about every member of caucus is in line for some sort of reward, or thinks he is.

But what is that reward, in the end? Cabinet ministers themselves have largely been reduced to courtiers. As their numbers have multiplied, their value, individually and collectively, has diminished; and as their value has diminished, fewer people of substance have stepped forward to take the job. Cabinet ministers are now tightly controlled by the Prime Minister's Office, in a way that previous generations of ministers, or ministers in other countries, would find intolerable. Not only does the prime minister appoint all of their deputy ministers, but in recent years the practice has been for the prime minister to appoint their chiefs of staff. Essentially, every minister now has a minder, reporting directly to the Prime Minister's Office.

And that's just the start. The prime minister alone decides when Parliament should be prorogued, and when it should be recalled, and when it should be dissolved in favour of fresh elections. Coupled with the power to declare any vote a matter of confidence, on any grounds, the prime minister has a metaphoric gun to the heads of individual members, on either side of the House, who might be tempted to defeat a government bill. The prime minister likewise decides which bills (other than private members' bills) to introduce and when, how much debate should be permitted on a bill, which bills might be combined with others into omnibus bills, who sits on committees and what business they will take up and when, etc.

Yet for all the concentration of power in the Prime Minister's Office it is at the same time draining power to the courts, to the bureaucracy, to the provinces, even to the Senate. Reforms instituted by Justin Trudeau, dismantling the party system in the upper house and requiring that Senate appointments be "merit-based," may have taken some of the partisanship and patronage out of that chamber, but at the cost of inflating senators' sense of self-importance. Senators may not have a mandate from the people but they can now tell themselves they have a higher mandate—a mandate of virtue.

The risk of confrontation with the Commons has grown accordingly. Senators rarely if ever defeat a bill outright. But they have taken to threatening to do so to back demands for amendments to bills passed by the Commons. The longer this goes on, the more it normalizes the idea that bills might be written by someone other than the people we elect to do the job. Until one day we wake up and find the unelected Senate is routinely defeating or rewriting bills.

All of which makes the more commonly heard complaint, that we are losing our democracy to the courts, seem quaint. The Supreme Court, it is true, may set aside a piece of legislation as unconstitutional. But the court does not have carte blanche to do so. It may do so only so far as the law in question conflicts with the higher law embodied in the Constitution, and then only in accordance with judicial precedent. Whereas senators can vote to kill a government bill for any reason they like.

There are, in short, legitimate and illegitimate constraints on executive power. The less the government is constrained by legitimate means—notably the House of Commons—the more encumbered it finds itself by illegitimate ones. The more powerful prime ministers have become within the precincts of Parliament Hill, the less their writ extends anywhere outside it.

* * *

To recap, a party, having been subjugated to the personal ambitions of a leader and his coterie of advisers—with the help of thousands of new members of dubious provenance—by a combination of false promises, venomous attack ads, and fortuitous media blunders succeeds in stampeding a little over one-third of the electorate into supporting it, which when processed through vote splits and other tricks of the first-past-the-post electoral system, is magically transformed into a majority. The prime minister, thus elected, rules with something approaching dictatorial powers until such time as he desires to repeat the process, ideally shortly after the opposition has exhausted its energies and its funds choosing another leader.

And we wonder why 40 percent of the electorate don't vote? Frankly, it's a mystery why so many still do.

So we have a crisis on our hands. It is a crisis of legitimacy, yes, but also an existential crisis. With so few real responsibilities Parliament is fast becoming irrelevant. And with so few Canadians bothering to take part in national elections it is debatable who Parliament is even answerable to, or what it represents. The very notion of Canadians as a self-governing people is dissolving before our eyes.

We are caught in a number of vicious circles. The more our democracy declines, the less shocking each new abuse becomes. The longer it goes on, the less anyone is conscious of what we have lost, or cares much about what remains. The weaker MPs grow, the less reason anyone can think why they should be given more power relative to party leaders—including MPs themselves. The less legitimate the federal government becomes, the more MPs are seen not, as the phrase has it, as representatives of the people in Ottawa, but as representatives of Ottawa to the people, and the more that the provinces are emboldened to fill the void. The more cynical and fatalistic people become about Canadian politics, the less likely they are to vote, or to pay attention, and the worse all these other ills become.

It is surely unnecessary to explain why this matters—why democracy matters. Without a functioning Parliament, we are denied adequate representation in or oversight of government. Error is more likely to go undetected, incompetence to go unpunished, abuses of power to go unchecked. As Parliament's legitimacy declines, people look to alternate sources of representation—the provinces, the courts, activist groups, charismatic demagogues, none of which have the unifying force of a national Parliament, where all parts of the community come together to debate the issues of the day. In time, as we have seen south of the border, the discrediting of democratic institutions can begin to nourish a desire for autocracy.

Or perhaps the better way of grasping it is to imagine a counterfactual: what if we had a parliament that mattered? What if we had elections that mattered? What if the candidates in each riding really were the choices of their communities as represented by their local riding associations? What if MPs had greater independence to represent their constituents in Parliament? What if leaders had to answer to their caucus, and governments had to answer to the House? What if Cabinet government were a reality and not a polite fiction?

What if parties had to battle for votes in every part of the country, in every riding in the country? What if all of us were represented in Parliament, and not that diminishing fraction of the voters in each riding that happen to support the winning party? What if 90 percent or more of the electorate showed up to vote, instead of 60 percent or less? What if governments really represented a majority of the voters, and not the fraction of a fraction that now passes for a mandate?

These are not idle questions. They do not describe some unattainable ideal, but democracy as it exists in other countries, and has in this country at other times. We do not have to accept the current degraded state of our democratic institutions as inevitable. Neither do we have to accept it in our politics. We do not have to put up with the flagrant and repeated breaking of solemn campaign commitments, any more than we do in other walks of life. We can have elections that are more than simply a parade of expensive attack ads. We can make televised debates the sort of illuminating democratic showcases they were meant to be, instead of the quadrennial embarrassments they have become.

There are solutions. Why, then, have they not been been implemented? Why does our democracy remain in such disarray? Two reasons.

One, because of the limitations to our imagination imposed by our self-image as one of the world's great democracies. Even as Canadians grow more and more detached from the political process and critical of particular institutions, they continue to tell pollsters they are generally satisfied with the state of our democracy[6].

The other reason? Because the reforms that are needed would reduce the powers and prerogatives of the people now in power, and require the consent of those same people to be put into effect. Change that would reduce the power of incumbents can only be enacted by incumbents. I wish I had an answer for this.

The Crisis of Canadian Democracy

But the beginning of change is to shed our illusions. Before we can start to fix our democracy, we need to realize how broken it is. That is the work of the remainder of this book.

2
Government vs. Parliament

DEMOCRACY IS NOT JUST what happens on election day, but every day in between. We do not hand our rulers a blank cheque. Elections may decide *who* governs us, but *how* they will govern is as much the work of a democracy.

Later in this book I argue that the way we conduct our elections is fundamentally broken, in ways that have profound implications for democratic politics. But if we had the most flawless electoral system imaginable, we would still be a long way from a fully functioning democracy. That is because the institution by which the business of democracy is transacted between elections—the institution it is the purpose of those elections to fill—is no less broken than the elections themselves.

I speak of the Parliament of Canada, the foundational institution in our democracy. On paper, its powers and prerogatives are formidable. It is the seat of authority, first. Although power is formally vested in the Crown, it is legitimated entirely by the support of a popularly elected Parliament. While we tend to think of parliaments as the bodies that debate and pass laws, their first responsibility is to choose who will run the government. This is no mere formality. No government may take office, or wield power, without the confidence of a majority of the House of Commons.

The government, composed of the prime minister, the Cabinet, and the civil service, is the executive side of our system. It is separate from Parliament, but connected. By convention, our prime ministers, though they lead the government, are also members of Parliament*, as are the Cabinet ministers chosen by the prime minister to frame government policy and oversee government departments. The executive and legislative branches are separate in a parliamentary system, with separate powers and responsibilities, they are also joined, via the Cabinet.

While the executive takes the lead in proposing legislation before Parliament, it remains the job of Parliament to decide what to do with that legislation: to examine, debate, amend, and ultimately pass it into law, or not, if it declines to do so. Foremost among its legislative responsibilities is the "business of supply," the ancient prerogative of Parliament to approve the raising of any and all revenues by taxation, together with how these are spent.

That is only one side of Parliament's powers. The other is to hold the government to account: to hear the government's plans and to give its opinion of them, and afterward to make ministers answer for the results; to investigate particular matters of concern through various parliamentary committees; and ultimately to express their judgment of the government as a whole, by the continued provision of, or occasionally the withholding of confidence in it. That is why our system is called "responsible government": the government is responsible—accountable—to the Commons.

---

* There have been prime ministers who governed for a time without a seat in the Commons: Sir Charles Tupper in 1896, Mackenzie King in 1925 and 1945, John Turner in 1984. But the expectation was that each would seek and win a seat before long, either in a byelection or a general election. Sir John Abbott and Sir Mackenzie Bowell each briefly served as prime minister in the 1890s from their seats in the Senate, a practice that would be unlikely to be accepted today.

Government vs. Parliament

Some of Parliament's powers are formal and legal. Some are more informal. They consist of the power to embarrass the government, or to delay its progress, or at the least to focus public attention on an issue. There is, it may be said, a large element of theatre in this. That is intentional. Parliament *is* a theatre. Its role, in part, is to dramatize the issues and events of the day, to make them relevant and intelligible. Parliament is the place where our great controversies are acted out for the public's instruction and approval. If its debates rarely change anyone's mind inside the House, they may influence the public at large.

That, as I said, is how it is supposed to work. But that is not how it actually works. The actual rather than theoretical powers of Parliament to debate, scrutinize, and amend legislation have been greatly attenuated. The actual, rather than theoretical powers of Parliament to hold government to account have been likewise circumscribed. Ours is a weak Parliament: weaker than it was, weaker than its counterparts in other countries, weaker than we imagine it to be, weaker than it can and should be.

* * *

I should stress how modest a standard I am proposing in this regard. Although there has been a decline over the years in Parliament's powers and prestige, it should not be imagined there was any golden age when members of Parliament were all-powerful and governments trembled before them. Politics has always been a grubby business for unscrupulous people, seeking power by whatever combination of flattery, catcalling, bribery, and extortion best advances their interests.

Neither is the aim here to reimagine Parliament on some utopian lines. Governments, in a parliamentary system, will always play a decisive role, and probably should. Parties, too, are essential; there is a reason that every parliamentary democracy is organized along party lines, as Parliament could not function without them. But we have taken things too far. We have allowed the powers of Parliament, and of members of Parliament, to decay to such an extent that it is hard to describe it as much more than a ceremonial body, of the kind we are careful to dismiss in other countries. Only force of habit prevents us from doing so here.

What I am proposing we should mourn are no more than the traditional powers and prerogatives of Parliament, the instruments through which, however imperfectly, it was intended to perform its historic legislative and oversight roles. These were once considerable. Democracy in Confederation-era Canada was far from perfect. Politics was a crude blood sport. Corruption was common. Votes were openly bought and sold (the secret ballot was not introduced until 1874[7]). Intimidation and other forms of voter interference were rife.[8] Most egregiously, the right to vote was still restricted to men—not until 1918 would Canadian women get the vote—and to property-owning men, at that.[9]

All the same, Canada at that time could fairly claim to be among the most democratic countries on earth.[10] Where property-ownership requirements in the United Kingdom meant that, even after the Second Reform Act in 1867, fewer than one-third of the adult male population[11] could vote, in Canada property was more widely held: despite broadly similar property requirements,* at least half the adult male population was eligible to vote at Confederation.[12]

Responsible government—an executive that was accountable to an elected legislature—was a freshly minted achievement. The rebellions of Upper and Lower Canada were barely thirty years in the past. People were acutely aware of how precious, and how hard-won self-government was. Leaders could not automatically assume that their caucuses (members of Parliament of the same party) would be with them on a given vote. At a time when the average riding held roughly

---

* These were largely provincial. There was no federal law regulating the franchise until 1885; it was abolished in 1898. The last remaining property requirement was not removed until voting regulations were again federalized in 1920. Elections Canada, *A History of the Vote in Canada*, 2021. https://www.elections.ca/res/his/WEB_EC%2091135%20History%20of%20the%20Vote_Third%20edition_EN.pdf

Government vs. Parliament

two thousand voters,[13] MPs took care to keep in touch with their constituents—certainly their constituents kept in touch with them—and did not shy from bucking the party line.

Public interest in the proceedings was keen. Debates were often memorable, frequently tumultuous, and on occasion decisive.* Commons debates were not officially recorded until 1875 (the Senate version of Hansard began in 1871), in part, as was said at the time, because newspaper reports of the debates were already so extensive. The Toronto *Globe* devoted fourteen columns of print a day to Commons business;[14] its rivals at the *Mail*, the *Leader*, the Montreal *Gazette*, and the upstart Ottawa *Times*, nearly as much.

Even as party leaders began to assert greater control in the decades that followed, Parliament remained the focus of national politics. A good speech in the House could still turn a few votes.† To be a Cabinet minister remained a position of some power and prestige, and attracted talent to match. Most important, the steady erosion of parliamentary norms and conventions that has done so much to weaken Parliament in recent decades had not yet begun in earnest.

An example: as late as the 1930s, a Member of Parliament, on being appointed to Cabinet, had first to resign his seat and run in a by-election. The reason? His role had changed: from being a

---

* The debate over the Pacific Scandal, involving the corrupt raising of funds from railway interests, is a spectacular example: Macdonald's government fell over it, although not before Macdonald had given a five-hour, gin-fuelled peroration in defence of his record.

† "The feature of this afternoon's debate was St. Laurent's magnificent speech," Mackenzie King recorded in his diary for December 6, 1944, at the height of the conscription crisis. "Magnificent in the sense that it was forthright, honest, sincere, straightforward and true. His decision to stand or fall with me was tremendously applauded in the House . . ." Libraries and Archives Canada, *Diaries of William Lyon Mackenzie King*, https://recherche-collection-search.bac-lac.gc.ca/eng/Home/Record?app=diawlmking&IdNumber=29567&ecopy=20003XSQ

To a modern reader, the passage is striking in several respects: The notion that the fate of a bill, indeed a government, might depend upon a Cabinet minister's decision "to stand or fall" with the prime minister; the notion that he might declare his position in the course of a debate in Parliament, and that on the strength of his speech might hang the votes of other MPs would be decided; or perhaps it is the notion that anyone would make a speech in Parliament that could be described, even by an admirer, as "magnificent." Parliament is not that place any more, and parliamentary debate has not that quality.

watchdog on the government—yes, as a member of the governing party—to being a member of it.* Before he could accept such a post, he was obliged to ask his electors' permission. It wasn't necessarily the most practical idea—more than one critical event in Canadian political history has turned on a prime minister in a narrowly divided Parliament losing his majority on appointing a Cabinet,† and shortly afterward losing power—but the thinking behind it is revealing, as is our inability to comprehend it. We have lost the sense that members of the governing party have any duty but to support the government, as uncritically as possible.

Another example: the famous Pipeline Debate of 1956, which consumed Parliament for weeks. The debate was nominally over a controversial‡ bill to build a natural gas pipeline across the country, but it soon was inflamed by the government's tactic of invoking closure, a motion cutting off debate in the House, at each stage of the bill's passing. The debate was passionate, at times close to violent,§

---

* Specifically, the member, by accepting an "office of profit under the Crown," might otherwise be suspected of having sacrificed his independence to the king's shilling. While MPs were prohibited from becoming ministers, it was nevertheless considered acceptable for ministers to become MPs. The requirement of ministerial by-elections neatly squared both principles. The rule was abolished in Britain in 1926, but remained in place in Canada until 1931.

    A vestige of it remains in Britain, only in reverse: by dint of a 1624 resolution of the House, a British Member of Parliament may not simply resign his seat, but must go through the elaborate ritual of accepting an office of profit, either Crown Steward and Bailiff of the Chiltern Hundreds, or Crown Steward and Bailiff of the Manor of Northstead, thus making himself ineligible to sit as an MP.

† It explains, for example, why Macdonald was prime minister of the Province of Canada in 1864: see Christopher Moore's description of the "double shuffle" of that year. It was also central to the King-Byng Affair, described later in this chapter. Prime Minister Arthur Meighen, assuming power on King's resignation, was immediately faced with the familiar dilemma: his wafer-thin majority, dependent as it was on the support of the Progressive Party, would vanish the minute he appointed a Cabinet. His solution was to appoint several ministers as "acting ministers," on the theory that the resignation-byelection rule did not apply to them. The Progressives, upright types that they were, cried foul, and that was the end of Meighen.

‡ The initial source of controversy was the project's heavy reliance on American capital.

§ It culminated in what became known as "Black Friday," June 1, after the Speaker reversed himself on an earlier ruling extending debate. As enraged MPs spilled into the centre aisle, the leader of the Co-operative Commonwealth Federation, M. J. Coldwell, charged the Speaker's chair, shaking his fist. Craig Baird, *The Trans-Canada Pipeline*, June 11, 2022. https://canadaehx.com/2022/06/11/the-trans-canada-pipeline/

and why not: the government had had the nerve to propose curtailing debate in the House! In peacetime! Whereas nowadays governments do something similar every other day. No one bats an eye.

The fall of Parliament is the result not of any cataclysmic event or (for the most part) of deliberate changes in the rules (the Standing Orders, as they are called), but rather of the gradual erosion of a number of unwritten conventions. These conventions are critical to our system of government. Indeed, most of the institutions by which we are governed have no formal standing in law. The Constitution* does provide for a Parliament, for instance, but it says nothing of political parties, or prime ministers, or Cabinet, as such: the reference, rather, is to "the Governor in Council."

In the same way, the checks and balances on executive power in our system are mostly matters of convention rather than, as in the United States, formal rules. It is convention, not law, that dictates that the Crown, in Canada represented by the governor general, governs only on the advice of the prime minister, and that a prime minister governs only so long as he enjoys the confidence of the House. How the various players behave within it is likewise governed by convention—by what people in similar positions have done in similar situations in the past.

But conventions are only as strong as the players agree they should be. If one side or another chooses to ignore a convention, and gets away with it, a new convention is born: what was previously forbidden is now permitted. Understanding the conditions that allow conventions to be flouted, therefore, is as important to explaining Parliament's decline as the changes in conventions themselves. When a piece of

---

* The original Constitution, that is, which came into effect at our founding in 1867. An act of the British Parliament, it established our system of government, along with the division of powers between the federal government and the provinces. Originally called the British North America Act, it is now known as the Constitution Act, 1867. The set of amendments passed in 1982, including the Canadian Charter of Rights and Freedoms, and a formula (several, actually) for amending the Constitution, is known as the Constitution Act, 1982. Or as I will refer to them here, the 1867 Constitution or 1982 Constitution.

the parliamentary firmament gives way, it is usually because other pieces have already deteriorated.

That is the reality of Parliament today. MPs are so tightly controlled that a prime minister in possession of a majority is in no serious jeopardy of losing any vote in the House, or even of significant numbers of his backbenchers voting against it. Neither can any amendments pass that he does not accept. Debate on any matter lasts for as long as he permits, and no longer. The same applies to the work of most House committees, for he controls those as well.

It is different, to be sure, in a minority Parliament, as have become common in recent years. But even then, Parliament has little power to call a prime minister to account; if he is less able to impose his will on the Commons, neither can the Commons do much to impose its will on him. In the absence of effective oversight by the Commons, other institutions have stepped in: the Senate, the provinces, the media. But none of these has the democratic legitimacy to be an appropriate instrument of accountability.

Some of this erosion, I think, can be traced to the influence of the Great Republic to our south, and the growing presidentialization of our own politics.[15] American politics is obsessively focused on the president because the presidency is central to their system of government: it was intended from the start that executive power should be concentrated in one person, elected independently of the Congress and with separate powers and responsibilities (though Americans themselves complain of the rise of the "imperial presidency," usurping the prerogatives of Congress). It is understandable, if unwelcome, that this should have informed our view of our own head of government, even if our systems are entirely different.

But much is also attributable to the long history of Liberal dominance in federal politics—the Liberals having governed for eighty-seven of the last one hundred twenty-nine years—what the late journalist and historian Richard Gwyn used to call "one-and-a-half party rule." In brief, the Liberals tend to undermine and override parliamentary conventions because they can—because people have become so accustomed to the Liberals' habitual disdain for the rules, they have forgotten there is any other way to govern. And the Conservatives do it because, they tell themselves, they must: the system, after so many years of Liberal rule, is hopelessly stacked against them. Each party comes to power vowing to correct the abuses of the other. And each then piles on fresh abuses, each excusing its own sins by comparison to those— far worse!—of its predecessor. Thus has responsible government been ratcheted ever downward.

* * *

How, specifically, has Parliament been weakened? How has the executive secured its ascendancy? The simplest and most direct way is by causing Parliament not to sit. The ordinary schedule of sitting days is set by the Standing Orders, but the schedule can change, as can the Standing Orders, if the prime minister wills it. The prime minister also decides when one session of Parliament should end, and another one begin; when Parliament should be dissolved for an election, and when it should return afterward. Not coincidentally, perhaps, Parliaments have been sitting for shorter and shorter periods each year, though the size and scope of government, and the volume of government business, has ballooned.

The Canadian and British Houses of Commons used to sit about equally often: roughly 150 days a year. Over the last three decades, while Britain's House has continued to meet more or less at the same pace, Canada's has fallen off by nearly a third, to 112 days annually, on average. The US Congress maintains about the same work schedule as Westminster. So does the French National Assembly.[16] But our MPs are obliged to show up fewer than one calendar day in three.*

---

* In fairness, the lower houses in Germany, Japan, and Australia sit for roughly sixty days a year. Of course, given the Canadian House's insistence on maintaining hybrid or virtual sittings, years after the pandemic ended—the only G7 country to do so—it's debatable what counts as a sitting day.

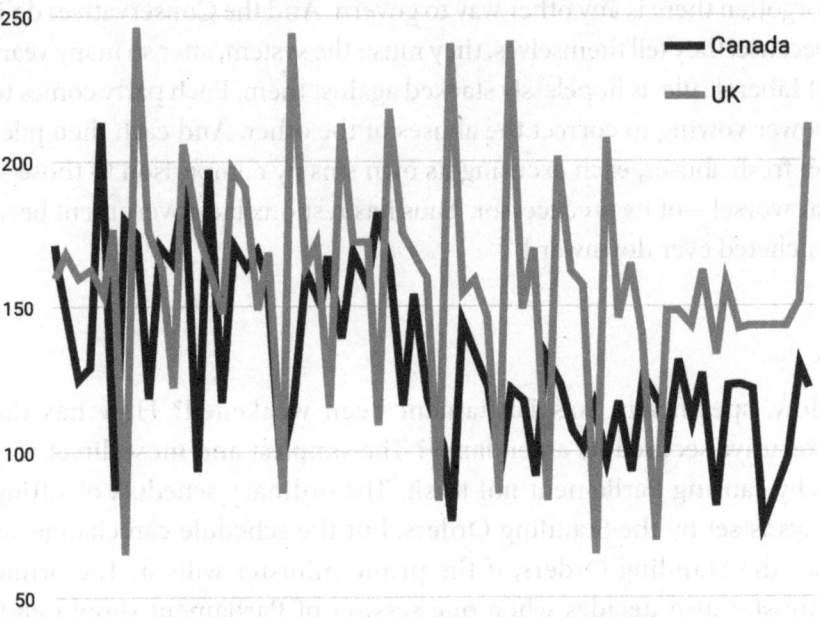

Sitting days, Canada and UK Parliaments, annual

Canada: https://lop.parl.ca/sites/ParlInfo/default/en_CA/Parliament/SittingsByYear
UK: https://commonslibrary.parliament.uk/research-briefings/SN04653/

Is this a big deal? The premise of responsible government is that the government must hold the confidence of the House at all times, and should be prepared to meet the House on any day of the year. Any day that Parliament is not sitting is a day that the government does not have to answer to the House: to face embarrassing questions, or be taken to task in debate. Fewer days per session also leaves less time for Parliament to examine each bill. For as long as a government refuses to meet with Parliament, then, under whatever pretext, it is hamstringing democracy.

Government vs. Parliament

One reason Parliament has not sat quite as often in recent years has been the greater frequency of elections, spurred in part by a series of minority parliaments in which no single party has a majority (a phenomenon we'll examine in chapter 7). Each time an election is called, Parliament is dissolved for the duration of the campaign. That much is understandable. Less understandable is the prolonged delay in recalling Parliament after the election is over. The average interval between election day and Parliament's return is sixty days[17]—longer, in most campaigns, than the election itself. In some election years, the gap has been much longer. Joe Clark set the modern record in 1979, waiting 140 days to recall Parliament rather than subject his minority government to its scrutiny.

There is no necessity for this. In Britain, Parliament typically reconvenes within a week or two of an election. In Australia, Parliament must resume sitting no more than thirty days after the writs are returned.[18] In New Zealand, likewise, Parliament must resume within six weeks of the writs' return—as in Australia, it's in their Constitution. The same is true after prorogation: the procedure, between elections, by which one parliamentary session is terminated and another begun. In Canada, this can result in Parliament going dark for weeks or months at a time. In Britain, the gap is no more than a few days.[19]

The frequency with which parliaments have been either dissolved or prorogued of late has given rise to a growing sense that these practices are being abused. There is nothing wrong with either dissolution or prorogation in itself: they are legitimate parts of the royal (in practice, prime ministerial) prerogative. But when Parliament is dissolved at a time purely dictated by the prime minister's electoral interests, or prorogued to avoid a confidence vote he knows he will lose, basic democratic principles are being violated.

Why a prime minister (or premier) should have the sole power to decide the timing of an election has never been clear: it is obviously to the government's advantage to be able to defer an election when public opinion looks inclement, or to hasten a vote when the electoral sun is shining. It is not a requirement of parliamentary democracy that prime ministers wield this power: New Zealand and Australia hold elections on fixed three-year timetables (in Britain, under the Fixed Term Parliaments Act 2011, they were to be held every five years, but the act was repealed in 2021).

Over the last two decades, efforts have been made to limit this prime ministerial advantage. Possibly spurred by Jean Chrétien's snap election call in 2000, just three years after the previous election, Parliament and all ten provincial legislatures passed laws requiring elections to be held on fixed four-year timetables. Yet scarcely had federal legislation been enacted in 2007 when Stephen Harper chose to call an election anyway, after only two years in government. How was this legal? A proviso in the bill stipulated that, notwithstanding the bill's intent, nothing in it limited the governor general's prerogative to call an election at any time. And since the governor general acts only on the prime minister's advice, neither could the bill limit the prime minister's prerogative.

That was the argument then. But that was not the understanding at the time the bill was passed. At the time, the clause was expressly presented as a mere formality, a constitutional nicety intended to ward off court challenges. Ministers, including the prime minister, were at pains to boast of how they had levelled the playing field between government and opposition. Passage of the bill, we were to understand, meant the end of snap elections.* Yet when it suited Harper to call

---

* Here, for example, is the minister responsible for the bill, former Minister for Democratic Reform Rob Nicholson, testifying before the Senate legal and constitutional affairs committee on December 6, 2006: "A prime minister who called an election [without having lost a confidence vote] would be into a very difficult constitutional situation that would require perusal by the governor general." He clarified: "If a prime minister, after three and a half years, for no reason understandable to the public, demanded a dissolution of Parliament by the governor general, *I believe that under this legislation the governor general would be within his or her rights to deny that.*" (Emphasis mine.)

The governor general's discretion might not have been circumscribed by the legislation, in other words, but the PM's was—by the governor general's. "It is a true restriction of the powers of the prime minister," Nicholson commented, "and a good one." https://sencanada.ca/en/Content/SEN/Committee/391/lega/18evd-e

a snap election, he did. The precedent having been set, so did his successor, Justin Trudeau. Although he came to power denouncing this and other democratic abuses under Harper,[20] Trudeau called his own snap election in 2021.

The pattern was repeated with prorogation. Harper prorogued Parliament in December 2008, to avoid being defeated on a confidence vote on the Fall Economic Statement; and again in 2010 to shut down a Parliamentary committee's hearings into allegations that the Afghan armed forces, our allies in the war in Afghanistan, had tortured prisoners in their charge—prisoners captured by Canadian troops. Trudeau, likewise, reached for the prorogation lever in 2020,* as a means of cutting short a committee inquiry into his involvement in the decision to award a large government contract to the WE Charity organization, an agency that, among other personal and political entanglements, had hired his mother; and again, to avoid a confidence vote, in 2025. (This is discussed further in chapter 8.)

Of course, the greater part of the power of dissolution consists not in the actual use of it, but in the threat of it, particularly in minority parliaments, as a means either of corralling recalcitrant government backbenchers or beating back opposition challenges. Should this bill be defeated, a prime minister will announce gravely, the government would have no choice but to view it as a question of confidence, meaning MPs would risk the defeat of the government if they were so foolish as to vote against it. More to the point, they would risk losing their seats.

That would be fine, were governments not in the habit of viewing virtually *every* vote, implicitly, as a confidence matter. They are entitled to do so. But they stretch credulity, not to say common sense, when they pretend the slightest expression of formal parliamentary opposition to the government's agenda, on however trivial a question, implies a general loss of confidence in it as a government.

---

* "Stephen Harper has used prorogation to avoid difficult political circumstances," the Liberals' 2015 platform complained. "We will not." https://liberal.ca/wp-content/uploads/sites/292/2020/09/New-plan-for-a-strong-middle-class.pdf

No constitutional principle obliges them to do this. A budget bill would be considered a confidence matter: it could hardly be expected that a government would carry on after its entire fiscal plan had been rejected. Likewise for a vote on the Speech from the Throne. And obviously an explicitly worded motion of non-confidence would count. But for the rest? Governments are routinely defeated on legislation in other parliamentary democracies, without it precipitating their downfall. For example, Theresa May's minority Conservative government was defeated on thirty-three votes in the House of Commons; Boris Johnson's two governments, sixteen more. Since 1974 British governments have lost a total of one hundred thirty-six votes in the House.[21] Only one, the defeat (by one vote!) of the Callaghan government on an explicit confidence vote in March 1979, precipitated an election.

Even in Canada, governments often suffer parliamentary defeats without either resigning or calling an election.[22] Only six times in our history has a government fallen after losing a confidence vote.*[23] Which is not to say that those are the only confidence votes a government has lost. If governments are in the habit of declaring votes to be matters of confidence that were not intended and ought not to be considered as such, there have also been examples, thankfully rare, of the reverse: a government refusing to acknowledge it has lost a confidence vote, when it in fact has. It happened, arguably, in 1968, when the Pearson government, having been narrowly defeated on an important tax bill, persuaded the courtly Conservative leader Robert Stanfield to give them a do-over, via a formal confidence vote.[24] It happened again in 2005, when Paul Martin's government, having been defeated on what was certainly intended as, and almost certainly

---

* These were in 1926, 1963, 1974, 1979, 2005, and 2011. The 1974 and 2011 losses are considered to have been deliberate. The last two, 2005 and 2011, were the only ones explicitly-worded as non-confidence motions; 2011 was unique in also finding the government in contempt of Parliament. In no case has a government simply resigned after losing a confidence vote, rather than call an election, though in a couple of cases (Macdonald, 1874, King 1925) they have resigned in anticipation of losing one.

was a confidence vote[25]—even the suggestion meant it should have immediately put a formal confidence motion before the House, to resolve any doubt—spent the next nine days trawling for votes on the opposition benches, dangling Cabinet posts and other goodies it was no longer constitutionally authorized to offer, until it eventually persuaded Belinda Stronach to cross the floor and save the government.[*]

A still more troubling example was the "coalition crisis" of December 2008. As noted earlier, Stephen Harper's minority government faced almost certain defeat in the House over the Fall Economic Statement, just two months after that year's election. The opposition parties had informed the governor general, not only that they were ready to defeat the government, but that they had agreed to form a coalition government in its place. Rather than submit to the vote, however, Harper demanded the governor general prorogue Parliament, hoping (successfully, as it turned out) that with the passage of time the cracks in the coalition would begin to show. The governor general reluctantly agreed, putting an end to the crisis.[†]

The situation recalled one of the most famous constitutional crises in our history, the King-Byng Affair. In the 1925 election, William Lyon Mackenzie King's incumbent Liberals had been returned with fewer seats than the Conservatives under Arthur Meighen. Nevertheless, King resolved to continue governing, as was his right,[‡] and informed the governor general, Lord Byng, of his intention. Byng assented,

---

[*] By one vote: the margin of heiress.

[†] She was probably right to do so. Harper had not yet lost a confidence vote, and was still her prime minister, on whose advice she was constitutionally bound to rely. Moreover, there was reason to doubt whether the coalition was any more likely to maintain the confidence of the House for long, with a divided and defeated Liberal party at its head, and depending as it did on the support of the separatist Bloc Québécois. It was, to say the least, a highly unusual situation. Harper arguably did her a favour in asking for prorogation, rather than dissolution. Had he asked for the latter, her choice would have been between defying convention and plunging the country into another election, so soon after the last, or defying her first minister and handing the government of the country over to an unstable coalition at the mercy of a separatist party. As it was, she could accept his advice while registering her displeasure at being put in such a position, forced to bail a prime minister out of a mess of his own making.

[‡] The prime minister remains the prime minister so long as the House has confidence in him, or at least until it has said it has no confidence in him.

but informed King that should his government fall, he would call upon Meighen to form a government, as was *his* right. King agreed but, on the verge of losing a confidence vote, reneged, demanding Byng dissolve Parliament and call an election. When Byng refused, calling on Meighen instead, a wholly fabricated constitutional crisis was upon us — just in time for King to win the next election. Who governed Canada, King demanded to know: the people, through their elected government, or some unelected foreign potentate? It did not seem to bother him that he had himself attempted to get King George V to overrule his governor general.

To the degree there is any ambiguity about the proper course to follow in such circumstances, there is the potential for recurring crises. Recent Canadian elections have yielded a succession of minority parliaments: five of the last seven, eleven of the last twenty-two. It is entirely likely they will do so again, if not in the election to come then in the not-too-distant future.

There are two possible crisis scenarios in that event. In one, a prime minister loses a confidence vote, or is about to, shortly after an election. Rather than yield power to his opposite number, he demands the governor general call another election. In the other, the governing party wins fewer seats than its nearest rival in an election, but attempts to hold on to power, believing it can govern with the support of another party or parties.

But what is common to both is the question of who has the right to govern: is it always the party with the largest number of seats, or is it whoever can command a majority of the House? And a second, related: is it acceptable for power to pass from one party to another by invitation of the governor general, rather than by a vote of the people?

To most constitutional scholars, the answers are obvious. There is no legal principle or convention that the party with the most seats always forms the government: the issue is strictly who can command the support of a majority of the House. Neither is there any rule that defeat on a confidence vote must always and everywhere lead to an election, rather than a simple change of government. We elect

Government vs. Parliament

parliaments in this country, not governments. Members of Parliament decide who governs.

Usually, to be sure, the party with the most seats forms the government. And usually when a government loses a confidence vote, an election follows, but not always or inevitably. It depends on the circumstances, and the governor general's judgment of how circumstances should inform convention: part of the viceroy's reserve powers. Convention dictates a governor general should not agree to a new election if it is too soon after the last, but how soon is too soon? Also, before calling on the opposition to form a government, a governor general might wish to be assured that it will not soon collapse in turn. There is some debate among scholars about how far the governor general's discretion extends.[26] But as to the basic principle, there is no reasonable dispute that the right to govern rests with whoever has the confidence of the House.

The only reason there is any uncertainty on this score is that, following Harper's example, and inspired by his success in rallying public opinion against the coalition, a number of Conservative politicians and thought leaders have pretended there is reason for dispute. The only party that has the right to govern, they insist, is the party that got the most seats. The only legitimate way in which a new government may take power is after an election. Should a party or combination of parties defeat the sitting government in the House and attempt to form a government in its place, it is not parliamentary democracy working as it should, but an "undemocratic seizure of power."[27]

And yet this is contradicted by multiple precedents. Meighen was not the first opposition leader to become prime minister without an intervening election: after Sir John A. Macdonald was forced to resign over his part in the Pacific Scandal, the governor general, Lord Dufferin, invited the Liberal leader, Alexander Mackenzie, to become prime minister (he called an election almost immediately after).

Provincial politics offers more recent examples. In the Ontario election of 1985, the incumbent Progressive Conservatives won the most seats, but were defeated shortly after recalling the legislature; the

Liberals took over from them, with the support of the NDP. Similarly, after the 2017 British Columbia election, the incumbent Liberals, although they, too, had won the most seats, were soon replaced by the NDP, who had obtained the support of the Greens. And after the 2018 election in New Brunswick, the Liberals attempted to continue in government, despite having won fewer seats than their Conservative opponents.* It did not last: a little over a month later, the government went down to defeat in a vote on the throne speech. A week later, the Conservatives were sworn in.

In all three cases, the incumbent premier remained the premier, regardless of which party had the most seats, until the legislature had met to decide the matter. In all three cases, the question of who had the right to govern was resolved by a simple test: who had the support of the majority of the legislature? In all three cases, after it became clear the government could not carry on, power passed smoothly from one party to another, without the need for another election. No crisis ensued.

But conventions depend for their power on observance. If a party is prepared to press the issue as far as some Conservatives seem determined to—at the height of the coalition crisis there was talk of "going over the head" of the governor general, whatever that might mean, in the event she had ruled against them[28]—we could be in for a major constitutional crisis. At base, our system depends upon everyone involved agreeing to be bound by convention—the prime minister abiding by the convention that he holds office at His Majesty's pleasure (via the governor general), the governor general abiding by the convention that she governs only on the advice of the prime minister, all sides abiding by the convention that the right to govern rests with whoever has the confidence of a majority of the House—behaving, as the phrase has it, like "good chaps."[29] If they don't, we are lost.

* * *

---

* They did, however, win the popular vote by six percentage points.

But we are getting ahead of ourselves. A prime minister need not invoke the confidence convention to ensure he gets his way in the House. He has many other powers at his disposal. One of these is the power to curtail debate. This can be done by passing a motion of closure, under which debate is abruptly cut off (not for nothing is it known as a "guillotine" motion) at the end of the current sitting, followed by an immediate vote on the question. Or, as governments now prefer, it can be done by means of "time allocation," a later invention setting less stringent limits on debate, meaning it is allowed to continue at least until the next day. In practice they amount to much the same thing.

In the first decades after Confederation, Parliamentary debates were under no formal time limit; the length of a debate was, rather, determined by a kind of gentleman's agreement between party leaders. As the business of government expanded and parliamentary time grew short, governments began searching for some means of curbing debate in the interest of "efficiency." Robert Borden brought in Canada's first closure rule in 1913[30] (Britain adopted one in 1881; Australia in 1905). It was used sparingly, just eleven times in the first nineteen years after it was brought in, and not at all between 1932 and 1956. Hence the outrage that attended its use in the case of the pipeline bill.

In the bitter aftermath of that debate, governments were again wary of using closure; there was talk of abolishing it. But by the late 1960s, the patience of the executive was again wearing thin. In 1969, the Pierre Trudeau government proposed changes to Parliament's Standing Orders allowing for the imposition of time allocation.[31] It proved extremely contentious, and was not passed until late at night on the last full day of the session—naturally, with the help of closure. At the time this was regarded as a shocking power play: longstanding parliamentary convention held that such changes could only be made by all-party consensus. But the government insisted it was merely a stopgap, a measure that would in all likelihood never be implemented.

That changed in December 1971, when the government used its newfound powers for the first time, to speed passage of a massive tax reform bill. Against opposition warnings that this would hasten the decline of Parliament,[32] the government argued that this was a special case and "would not constitute a precedent." But, as the years passed, more and more such special cases seemed to arise. In the fifty-odd years since, governments have imposed time allocation over opposition party objections[*] more than three hundred times. Just under half of these (one hundred forty-six) occurred in the first forty years, 1971–2011. The other half have occurred since then: ninety-one under the Harper government of 2011–15, plus another fifty-nine under the first Justin Trudeau government, 2015–19.[†] Not coincidentally, both were majority governments: 96 percent of all time-allocation motions were passed under majority governments.

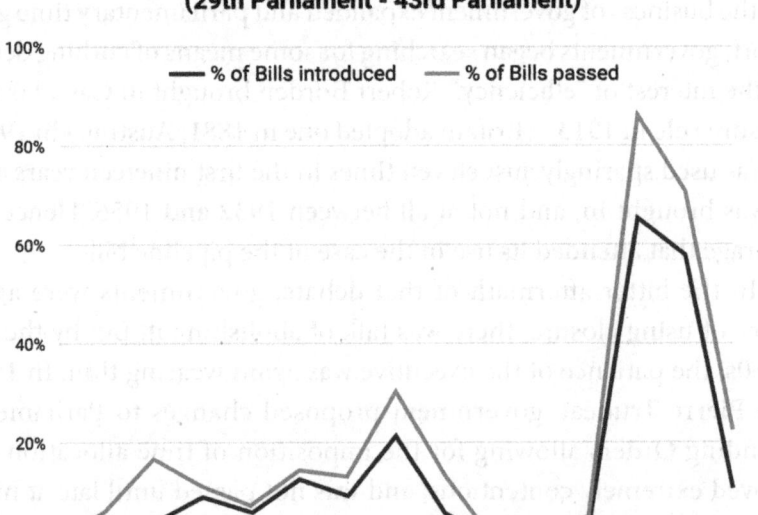

Source: Canadian Parliamentary Review https://www.revparlcan.ca/en/governing-by-time-allocation-the-increasing-use-of-time-allocation-in-the-house-of-commons-1971-to-2021/

* That is, using the draconian Section 78 (3), where time allocation is passed by a vote of the House, rather than the softer variants: 78 (1) with the agreement of all the parties, and 78 (2) with the agreement of a majority of the parties. There were twenty-nine uses of the latter two in the period studied.
† In addition, the two governments formally *threatened* to impose time allocation, by tabling time-allocation motions, thirty-five more times, without subsequently acting upon them. The point was made.

Government vs. Parliament

It is not unreasonable to argue that, as the time of the House is not unlimited, neither should its debates be. But the practice has been taken to such an extreme that debate has become almost an afterthought, a brief formality on the way to a bill's inevitable passage. Was this increased recourse to time allocation driven by the need to accommodate a heavier legislative workload? Hardly. The Mulroney majority governments of 1984–88 and 1988–93 imposed time allocation just forty-six times in total, yet passed 433 bills. The Harper and Trudeau majorities passed fewer than half as many bills, 188, yet imposed time allocation more than three times as often. What was once the exception has become the rule.

In no major democracy is debate cut short more routinely, or more high-handedly. The UK has "programme motions,"[33] which set out a timetable for how long a bill will be debated at each stage, but these are usually negotiated with the opposition parties, not imposed unilaterally by the government. Governments in Australia and New Zealand can curtail debate in certain circumstances, but do so less often[34], or less brutally[35], or with the agreement of the other parties. Closure is not unknown in the French National Assembly; more common is "programmed legislative time"—again, as negotiated among the parties*. Canada is unusual in the degree to which it reserves the right to limit debate exclusively to the government, and in the enthusiasm of governing parties to exploit this advantage.

Does it matter? So what if opposition MPs don't get to debate as long as they'd like. Maybe that puts their noses out of joint, but why should the rest of us care? Aren't the debates in Parliament pointless and futile? No one's mind is changed; no votes are changed, certianly, given our ferocious system of party discipline. What, then, is the point?

First, we should not use one failing of Parliament to justify another. If votes were not so strictly whipped, debates might matter more.

---

* Canada has nothing like France's Article 49.3, which allows a bill to pass without a vote (as long as the government survives a subsequent no-confidence vote). It is rarely invoked.

And second, the point of parliamentary debate is not just to assist in Parliament's internal deliberations.[36] It is to engage and represent the country, to educate the public on an issue, but also to give voice to their opinions.

Debate is important, but as important is who is debating, and where. No doubt bills are subject to extensive debate behind closed doors, among the civil service or the prime minister's staff—who knows, maybe even in Cabinet. But in Parliament, a much wider range of views and interests and values can be brought to bear, not only those of MPs, but also those of the citizens who elected them. Yes, debate can expose weaknesses in a bill before it is passed, that they might be remedied in time. Yes, it can potentially sway public opinion, if public opinion is swayable (and if the public is paying attention). But it can also simply remind governments of facts or opinions they might have overlooked, from corners of society they might not always think to consult.

At the very least, it can let governments know they are passing legislation that is objectionable to sections of the community. It may still be in the public interest to proceed, but we would be worse off if governments were not at least aware of whom they had just run over. And yet it is through just this sort of robust parliamentary debate that we may best hope to knit society together again, afterward, from that sense of everyone having at least been fairly heard and fairly represented. By sending our MPs to do battle on our behalf, we avoid the more grievous wounds that would result if we took it upon ourselves to air our differences directly. That disputatious body is *us*. As it, despite its divisions, remains one and whole, so do we.

* * *

That there have been fewer bills passed in recent years may owe in part to the growing tendency to bundle a number of different bills together to form gargantuan "omnibus" bills. As with most things, there is a question of balance involved. Omnibus bills, in themselves, are neither new nor controversial—most budget bills could be described as such—provided there is some valid reason to yoke the various bills together: that is, provided they are connected, in the language of Speakers' rulings over the years, by a "single purpose" or "unifying principle." A valid unifying principle would not include "we wanted to push through our entire legislative agenda for this session in a single vote." But that is close to where we have landed.

Bill C-38, for example, 2012 legislation titled the Jobs, Growth and Long-term Prosperity Act, was 425 pages long[37] and amended or repealed seventy existing acts. Supposedly a budget implementation bill, the act, among other things: substantially overhauled a number of federal environmental laws; repealed the Fair Wages and Hours of Labour Act; moved responsibility for monitoring CSIS, the federal spy agency, to the department of Public Safety; gave Cabinet the power to adjust Employment Insurance rules by order in council (that is, without having to pass legislation through Parliament); raised the retirement age for federal pensions, and more. Naturally, it was passed with the help of time allocation.

One of three omnibus bills the Harper government passed that year—there was also the omnibus crime bill and the omnibus refugee bill—Bill C-38 was followed the next year by Bill C-4, an omnibus budget implementation bill that weighed in at 309 pages,[38] with 472 sections. In fairness, that was only slightly more than the average length of a budget implementation bill under the Harper government (four times as long as the average in the Chrétien years[39]). It passed the House in seven days.

The practice has continued under the Trudeau Liberals. Their first budget implementation act, 2016's Bill C-15, ran to "only" 179 pages.[40] But by 2018's Bill C-86, it had rebounded to 854 pages.[41] And that wasn't the only omni-budget bill that year. There was the earlier Bill C-74, at 559 pages,[42] which included, among other measures: the Greenhouse Gas Pollution Pricing Act (enacting the federal carbon tax), and a provision allowing for deferred prosecution agreements for corporations accused of economic crimes. Alert readers may recall this set the stage for the SNC-Lavalin affair.*

The 2022 budget bill, in case anyone thinks this is old news, clocked in at 420 pages[43]; the 2023 budget bill, another 408 pages[44]; the 2024 edition, an epic 656 pages.[45] A look back at previous omnibus bills that were controversial in their day shows how far we've fallen. Bill C-150, the landmark 1969 package of Criminal Code amendments that legalized homosexuality and abortion, passed after nearly two years of debate. It was all of 118 pages.[46] A 1994 budget implementation bill, C-17,[47] attracted considerable wrath from Stephen Harper, then the opposition Finance critic. "The subject matter of the bill," he complained in Parliament, "is so diverse that a single vote on the content would put members in conflict with their own principles . . . How can members represent their constituents on these various areas when they are forced to vote in a block on such legislation and on such concerns?"[48] That bill was twenty-one pages long.

Harper's hypocrisy is not unusual. The Trudeau Liberals came to power in 2015 vowing to "bring an end" to the "undemocratic" use of omnibus bills.[49] And rightly so. Omnibus bills *are* undemocratic. When legislation runs to such length, with so many parts, it is inevitably less closely examined than it would be if each of its constituent bills were debated and passed separately. When, worse, a bill attempts to legislate on so many different subjects at the same time, all to be decided in a single vote, it makes it impossible to know what MPs really intended. Perhaps they were in favour of the measure mandating hammocks on seagoing vessels, but were they really in favour of the one banning the sale of ice cream to minors?

---

* In 2019, it was revealed that Prime Minister Justin Trudeau and his officials had improperly pressured then-Minister of Justice and Attorney General Jody Wilson-Raybould to intervene in a criminal case against SNC-Lavalin, a Quebec-based construction company with Liberal ties. Specifically, she was pressured to advise prosecutors to offer SNC-Lavalin, in lieu of a trial, a deferred prosecution agreement. The scandal led to the resignations of top government officials and findings of improper influence by the ethics commissioner. See chapter 4.

While omnibus bills have always been with us, the problem, like much else in Parliament's decline, has grown far worse in recent years. And it is worse here than in most other countries, the US being the notable exception. Among the Westminster democracies omnibus bills are a uniquely Canadian ill: Britain's Parliament does not allow them, nor does Australia's (New Zealand's does, but under restrictive conditions)[50]. In France, Germany and Italy they are limited by "single subject" rules. They are permissible in Japan, but discouraged.

Why have they tended to metastasize here, and not elsewhere? Again: once conventions are allowed to decay, the rot spreads. Had opposition parties put up more of a fight over the use of omnibus bills, as once they did—the 1982 "bell-ringing" episode, in which the opposition refused to enter the House to vote for fifteen days in answer to the division bells, was in protest at an omnibus bill*—governments might have thought twice about it. Instead, they appear to have quietly resolved to do the same once they are in power.

One of the worst effects of omnibus bills is the burden they place on Parliamentary committees. Parliamentary committees are commonly described as the jewel in the parliamentary crown, the one area where MPs set aside some of their partisan enmity and work together across party lines. Away from the limelight, it is said, committees do much useful work improving legislation, without the grandstanding that so often hinders parliamentary proceedings.

But which committee should review a bill that might fall under the responsibility of half a dozen of them? And whatever committee is chosen, how can it properly apply its members' specialized expertise to legislation that touches on a number of entirely different subjects?

At the best of times, committees are far weaker than their reputation makes out. Yes, there are examples of committees doing bipartisan work in the public interest. But there are too many examples to the contrary, where the governing party majority on a committee simply

---

* Bill C-94, also known as the Energy Security Act, 1982. The protest was resolved when the government agreed to divide the legislation into eight separate bills. It was 149 pages long. https://parl.canadiana.ca/view/oop.HOC_32_1_C94_C105/5

falls into line with the executive (Bill C-38, for example, was passed without amendment).

One of the "undoubted privileges" of a Parliamentary committee is its power "to send for persons, papers and records"* in pursuit of its inquiries. Yet successive Conservative and Liberal governments have used their majorities on committees to refuse the production of witnesses or documents, and run out the clock. When the SNC-Lavalin scandal blew up, the Liberal majorities on the relevant Commons committees limited their inquiries to a short list of witnesses, gave extra time to those favourable to the government's position, and abruptly shut down the hearings without ever having gotten to the bottom of the matter. A committee looking into the WE Charity affair was similarly stonewalled, as was another examining sexual misconduct allegations against the Chief of Defence Staff and what the prime minister or his officials might have known about it. The Harper government did the same in the Mike Duffy affair.† Even the sponsorship scandal,‡ perhaps the greatest federal corruption scandal of modern times, received only a cursory look from the Public Accounts committee before it, too, was shut down. Needless to say, there were no committee hearings into Jean Chrétien's business dealings in Shawinigan.§ (Par for the course, I suppose: Chrétien shut down a *judicial inquiry*.)¶

---

* The American version of this is "persons, papers and things."
† Duffy, a Harper appointee as senator, had run up a massive expense bill of dubious propriety, then threatened to go public when pressured to pay the money back. To keep Duffy quiet, the prime minister's chief of staff, Nigel Wright, had personally paid his expenses; the payment was later concealed from an outside auditor. Among other subplots.
‡ The sponsorship scandal, also known as Adscam, involved the diversion of roughly $100 million in federal funds from a program to promote Canadian unity in Quebec to Liberal Party–affiliated advertising agencies and the Quebec wing of the Liberal Party. The scandal led to multiple investigations, criminal charges, and contributed heavily to the Liberal Party's defeat in the 2006 federal election. Incidentally, I am the originator of the name Adscam.
§ In 1988, before his return to politics, Chrétien and some partners had purchased a golf course and adjoining hotel in his hometown of Shawinigan; the hotel was later sold to a friend of Chrétien's. As prime minister he pressured the federal Business Development Bank of Canada to finance an expansion of the hotel with a $2 million loan. The loan would not only have benefited his friend, but arguably would have increased the value of the golf course, in which Chrétien retained an interest.
¶ The inquiry was concerned with abusive behaviour by Canadian soldiers stationed in Somalia in the early 1990s, including the beating death of a Somali teenager.

Government vs. Parliament

Opposition committee members have found themselves no less stymied when they are in the majority on a committee (ie when the government has a minority of the seats in Parliament). It requires no great parliamentary wile for the government to avoid compliance, given the weak enforcement powers of committees. In 2009, under the Harper Conservatives, the "papers" in question had to do with the Afghan prisoners affair. In 2021, under the Trudeau Liberals, the "papers" related to the mysterious dismissal of two Chinese nationals from a top-security infectious disease research laboratory in Winnipeg.*

In each case, the government faced formal demands from the relevant committee, and from Parliament as a whole, to produce documents. In both cases, the government refused, citing national security considerations. Under pressure and seeking to buy time, each government took extraordinary evasive action: Harper, by proroguing Parliament; Trudeau, by dissolving it. Each attempted to stall with offers for an independent arbiter to decide which documents Parliament could see, or by releasing documents in heavily redacted form. Each was rebuked by rulings from the Speaker of the House, who upheld Parliament's absolute right, sanctioned by centuries of precedent, to see whatever documents it pleased[51]. Each government offered a compromise, wherein selected members of Parliament would be given access to certain documents, with a panel of judges deciding which might be released to the public. And in the end—well, MPs did finally see some of the Afghan documents. As they did in the Winnipeg lab business, eventually: after the Speaker ruled that the government was in violation of Parliamentary privilege, after the government was found in contempt of Parliament by a vote of the House, after the government sued the Speaker to prevent the documents' release, and after the election.†

---

* It was later determined they were, in fact, agents of the People's Republic, but not before they had fled back to China.

† In the fall of 2024 the business of the House of Commons was held up for many weeks over the government's latest refusal to provide it with the documents it has demanded, this time in the matter of a scandal at Sustainable Development Technology Canada, a federal agency. The details need not detain us here, but the pattern should.

That wasn't the first time a government was found in contempt of Parliament. That honour belongs to the Harper government, in 2011* for failing to release documents Parliament demanded in relation to the cost of the F-35 fighter-jet contract. Part of the problem is the extraordinary deference accorded to Cabinet confidences in Canadian law—a near-total immunity from judicial scrutiny that, once again, is found in no other parliamentary democracy.[52] It seems plausible this has emboldened successive governments to take the same attitude with Parliament.

But part of it is the general weakness of our parliamentary committees.[53] Committees in the US Congress or in the United Kingdom have real power and prestige, with broad authority to launch investigations and significant powers to compel evidence. They are better funded than their Canadian counterparts, more independent of the executive and have less restrictive terms of reference.

Committees of the Canadian Parliament, by contrast, tend to be either rubber stamps for the government, in a majority Parliament, or toothless talking shops in a minority. There are too many of them, for starters. With twenty-five standing committees, each with twelve members, some meeting twice a week, MPs are stretched thin, especially on the government side, often rotating onto and off committees in quick succession, without the time or the resources to develop the kind of individual and collective expertise that make committees in other legislatures so formidable. Government MPs are further deterred from any latent stirrings of independent action by the presence of ministers' parliamentary secretaries on committees, who act, essentially, as watchdogs for the PMO—part of the all-embracing apparatus of party discipline we will examine in chapter 3.

Committee chairs could potentially offer a bulwark against prime ministerial control, but unfortunately, they have long been co-opted. Since 2002 committee chairs have theoretically been elected by

---

* Not just the first time in Canada: the first time in the Commonwealth.

committee members, but the reality is that they are chosen by the prime minister[54] (or the opposition leader, in the case of the four standing committees where the opposition holds the chair). Committee members, all of them appointed by their respective party leaders, take their cues from them, not least since votes are a matter of public record.*

This cursory sketch of parliamentary futility reaches its nadir with regard to "the business of supply," the fundamental prerogative of parliaments. With MPs handed the estimates weeks before the budget they are supposed to explain, the numbers in each document based on a different accounting system, the process would appear to have almost totally collapsed.[55] There was some attempt a few years ago to repair it, but with limited success: the estimates and the budget are still on different accounting systems (an attempt is now being made to reconcile them via yet a third document). An experiment in publishing the estimates after the budget appears to have ended: as of 2022, the estimates were back on their usual March 1 publication date, well before the April budget.

Budgets, in any event, have ceased to have much relevance, but are simply bloated propaganda sheets. Once, not so many years ago, budgets offered a relatively straightforward rendering of the nation's accounts, together with a few plans and projections for the coming year. Now they are hundreds of pages of bragging salted with dubious accounting and impenetrable bureaucratic jargon, the whole wrapped in colourful photographs of active, smiling families, like a brochure selling life insurance. The spending projections in any given budget almost invariably prove to be ludicrous underestimates, to the tune of billions or tens of billions of dollars, not only in future years, but for the fiscal year in which they are published.

So if MPs were of a mind to exercise the custodial role over the public purse that was the founding purpose of the institution, they couldn't. If, some months after the budget, the government finds

---

* Not that it often comes to that: the chairs are usually chosen by acclamation.

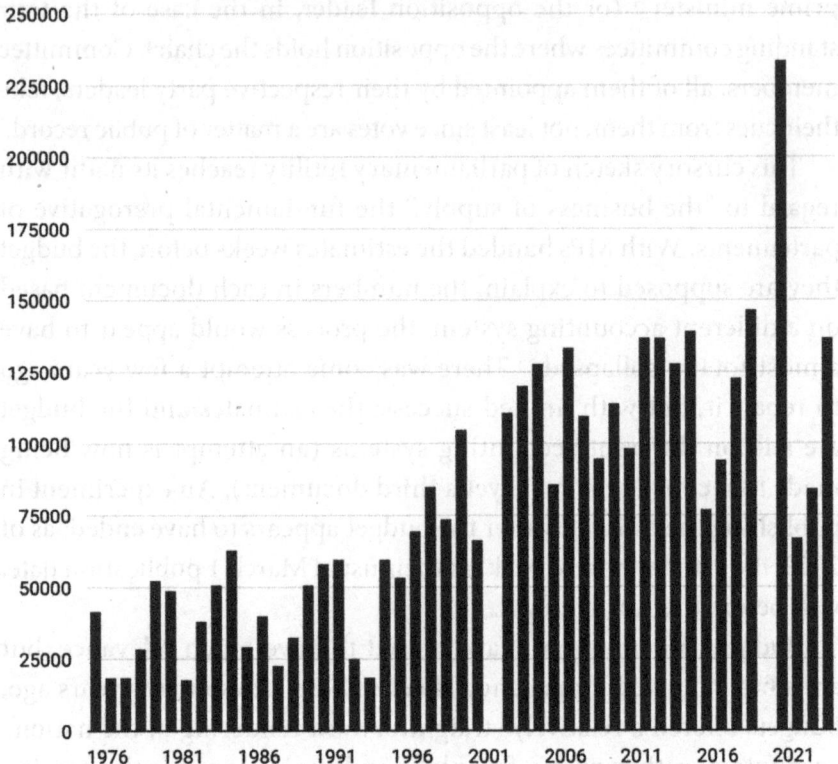

Source: Dept. of Finance Canada, https://budget.canada.ca/home-accueil-en.html

it wants to spend more money than the amount for which it had previously secured Parliament's approval, it has only to introduce a set of supplementary estimates, and another, and another, to be waved through by the same group of befuddled MPs that barely had time to look over the first batch of numbers. Leviathan has left the building.

* * *

In sum, the House of Commons has become little more than an appendage of government, an electoral college that meets to confirm the government in power and is never heard from again, or might

Government vs. Parliament

as well not be, for all the influence it wields. A prime minister in possession of a majority can summon, prorogue, or dissolve Parliament more or less at will, and push through whatever legislation he likes without fear of defeat, amendment, or significant delay. Even in a minority, as we have seen, the prime minister can evade being called to account without much difficulty.

The problem is not that the prime minister has all these powers. It is that they are, every one of them, abused—repeatedly, flagrantly, without remorse, and without consequence. And yet it is hard to separate the one from the other. I suppose it is possible to conceive of a prime minister possessing such vast and unilateral powers—control of the legislative timetable, control of debates, control of committees—without abusing them. But then, as Valéry said, power without abuse loses its charm.

It is difficult to think how any of this could be reformed. Whenever remedies are proposed for this alarming concentration of power, they lean heavily to suggesting that power should be less concentrated. Powers that are now the exclusive preserve of the prime minister, it is often proposed, should be distributed to others, whether the Speaker of the House, or MPs themselves.

How do we stop prime ministers abusing the power of dissolution and prorogation? The authors of *Democratizing the Constitution: Reforming Responsible Government*[56] have an answer: make these subject to votes of the House, by a two-thirds majority, rather than the personal prerogatives of the prime minister.

Is there ambiguity in the confidence convention, such that governments may either declare votes to be matters of confidence that aren't, or ignore votes of non-confidence that manifestly are? Spell these out in law*, they advise, perhaps with a provision for

---

* Alternatively, in a Cabinet Manual, of a kind in use in New Zealand and the UK: an authoritative statement on constitutional conventions and government procedures. This could help clarify several contentious issues, including dissolution and the formation of governments, prorogation, and the role of the Governor General.

"constructive non-confidence" votes—explicit motions of non-confidence, accompanied by a declaration of who would form the government were it to pass.

Are debates cut off too soon, purely to suit the government's interests? Give the power to decide when debate has become dilatory to the Speaker. Are MPs placed in an invidious position by mammoth omnibus bills, bound by no unifying purpose? Give the Speaker the power to order them split.

How do we protect the independence of committees? Elect the chair from a list of all committee members by secret ballot, proposes Michael Chong, the reformist Conservative MP. Let party caucuses, rather than party leaders, decide which members should represent them on committees. Ban parliamentary secretaries from participating. And so forth.

All of these proposed reforms would, in one way or another, limit the powers of the prime minister. Yet they all face the same practical obstacle: they can only be implemented with the prime minister's approval. That doesn't mean reform is impossible. It just means no reform is probable that significantly limits the prime minister's powers.

Indeed, some of these reforms *have* been implemented. But each, in one way or another, was crafted in such a way as to be either ineffective or short-lived. The Speaker was given the power, under a package of reforms introduced by the Liberals in 2017, to sever omnibus bills. Except the reform did not apply to budget implementation bills[57], which are by far the worst offenders. Parliamentary secretaries were dropped from committees, for a time, but were restored after a couple of years. Changes were made to the budget process, as mentioned, but didn't stick.

Or rather, no: the problem isn't the prime minister. Granted, reforms can only be implemented if the prime minister agrees, but reforms are only *necessary* because government MPs refuse to do their job, as members of the legislative branch, of holding the executive to account. Were they to take a more constructive view of their role as members of Parliament—broadly supportive of the direction of government policy, but watchdogs nevertheless against waste, incompetence, and arbitrary rule—prime ministers might not be so quick to abuse their powers, and reform would not be so imperative.

Alternatively, were government MPs more willing to enlist on the side of reform, the prime minister's views would not matter: reform would be imposed upon him. Instead, they have become foot servants to the PM. Opposition MPs are no less obedient to their party leaders. But at least opposition MPs, pious and predictable frauds though they are, have a professional interest in serving as a check on the government's abuse of power. Whereas government MPs seem to think it is their job to collude in it.

Why MPs on either side of the House have become such pliant tools of their respective party leaders is a fascinating story—a mix of institutional design, learned helplessness, self-selection, and ambition—and it is to that we turn next.

3

Leader vs. Caucus

THE PLIGHT OF THE ordinary Canadian Member of Parliament, summed up in one image. The leader of one of the parties rises to speak in Parliament; immediately, all of his MPs leap to their feet, applauding maniacally. At length the applause subsides, and the leader begins to speak. Hardly has he uttered a couple of sentences, however, before his MPs, overwhelmed by the molten brilliance of what they have just heard, again leap up to applaud. A few sentences later, up they pop again. And again. Whenever any of the party leaders so much as open their mouths, the result is standing ovation after standing ovation after standing ovation from their exhausted MPs. They must have thighs of steel by now.

To be sure, MPs will often award each other this accolade, especially during Question Period, where furious ovations, many of them standing, erupt after virtually every question, and some answers—dozens of times, every single day.[*] The same ecstatic response is observed during the part of the parliamentary day devoted to statements from members, when MPs are permitted to make brief

---

[*] After one 2016 Question Period, a reporter counted eighty-five rounds of applause, "twenty-four of which were either full or partial standing ovations." https://www.cbc.ca/news/politics/applause-question-period-wherry-1.3422691

declarations on a variety of subjects. But these are almost peremptory, compared to the adulation showered upon the leaders.

It was not always thus. Until the 1970s, MPs signalled their approval of a speaker via the time-honoured Canadian tradition of thumping the desks in front of them. Television put an end to that: innocent viewers were apparently shocked by the ruckus, prompting the Joe Clark Conservatives to discard the practice. But whereas desk-thumping had limits—you either banged your desk or you didn't—its replacement has been vulnerable to "applause inflation." The ovation that once seemed sufficient in time seems inadequate to the historic greatness of the occasion. So it must be made more vigorous. Then lengthened. Eventually only a standing ovation will do. I expect jumping ovations will be next.

No other democratic country's legislature carries on this way. The British House of Commons is a notoriously raucous place, yet applause (let alone standing ovations) is all but unknown. In fact, it is officially banned, and has been for more than three hundred years.[58] Members instead confine themselves to a brief "hear hear" after a statement that finds their approval. The same is true in Australia and New Zealand. The nearest international equivalent, at least in the democratic world, would be the president's State of the Union speech before the US Congress. But that's only once a year!

If other democratic countries have not succumbed to this disease, it may be because their legislators have not reached the same degraded state as ours. Applause inflation does not fully explain it: there first has to be a culture that validates and requires such extravagant displays of leader-love. It has to be normalized and expected. That Canadian MPs feel peculiarly anxious to fulfill that expectation, and to be *seen* to fulfill it—a chorus of "hear hears" conveys a certain anonymity, whereas it is painfully obvious whether or not an individual MP has jumped to his feet—is a statement of their uniquely servile relationship to their leaders.

Parties have their place, of course, and a party with no ideology or identity would serve little purpose. Political party affiliation helps voters understand what a candidate stands for; research shows a candidate's individual merits lag far behind party and leader as factors in determining voter choices. It is natural to expect that a candidate elected under a party banner should broadly support the party and the policies once elected.

Clear party identities provide voters with distinct choices. When it is evident which party stands for what, it is easier to hold them to account. Parties also facilitate bargaining and compromise among their members, without which it would be difficult, if not impossible, to assemble majority support behind a particular proposal, or to govern. Without the discipline of party, at worst, MPs would be free to sell their votes to the highest bidder, or trade them for favours. A House made up of three hundred forty-three (as of the next Parliament—there are three hundred thirty-eight currently) fully independent operators would be a madhouse.

The argument here is not that parties are unnecessary, or that MPs should never be obliged to vote the party line—only that in Canada we have taken party discipline to an absurd extreme. Experts agree[59] that Canadian members of Parliament have less independence from party control, enjoy fewer opportunities for individual agency or initiative, and are generally more in the thrall of the party and the party leader than their counterparts in other democratic countries. As the political scientist Alex Marland writes, in *Whipped: Party Discipline in Canada*,[60] "Political parties are essential for keeping large numbers of politicians organized; however, the systematic integration of politicians is so successful that some believe Canada has the most rigid party discipline of any liberal democracy."

Just as a party without unity has little purpose, MPs without autonomy are superfluous. What is the point of sending a representative to Ottawa from each riding if they are all obliged to vote the same way? What is the point of electing humans if they are not permitted to exercise their human faculties? What character of representative is likely to volunteer for such an assignment? Whether MPs should represent the wishes of their constituents or their own judgment and conscience—whether they should be "delegates" or "trustees"—is an old debate. But they cannot represent either their constituents or their own judgment so long as they are slaves to the party whip.

The usual measure of this is how much or how little MPs deviate from the majority of their party in votes in Parliament. A 2020 study of voting records in the 42nd Parliament (2015-19), carried out by the Samara Centre for Democracy, found the average Canadian MP voted with his or her party fully 99.6 percent of the time.[61] Only one in five MPs went against their party on even half a dozen votes, out of nearly a thousand in total. The most independent-minded MP in the House bucked his party on just 3.4 percent of votes; no other MP dissented so much as 2 percent of the time.

Contrast with the UK's Parliament. The 3.4 percent anti-party voting record that marks the height of rebelliousness in Canada's Parliament would not rank among the top fifty in the typical British Parliament.[62] On average, nearly one in five British MPs in any given Parliament break with their parties at least 2 percent of the time—a mark surpassed by just one MP in Canada. In the US, likewise, data showing members of Congress now vote with the majority of their party roughly 95 percent of the time—an increase of 20 percentage points since the 1970s—is seen as evidence of the growing polarization of American politics on partisan lines.[63] What on earth would they make of the near-unanimity found in Canada?

Here again, current practice departs not just from international norms, but from our own past. In the first decades after Confederation, MPs often declined to follow the whip. Sir John A. Macdonald famously referred to those independent-minded MPs as "loose fish." Macdonald's first government was defeated eighteen times in the House. This was not necessarily out of an abundance of principle: members seemed concerned mostly to trade their vote for the patronage and pork barrel benefits that were presumed to follow.[64]

Party discipline increased after the turn of the century, spurred partly by rule changes in the House[65], partly by the rise of third and fourth parties: with less margin for error, MPs were given less room to stray. All the same, it was not until after the Second World War that party-line voting became the universal norm. And, by all accounts, it has grown more absolute since then. We have the most severe regime of party discipline of any of the democracies, and it has never been as severe as now.

The remarkable thing about this insistence on absolute conformity has been that it has occurred at a time when successive governments have gone to considerable lengths to disavow it. The Conservatives came to power in 2006 promising "all votes in Parliament, except the budget and main estimates," would be "free votes,"[66] meaning ordinary members (outside Cabinet) would not be required to vote with the government. When the Liberals replaced them in government in 2015, they, too, promised to "make free votes in the House of Commons standard practice," albeit with several exceptions: not only budgets and other traditional confidence measures, but also bills that enacted items in the Liberal election platform and "those that address our shared values and the protections guaranteed by the Charter of Rights and Freedoms."

(That's neat: by the time you've got through the platform with its hundreds of commitments, plus the budget—especially given the tendency of governments, as noted in chapter 2, to stuff much of their legislative agenda into a single omnibus budget bill—plus whatever "our shared values" means, there's not a great deal left. Still, in principle it marks an expansion of the traditional domain of free votes, which have hitherto been limited to so-called conscience issues[67]: capital punishment, abortion, assisted suicide, and, er, the design of a new flag.)

How to square this bipartisan commitment to allowing MPs to vote more freely with the bipartisan record of near-total uniformity? Free votes, it seems, are never truly free. The party leadership may have notionally relaxed the usual requirement to vote as the party instructs, but members of caucus will know that any display of disloyalty will be noted and remembered. If they are unlikely to be subject to the rougher sorts of penalties for voting against the party line (a veto on their candidacy in the next election, or even expulsion from caucus) they may nevertheless find themselves cut out from plum committee assignments, say, or the better office locations, or appointments as Cabinet ministers or parliamentary secretaries—or, on the opposition side, as critics ("shadow ministers"). Ambition, I repeat, more than the whip, is the real enforcer of party discipline.

There is also a strong element of self-selection involved. Given all that has been written about the diminished role of MPs, anyone who is willing to run as a candidate for one of the major parties has displayed, in so doing, a certain taste for subservience. Those who retain a lingering independent streak will soon find themselves winnowed out by one means or another, either in the course of being vetted by party officials, or in the arbitrary, opaque, and sometimes corrupt process by which the parties contrive to nominate candidates in the ridings (more on this in chapter 7).

And any who survive *that* with their self-respect intact will have it beaten out of them, not necessarily by the leadership, but by their fellow MPs. Peer pressure has at least as much to do with keeping MPs in line as any edict from the party hierarchy. MPs who feel an urge to rock the boat will soon find themselves confronted by other members of caucus, gently reminding them that politics is a "team sport" in which it is essential to be a "team player." This is a formidable incentive for compliance. A person of conscience may be willing to sacrifice his or her own career for a principle, but it takes a much stronger constitution to be willing to jeopardize the careers of others, and to suffer the blowback that ensues. When Justin Trudeau expelled Jody Wilson-Raybould and Jane Philpott from the Liberal caucus for calling out his abuse of power in the SNC-Lavalin affair, it met with enthusiastic cheers from other caucus members[68].

This culture of conformity did not spring from nowhere. It is a form of learned helplessness. The MPs who take it as their duty to enforce party discipline on their colleagues are themselves the product of a system in which they are under the constant surveillance and control of the party from before they are even nominated. Votes in Parliament are only a small part of it. In the modern era, Marland argues, much more importance is attached to "message discipline," in which the party seeks to control an MP's every utterance, inside Parliament or out[69]. Caucus members are required to repeat party messaging not only in speeches (when they are not actually written for them), but also in press releases, panel appearances, social media posts, and the like. MPs are expected to parrot the party line, almost verbatim: the same "message tracks," the same slogans and catchphrases, the same buzzwords. Those who do are rewarded. Those who do not find that politics is a lonely business.

"Discipline permeates almost all aspects of politics in Canada, especially communications," Marland writes. "The corollary of communications technology focusing more attention on party leaders is that most of Canada's elected representatives are increasingly peripheral actors. . . . The anthropomorphism of parrots who learn to repeat phrases and buzzwords is replacing the time-worn comparison of Canadian backbenchers to trained seals who vote according to the party whip's instructions."[70]

(Party officials blame the media. If the media were not so quick, they say, to demand leaders account for every gaffe or glitch by every MP, candidate, or official, then leaders would not have to keep them on such a tight leash. There's some truth in that. On the other hand, if party leaders were not so visibly determined to police their MPs' public statements, they would not be held responsible for the odd remark that might come out of the odd mouth.)

The most visible expression of this is in the daily Question Period. What once was an opportunity for individual members to question ministers or flag issues of concern to their constituents has become yet another vehicle for party branding, with MPs as willing messengers. The questions are rarely questions, in the sense of requests for information, but statements— "when will the minister resign?"—masquerading as questions. The answers are almost never answers, but opportunities to talk about whatever else the minister would prefer to talk about, or to make tu quoque attacks on the opposition. While the speaker may rule out a question that does not address an issue within a minister's administrative responsibility, ministers are not held to a similar standard of relevance in their answers.

The absurd time limits on both questions and answers—just thirty-five seconds for each—adds to the frenetic air: where the UK and Australian equivalents of Question Period run to about twenty questions a day[71], it is not uncommon to see Canadian parliamentarians rip through more than forty[72]. But as many of these amount to repetitions of the same question two or three times—MPs in Canada are allowed follow-ups—perhaps it amounts to the same thing.

The strong impression that everyone is going through the motions is reinforced by the modern practice, once frowned upon, of reading from prepared notes. The effect is particularly comic in those egregious lobs from government backbenchers, inviting the responsible minister to tell Canadians what a magnificent job the government is doing on this or that file. Both the question and the response were likely written by party communications staff; it is entirely possible they were written by the same person.

Worse still is the behaviour of MPs while this is going on: braying, catcalling, heckling witlessly, shaking their jowls in feigned outrage, nodding their heads in feigned approval, gasping in feigned astonishment at pretended "revelations," like characters in a Christmas pantomime. The whole performance is profoundly alienating, and disturbing. These are, after all, adults behaving in this degrading fashion, and being encouraged to do so. It's the kind of behaviour no self-respecting person would engage in, the self-destructive "acting out" of people who have lost any sense of purpose or meaning in their lives, with neither the respect of their peers nor useful work to sustain them—hysteria, born of despair.

And yet this is the part of the parliamentary day to which the most attention is paid, the part for which the parties spend the most time preparing in advance, and reviewing afterward. Was ever so much labour expended to such self-destructive purpose? For as much as the parties might think to poke holes in their opponents' position, the greater consequence is to cast them all into disrepute. Certainly it does little, in its present form, to hold the government to account, or to illuminate much of anything, other than the slough into which MPs have descended. The public sees it for the phony partisan spectacle it is and tunes it out.

* * *

The easiest way to see how uniquely awful Canada's Question Period has become is to watch the British equivalent. The contrast is stunning. At Westminster, the questions are generally questions, the answers something at least resembling an answer. The two sides seem to be listening, and talking, to each other, rather than to the air, framing their thoughts in response to what was said rather than reading what is written on the paper in front of them. It's contentious, even brawling, but in a high-spirited, respectful way—the respect accorded others by people who respect themselves.

Why the difference? Part of the explanation lies in the different layouts of the two chambers. The British House of Commons is significantly more compact, not to say crowded, than its Canadian equivalent. While the centre aisle separating the two sides is the same width, at 13 feet (3.96 metres, supposedly two sword lengths)[73], frontbenchers in the British House actually sit several feet closer together than their counterparts in the Canadian House, without the heavy wooden desks that guard every Canadian MP's seat. (British MPs, from the prime minister to the lowliest backbencher, sit on simple padded benches, without accoutrements of any kind.) The British House, moreover, while about the same length as the Canadian House, is appreciably narrower: only 45 ½ feet (13.8 metres) in width, versus the Canadian House's 52 ½ feet (16 metres). Indeed, it is too small to hold all of its 650 members, there being space for only about about two-thirds that number. This is deliberate. After the House was destroyed by a bomb in the Second World War, Churchill gave instructions that the rebuilt House should have fewer places than members, in order that there should be "on great occasions a sense of crowd and urgency."[74]

The result is to make the British House a more intimate space than ours, with palpable effect on its inmates' conduct (as Churchill observed, "We shape our buildings, and afterwards our buildings shape us.")[75] Notably, it seems to encourage a greater civility, or at least a rough comity. It is harder to shout down your opponents when they are, as it were, in your face, rather than halfway across a vast expanse. The absence of desks also plays a part. The benches in the British House are reminiscent of church pews, or councils of elders—places for humble rumination and deliberation. Rows upon rows of desks, by contrast, suggest nothing so much as a middle school classroom. Is it purely coincidence that MPs so often behave in kind?

Another factor may be the differences in how television cameras are deployed in the two parliaments. Television has arguably done great harm to the Canadian House, the first in the world to broadcast its proceedings live[76] (Britain followed more than a decade later). It is surely significant that the age in which Parliament last mattered predates its broadcast.

Why? Look at it from the point of view of a Member of Parliament asking a question or giving a speech in the Commons. Before 1977, when the television cameras first intruded, who was your audience? Who were you trying to persuade, or impress? Who graded you on your performance? It was the people within its walls—your fellow MPs, plus the press gallery. That was your world: people who were committed to Parliament, and knowledgeable about its traditions, and who themselves believed in its importance. For it was their world, too.

Perhaps they were wrong to believe this. Perhaps it was no more important, objectively, than it is now. But they believed that it was and, believing it to be so, acted accordingly. And as it was important to its participants, so that importance was communicated to the country, which, not having been exposed to the more mundane reality, had no evidence to the contrary. If it was a delusion, it was a shared delusion. More, it was a *necessary* delusion.

Consider what it means to speak in Parliament today. You are only notionally speaking to your fellow MPs. You are acutely aware that your real audience is the viewers at home, or at least the television producers waiting to select a clip for the news—or today, social media. So much of what goes on in Question Period these days seems designed to generate clickbait for online partisans, little snippets of dialogue that can be ripped out of context to make your guys look good or, ideally, the other guys look bad. As the outside world intrudes, the chamber itself dwindles in significance, along with everything that happens within; it is not the world, just a particularly shouty corner of it.

To make matters worse, the rules governing the parliamentary television service allow only a single, fixed camera on whoever is speaking at the time. This presents a stilted, distorted version of what is going on. Witness the little charade wherein a platoon of a speaker's colleagues rearrange themselves to occupy the empty chairs around him, to create the illusion that he is speaking to a packed House, and not the handful of MPs usually in attendance. The public has been given the pretense of a direct, unfiltered broadcast of Parliament; in fact, it is as if we were viewing it through a straw.

In other parliaments, Britain's among them, cameras are allowed to cover the proceedings more as they do other events, with cutaways, reaction shots, and movement. If an MP makes a slighting reference to another member, there is a quick cut to the face of the intended target. It is both more compelling to watch, and more real. It makes flesh and blood out of what otherwise comes across as two-dimensional. The lesson is clear. Having let the cameras in, we should let them all the way in.

There is a more fundamental reason for the differences in the two parliaments, however. British MPs are in a variety of ways less under the thumb of their respective party leaders. They can, for example, pose their own questions at Question Time. To do so, they have only

Leader vs. Caucus

to "catch the Speaker's eye"—that's why you see them bobbing up and down in their place after every question.* The Speaker decides who to call next. To ask a question in the Canadian House, on the other hand, you have to get on one of the lists compiled by the party whips in advance of each session, to which the Speaker is obliged to adhere—the rule since the 1970s. In this as in all things, in Canada, the party decides.

The same applies to members' statements. Formerly the Speaker's prerogative, the lists of members eligible to make statements on any given day are now maintained by the party whips. As a result, MPs now commonly use these opportunities not to raise issues of concern to their constituents, as they might have in the past, but to slag off their opponents, repeat party catchphrases and talking points, and otherwise beclown themselves.

Even private members' bills have been consumed by the all-devouring leader's office. There was a time when private members' business—the consideration of bills and motions presented by ordinary MPs—was a good part of what Parliament did. From 1867 to 1906, private members took precedence over government business three days a week, to the government's increasing displeasure. As the role of government grew, and government business began to occupy more of the House's time, private members' business was whittled back: to two days a week, to eight days per session, to one hour per day, to one hour some days.[77]

In parallel with the shrinkage in the speaking time allotted members is the shrinking proportion of the legislative agenda they are permitted to occupy. Members of the US Congress are judged by the number and significance of the bills they manage to pass. Canadian members of Parliament are lucky if they get one bill put to a vote—in their careers, never mind in a given year. It's not hard to see why. To

---

* The practice is broadly the same in Australia. MPs in the UK can also submit questions through a lottery, known as a "shuffle."

be eligible for consideration, a private member's bill has to be picked in a lottery, held at the beginning of each session; to get to the floor of the Commons, it must survive a special committee's ruling on its "notability"; and once on the floor, it often falls victim to the vagaries of the parliamentary schedule, held in abeyance while government bills are given higher priority, only to die on the order paper at the end of a session. Of the dozens of bills that might be passed in the course of a typical Parliament, only a handful originate with private members,[78] most of them fluff along the lines of "An Act Respecting National Seal Products Day." Over the last four decades an average of just over three private members' bills have passed in the Parliament of Canada each year, versus the more than eight that passed annually in the British Parliament.*

* * *

A Canadian Member of Parliament, then, would seem a curious sort of representative. Their job is not to represent their constituents, but to represent the party: to vote as they are told, to speak the lines they are given, to applaud on cue. Tellingly, MPs themselves seem neither to understand their role, nor to be able to articulate it.

In 2014, the Samara Centre published a landmark report entitled *Tragedy in the Commons* based on exit interviews with eighty former members of Parliament on their experiences of public life. Authors Alison Loat and Michael MacMillan were surprised to find that the former MPs "held often-conflicting ideas regarding the role and purpose of a Member of Parliament." They had served, on average, more than ten years in the House of Commons, yet they could not agree on the basic question of "what they were elected to accomplish or what the essential purpose of their role was intended to be."[79]

---

* The figures in both cases refer to bills introduced in the House of Commons, that were then passed by both houses. https://lop.parl.ca/sites/ParlInfo/default/en_CA/legislation/privateMembersBills; https://commonslibrary.parliament.uk/research-briefings/sn04568/

Some said it was to represent the views of the people in their ridings. Some thought it was to exercise their own best judgment. For others, it was to advance the interests of their party. Still others said it was to "bring their own personal identities into Parliament," or to change how politics was done. Altogether, Loat and MacMillan reported, the former MPs used an "astonishing variety of terms and concepts to describe the position," likening it variously to being an "administrator, doctor, priest, teacher, ambassador, social worker, messenger, spokesperson and lobbyist." [80]

What almost none of them did was to describe themselves as *legislators*, or their job as involving any of a Member of Parliament's three historic roles: to "consider, refine and pass" legislation; to hold government to account, notably for how it spends public funds; and to decide whether the government should remain in office. "None of the MPs," Samara's authors write, "described their jobs in terms consistent with the traditional Westminster definition, and only a few were even close."

Pressed on what actual purpose they served, MPs typically retreated into what might be called the constituency-office defence. As in, I may not get much done in Ottawa, but think of all the good work I do back in my riding, writing letters on behalf of constituents, helping them navigate the bureaucracy and whatnot. But are these really the sorts of things we elect people to Parliament to do? Most could be more efficiently handled by a junior assistant.

Indeed, it is arguably improper. It is hard to square the idea of MPs poking their noses into decisions about immigration or employment insurance and throwing their weight around on behalf of their constituents, with the ideal of an independent and impartial bureaucracy, immune from personal or political influence. As Loat and MacMillan observe, "in other countries where politicians interact with government in such a manner, those activities are referred to as corruption."[81]

If the process of government has become too complex and impenetrable for the average person to deal with on their own, the job of MPs is to fix the process: to change the laws, or reform how they are administered, not to act as "customer service rep for the federal government." That MPs nevertheless conceive of their role, or feel the need to justify it in such terms is a reflection of how little function is left to them as legislators.

How did it come to this? How did members of parliament, once so independent, become so wholly the creatures of the party, such obedient servants of the party leader? It has been a gradual process, to be sure, but two dates stand out in particular.

The first is 1919, the year the Liberal national convention elected Mackenzie King as leader[82]. It was the first convention of its kind (the Conservatives were to follow in 1927). Previously, party leaders in Canada had been chosen by the caucus, as they are in the classic Westminster model, if not by a formal vote, then by an informal sounding.* Since the King convention, leaders have been chosen by the party at large. At first, this was the task of delegates, elected from each riding, at a party's national convention. Latterly, the choice has been entrusted to direct election by the membership—or rather, by the membership plus the tens of thousands of new members recruited by the various candidates in the course of the campaign. The Liberal leadership race that elected Justin Trudeau in 2013 did not even require that voters be members. It was sufficient that they declare themselves "supporters."

Direct election may seem more democratic. But the practical effect of it is to make the leader accountable to no one. The members have their say and are gone, never to trouble the leader again. It's a presidential-style system for a presidential-style leader: the focus of media attention, the fount of authority, the centre of the political universe. Under the old system a prime minister had to pay close attention to the concerns of ordinary MPs, since he could be removed by caucus at any time, and replaced by caucus just as quickly. By

---

* Usually conducted by the previous leader, whose own preferences often proved decisive.

contrast a leader in possession of a mandate from the membership is free to thumb his nose at the caucus for years at a stretch, with only the occasional confirmation vote by the party, in which the leader typically runs unopposed, to disturb his Augustan reign.

Certainly, the leader is not accountable to the party's MPs, the people it is his job at most times to lead: though he controls every aspect of their working lives, *they* have no say in choosing *him*. Party caucuses in Canada are regularly saddled with leaders they cannot abide and would not have chosen if it were left to them. Government with the consent of the governed is democratic holy writ, everywhere except in the seat of democracy, Parliament.

Leadership-races-as-membership-drives have many failings, which we'll revisit in more detail in chapter 7. They are lengthy, costly, divisive, and prone to corruption. They expose the party to takeover by extremists and single-issue interest groups. But the biggest impact of choosing the leader this way has been to irrevocably alter the relationship between the leader and the caucus—although its impact would not have been so profound without a second, complementary change in the rules, this one governing how MPs are elected.

The date to remember here is 1970: the year the Elections Act was amended to require, for the first time, that the name of the party appear on the ballot beside the name of the candidate. Until then—it seems hard to imagine now—only the candidate's name (and occupation!) appeared. A second, crucial change required candidates to obtain the endorsement of the party leader before their name could appear on the ballot.

The result, if not the intent, was to give the party leader a personal and absolute veto over the nomination of every member of caucus. No longer was the selection of a party's candidate in a constituency up to the local riding association—not even when it came to incumbent MPs. It didn't matter how long they had represented the riding, or how popular they were with the members. Without the leader's signature on their nomination papers, they could not run. The implication was, and is, clear: step out of line and you will not be an MP.*

The leader dominates caucus, then, not just because members of caucus do not choose the leader, but because the leader, in essence, chooses them. Members owe their seats entirely to the leader, dependent for their very livelihoods on the sunshine of his love. Caucus revolts are accordingly rare. Only when the situation is truly life-threatening, electorally speaking, can members pluck up the courage to face down the leader, and then only if enough of them manage to move together: otherwise, they will be picked off, one by one.

All of the other encroaching powers of the leader—to control how an MP votes, to dictate what an MP says, to decide what positions the party will take and so on—stem from these twin provisions, and the power imbalance they imply. Much of what is wrong with Canadian politics, in turn, flows from that leader dominance. When the position of the party at any given time is whatever the leader says it is, is it any wonder that our politics is so unprincipled, so lacking in definition? And is it any wonder that in the absence of principled differences between the parties, raw partisanship takes its place?

* * *

The many and various ways in which party leaders impose their will on their respective caucuses—the world's most rigid system of party discipline, surpassed only by the *suffocating* regime of message discipline—are therefore only the symptoms: the disease is the power imbalance between them.

How to treat the symptoms is simple enough: broadly, reverse what I have described above. Rather than leave it to party lists supplied by

---

* This provision was modified somewhat by the Reform Act 2014 (see below). As originally drafted the bill would have transferring this power to a "nomination officer," one for each province. As passed, however, the power is reserved to "the person or persons authorized by the party." Which, if it doesn't mean the leader, means the leader's designate.

the Prime Minister's Office to decide who gets to ask questions in Question Period or make statements in members' statements, entrust the matter again to the Speaker, as of old. Enforce the existing rule against reading speeches—again, a matter for the Speaker—and party staffers would soon stop writing them.

Question Period could be improved in other ways[83]. Allowing more time for each question, and each answer, would surely make for more thoughtful, less barky exchanges. Similarly, it might be worth adopting the British system of reserving days for questioning particular ministers, rather than obliging the entire Cabinet to show up every day on the off chance someone might lob a question their way.

We might even consider remodelling the Commons chamber on Westminster lines—rip out the desks, that is, and move the benches closer together—with a view to creating a more intimate, conversational tone. (We will be forced to confront this question someday, as the number of MPs expands.) We could also remove some of the more obtuse restrictions on television cameras in the House: allowing the cameras to capture a more accurate picture of what goes on would deter some of the bad behaviour, and dispel some convenient fictions.

Reform of the confidence convention, as discussed in chapter 2, would reduce the ability of prime ministers to use the threat of dissolution as a stick with which to beat government MPs into line. Increasing the ratio of backbenchers to frontbenchers, either by increasing the number of MPs, or by reducing the size of the Cabinet and Shadow Cabinet, would take care of the carrot side of the equation.

Last, we might ask, not why there should be so many whipped votes, but why should there be any? Cabinet members are obliged to vote with the government—Cabinet solidarity (see chapter 4) and all that—but why should that extend to MPs on the backbench? For a lot of people, this is self-evident. A party, they believe, is defined by the positions it takes on certain questions of policy. If MPs are free to vote as they please, voters might be confused about where a party stands. Worse, the party might be seen to be divided, lacking direction. Only the leader can provide direction, so it is not only the right of the party leader to enforce the party line, it is his duty—a test of his leadership, in fact. The media are prominent in promoting this line. When an MP or MPs dissent from the leader's position, we tend to report it in strongly negative, crisis-laden terms: the party is "divided," we say. The leader's position is "under challenge."

That is certainly one way a political party can function. It is just not the only way. It may be how our parties have tended to behave, but that does not mean they must continue to do so. Consider an alternative definition of party: simply, a group of people who share the same broad political outlook. That does not mean they must agree on everything, or that everyone must agree on anything. It just means that, on the whole, there is more that unites them than divides them, and more that they hold in common with each other than with members of other parties.

Nothing would preclude such a party from taking a stand on any given issue. Nothing would require it to insist on unanimity, either. If a small number of the party's MPs were to vote a different way, so what? It would not detract from the party's general support for the policy. If, on the other hand, the party were genuinely divided on an issue, what would be the point of pretending otherwise? Why take a stand as a party if the party, as such, does not have a view?

What about budgets? A government could hardly carry on if its broad program of spending and taxation had been rejected by the House; MPs should reasonably be expected to vote with their party on these and other matters of confidence. Another exception might be major platform planks. If an MP gets elected based on the party's position on an issue, shouldn't he be obliged, morally at least, to vote with it when it comes before the House? Yes, if that's the position the MP took at the time. But why should a party's candidates have to stand behind every line of its platform? Should they not be allowed to say: I support my party's position on *those* issues, but not on *these*?

But all of these, as I say, amount to treating the symptoms, rather than the disease—the underlying power imbalance that permits the

Leader vs. Caucus

leader to dominate the caucus. Indeed, unless you treat the disease, you *can't* treat the symptoms. The leaders won't allow it. Treating the disease means correcting the two main sources of that power imbalance: restoring the power of MPs to choose the leader, and removing the leader's power to veto their nomination, or expel them from caucus.

Yet both proposals run into opposition, not least from MPs themselves. Why, they ask, should the choice of the leader be left to . . . them? Isn't it more democratic to have the leader chosen by the rank and file rather than by a small clique of MPs? I suppose it depends in part on your concept of democracy. Each of those MPs was nominated by perhaps hundreds of party members, and elected by thousands or tens of thousands of citizens. It is their job to represent those people, and one of the most important ways they can do so is by holding party leaders to account. Most people aren't in a position to do that, at least on a day to day basis. MPs can. That's what they're there for: to ensure our leaders are accountable, not just on election day, every four years, but—again—every day in between.

That even MPs themselves cannot grasp this concept shows how fully they have absorbed the idea that they are, essentially, the leader's employees, insignificant nobodies with no business assuming such exalted responsibilities. The logic is, as usual, circular. The reason members of Parliament are regarded as insignificant nobodies is because our politics has become so leader-obsessed. And a big part of caucus's decline is due to the loss of the power to hire and fire the leader. Give that power back to caucus, and those nobodies will become somebodies in a hurry.

In the same way, they ask, why should a leader be expected to put up with an MP who was damaging the party's "brand"? There's a germ of truth to this: in theory, a riding could nominate a candidate so abhorrent to the party that it would have no choice but to withdraw its imprimatur. But why should that be the prerogative of the leader, or his designate? Why not, say, a vote of the other riding associations? Or of caucus?

Yet here we run into the same dilemma as in the previous chapter. Even if MPs were convinced of the need for these reforms, the leaders would still have to approve them—the very people who stand to lose the most from any such change. This is the ever-present paradox of reform: the same stifling control from the top that makes reform necessary also makes it impossible.

And while in theory it should be possible for MPs to rise up in revolt, in practice they generally choose not to. This is the other paradox of reform: the people who stand to benefit most from it show the least interest in it. The experience of the Reform Act, 2014 is instructive.* As drafted by Conservative MP Michael Chong, the bill aimed to redress the leader-caucus imbalance in four specific ways: by reserving to caucus the power to expel or readmit a member, to elect or remove a caucus chair, to remove the leader, and to elect an interim leader.

This immediately raised several objections. Some rejected the whole purpose of reducing the power of the leader. Others objected less to the ends than the means: they opposed regulating the internal affairs of political parties, which they maintained were "private organizations." But the most fundamental objection was rooted in the paradox mentioned above. What is the point, critics scoffed, of asking MPs to do by act of Parliament what they are unwilling to do on their own: defy their leaders? If they were willing to do that, you wouldn't need legislation.

That the bill passed, in the end, both proved and disproved this objection. Although every party leader professed support for the bill in public, behind the scenes word was put out that it should be gutted. To avoid defeat, Chong was forced to water the bill down in various ways. A clause that would have taken the power to approve or reject candidates away from the leader was amended in a way that left the leader in effective control (see note above). Another clause was added,

---

* As it is called: it was not passed until 2015.

making the whole thing optional: the only requirement was for each party caucus, in its first meeting after every election, to hold a vote on whether to arm itself with each of the bill's four powers.

Alas, the bill contained no provision for a secret ballot, nor any method of ensuring caucuses held the votes as required. The caucuses, accordingly, took instruction from their leaders. In the Act's first test, immediately after the 2015 election, the Liberal and NDP caucuses did not bother to hold a vote.* The Conservatives did, voting to give themselves three of the four powers; the exception was the power to remove the leader. After the disappointment of the 2021 election, however, Conservative MPs voted to acquire that tool, too. Almost immediately, they put it to use, removing Erin O'Toole as their leader.

So change is possible. The efficiency of O'Toole's toppling—it was all done inside of two days, start to finish—was a watershed moment in Canadian politics. Other party caucuses have forced out their leaders (as Justin Trudeau can now attest),† but only after long and debilitating internal conflicts, with no process, no rules, and no benchmark of what would be a sufficient level of caucus dissatisfaction to trigger the leader's exit. The whole caucus might want the leader gone, yet no one wants to be the first to put their head above the parapet. So everyone creeps about in the shadows, taking anonymous shots at the leader in the media, without dislodging him. This can go on for months, even years.

By providing certainty and structure to the process, the Reform Act reduced the cost of leadership changes; by making the caucus less hesitant to replace its leader, it made future Conservative leaders less likely to run roughshod over their MPs. In time, that might embolden Conservative caucus members to demand other reforms. And, in

---

* The NDP eventually got around to voting the following year, rejecting all four provisions.

† Although it is rare: Erin O'Toole was just the fourth opposition leader to be removed against his will, after John Diefenbaker, Joe Clark, and Thomas Mulcair. Prime ministers who were toppled by their party are even rarer. Prior to Justin Trudeau, there had been only two: Jean Chrétien and Mackenzie Bowell.

time, members of other party caucuses may come to wonder why they should not enjoy the same powers and freedoms as the Conservatives.

Still, the revolution is at best half complete. Caucus may have the power to remove the leader, but the power to elect a new leader remains with the membership at large. That poses an important continuing obstacle to leadercide. Dump the leader, and you tip the party into a costly, months-long bloodletting—it took seven months to elect a replacement for O'Toole, which was at least shorter than the previous two Conservative races*—with no guarantee the new leader will be better than the last. That suggests caucus's new power will remain the nuclear option: so awful as to be unusable.

Only when caucus also has the power to elect a new leader will the balance between caucus and leader be fully restored. Too radical? It's the way Westminster systems are supposed to work—the way our system did work, for much of our history. It's how it works in many other democracies. It's not unusual or outmoded. The majority and minority leaders in both the US House of Representatives and the Senate are elected by the members of their respective caucuses, and can be removed by them. The same is true of party leaders in Japan, as well as New Zealand and Australia[84]—although the Australian Labour Party now uses a hybrid system, combining the caucus and the membership at large. Similarly, in Britain both the Conservative Party and the Labour Party involve the parliamentary caucus in choosing the candidates to be put to a vote of the membership.

There are any number of other reforms that could be made to our democracy, but they all depend on ordinary MPs having the pluck to vote for them. So long as they remain the willing pawns of the party leaders, they never will. The Conservatives have taken a big step toward fixing that. But many more such steps will be needed.

---

* Between October 19, 2015, when Stephen Harper resigned as leader, and September 10, 2022, when Pierre Poilievre was elected as leader—a period in which the party went through three leadership races—the Conservatives were without a permanent leader for nearly thirty-six months, or 42 percent of the total.

4

Prime Minister vs. Cabinet

MOST OF OUR PRIME ministers have been scoundrels: the great ones, almost exclusively. From the brazen opportunist Sir John A. Macdonald, to the oily equivocator Sir Wilfrid Laurier, to that unctuous hypocrite William Lyon Mackenzie King, our greatest political leaders have been, if not utterly ruthless, then not, shall we say, overburdened with ruth.

On occasion, this habit of taking ethical shortcuts has tipped into outright corruption. Think of Sir John A. desperately pleading for "another $10,000" in illicit campaign contributions from his patron, Sir Hugh Allan, in the Pacific Scandal. Or Brian Mulroney's furtive receipt, weeks after leaving office, of $300,000 in cash from the lobbyist Karlheinz Schreiber, on whose behalf he had long been suspected of tilting a major Air Canada (at the time state-owned) jet purchase.

More often corruption has meant not outright criminality but abuse of power. Recent decades have witnessed an accelerating decline in political mores among our leaders, notably in the alacrity with which they have taken to betraying not only their principles or their friends, but the public. We have discussed some of these already. Jean Chrétien pressured the federal Business Development Bank to make a loan to a friend to renovate a hotel next door to a golf course in his riding in which he had a part interest. Stephen Harper's chief of staff paid $90,000 under the table to a Conservative senator, Mike Duffy, to keep his expense troubles from coming to light. Justin Trudeau leaned on his attorney general to improperly intervene in a criminal case on behalf of a Liberal-connected company, SNC-Lavalin.

All three incidents blew up into major political controversies, to be sure. And yet, no further consequences ensued. The prime ministers were not charged, or censured by Parliament, or even made to appear before a parliamentary committee. There was no question of them stepping down. We have had premiers driven from office by scandal in this country, but no prime minister since Macdonald.

Other world leaders are periodically brought to account for their misdeeds. In recent years, the current or former presidents of the United States, France, Brazil, South Africa, South Korea, Peru, Argentina, and Ukraine, among others, along with the prime ministers of Pakistan, Italy, and Great Britain have all either been prosecuted, forced out, or both in connection with corruption scandals. Nothing of the kind has happened in Canada.

It used to be said, at the time of Watergate, that a scandal of that magnitude could not happen in Canada—a prime minister caught doing what Richard Nixon did, if he were not forced to resign, would be swiftly deposed by a confidence vote in the House of Commons. But the opposite is true. He would very likely not be caught, and if he were, there would be no equivalent mechanism to the special counsels and congressional committees that brought Nixon low. Still less would he be subject to the humiliation of large numbers of his own party's legislators asserting his guilt and demanding his ouster.

On the evidence of recent political scandals, governing party MPs instead would be instructed to delay, deflect, and otherwise stonewall any investigation. Committee hearings would be prematurely shut down. Police investigations would be stymied. Occasionally, a prime minister might be shamed or bullied into calling a public inquiry. But always at his discretion, and on his terms.

Prime Minister vs. Cabinet

Is this because Canadians care less about ethics in government? Is it because we are more deferential to those in public office? Or does the explanation have more structural roots: in the chronic weakness of our institutions of accountability. Or, to say the same thing another way: in the unrivalled power of our prime ministers.

Prime ministers of Canada are unusually powerful—the most powerful, experts (mostly) agree[85], of the world's democratic leaders, with the fewest constraints. They've always been powerful, of course, ever since the days of Sir John A., but nothing like as powerful as they've become. "Canadian parliamentary democracy, as it has evolved, places more power in the hands of the prime minister than does any other democracy," argued Jeffrey Simpson in *The Friendly Dictatorship*, his 2001 critique[86]. If anything power has grown more centralized since then.

One expression of this is a certain de facto immunity from political or even legal scrutiny: so long as he controls a majority in the House, a prime minister of Canada is unlikely ever to be held to account for his actions, whether by opposition MPs, committees of Parliament, or the police. But a prime minister's powers extend far beyond that. These were described earlier as powers of government, but we can dispense with this euphemism: they are, for the most part, the personal prerogatives of the prime minister. He is not just the head of the government. For most practical purposes he *is* the government, to the point that the terms "government" and "prime minister" can be used interchangeably.

In part, this is explained by the conjoining of the legislative and executive, through the Cabinet, that is at the heart of the Westminster system. A president of the United States, under its system of rigorous separation of powers, controls the executive, but not the legislative branch. He can propose legislation, but cannot be assured of its passage, even where one or both houses of Congress are controlled by his party. And he is bound by other checks and balances that are not part of the Canadian system.

Prime ministers in a European parliament must typically share power with other parties in their governing coalitions, single-party majority governments being rare under the proportional-representation systems in use on the continent (see chapter 7). A prime minister in a Westminster-style majoritarian system like ours is more likely to have the guaranteed support of a majority of MPs.

Even among Westminster systems, however, the powers of a Canadian prime minister have become noticeably distended. In addition to our notoriously severe regime of party discipline, our prime ministers are no longer bound by many of the conventions that still constrain prime ministers in Britain, Australia, and New Zealand. Neither is there an elected upper house in Canada to check the PM, as there is in Australia.

That our prime ministers have grown so powerful should not surprise us. They stand at the intersection of two broad trends described in earlier chapters: the ascendancy of party leaders over caucus, and of the executive over the legislature.

As party leader, the prime minister enjoys all the control over his own caucus that other party leaders do, and for the same reasons: he does not need their approval to become leader, while they need his to be renominated; he cannot be removed or replaced, except by the most tortuous, divisive process imaginable, while they can be dismissed from caucus at his whim; he decides (or his lieutenants do) which of his MPs gets to speak or ask questions in the House, what committees they should sit on, and what perquisites they should receive. Needless to say, he also decides how they should vote.

With so much attention focused on the party leader, during elections and after, he has not just institutional power, but also moral authority: You are nothing without me, he can say to his caucus, with some justice. It is because of me, and me alone, that you were elected. Any leader can make that argument, but it is especially compelling coming from the leader of the party in power.

Now add to that the powers he enjoys as leader of the government, especially a majority government: the power to decide when Parliament will sit, and for how long; when to recall it after an election, and when to prorogue it; what legislation it should consider, and when, and for how long; what should be considered a confidence motion, and what should not, and so on. Other party leaders are powerful in their own right, but a prime minister's powers are unique in so far as they apply not only to his own caucus, but to Parliament.

And that speaks only to his powers within and over the legislature. He also has considerable power, as we shall see, over the judiciary. And, of course, he rules utterly over the executive.

It is a paradox that, as the size of government has expanded, power has become more centralized in the Prime Minister's Office. Conventional management theory teaches that the greater the size of the operation, the more important it becomes to delegate authority to subordinates. A small shop can be run by one or two people at the top. A larger operation requires a team.

Canadian governments have absorbed the opposite lesson. The growing complexity of government has led to ever more elaborate attempts to control everything from the centre: either through the Prime Minister's Office itself, or through the other great centralizing agencies of government, notably the Privy Council Office, which sits at the apex of the civil service and also reports to him.

The PMO exercises power across departments, but the PCO's reach extends deep within each. Combined, they allow a prime minister and his officials to take charge of virtually any file they like, without regard to departmental roles or the sensibilities of Cabinet ministers. It is often observed within the bureaucracy that a file is much more likely to move if the prime minister takes a personal interest in it. If he agrees with a proposal, he can see that it proceeds without anyone else's approval; if, on the other hand, he disagrees with it, he can easily kill it. Accordingly, anyone with sufficient clout will, on dealing with government, insist on speaking directly to the prime minister or his staff, knowing that the bureaucracy takes its cues from him.

As Donald Savoie writes in *Governing at the Centre: The Concentration of Power in Canadian Politics*:

> The prime minister alone . . . has access to virtually every lever of power in the federal government, and when he puts his mind

to it he can get his way on almost any issue . . . Indeed, all major national public policy roads lead one way or another to their doorstep. . . .

[Prime ministers] articulate the government's strategic direction as outlined in the Speech from the Throne; they dictate the pace of change, and are the main salespersons promoting the achievements of their government; they have a hand in establishing the government's fiscal framework; they represent Canada abroad; they establish the proper mandate of individual ministers and decide all machinery of government issues, and they are the final arbiter in interdepartmental conflicts.

Each of the above levers of power taken separately is a powerful instrument of public policy and public administration in its own right, but when you add them all up and place them in the hands of one individual, they constitute a veritable juggernaut of power.[87]

The dominance of the executive, and of the prime minister within the executive, is further reinforced by the increasing tendency of government business to be decided between heads of government, that is via agreements with the provincial premiers, or with the leaders of other countries—the terms of which, though they may have been negotiated without input from either Parliament or Cabinet, both are obliged to accept, and civil servants are expected to follow.

* * *

More important, nearly everyone who works in in the top ranks of government owes their job to the prime minister. As Savoie writes, the prime minister exercises "virtually all the powers of patronage and acts as personnel manager for thousands of government and patronage jobs."

The relative invincibility of our prime ministers is perhaps best seen in this light: most of the people who might theoretically be responsible for holding him to account are themselves appointed by him, if not reporting to him. Who or what restrains a prime minister of Canada from doing precisely as he pleases? The governor general, in whose name he serves? But she is his appointee.* The Senate? He appoints all the senators. The courts? He appoints every member of the Supreme Court, and all the federal court judges, too. The prime minister appoints the commissioner of the RCMP, the director of the Canadian Security Intelligence Service, and the chief of the Defence Staff, as well as other senior military personnel.

The clerk of the Privy Council, every deputy minister of every department, the governor of the Bank of Canada, the chair of the CBC, the CEOs of all the major Crown corporations, even the ambassadors—the PM appoints them all, too. Appointments to a wide range of federal agencies, boards, and commissions—from the Canada Council for the Arts, to the National Energy Board, to the Public Service Commission, and beyond—are likewise the personal prerogative of the prime minister.

Not all these appointments will be made by a single prime minister, but by prime ministers past and present. Nevertheless, the current holders of these posts will know that their chances of being kept on (or, if they are on a fixed tenure, of having their term renewed) improve, the more adroit they are at maintaining themselves in the PM's favour. The point is not that the recipients of prime ministerial appointments are necessarily toadies. But if they were likely to displease him, they would not have been hired in the first place. And the longer the PM is in office, the fewer such people there will be.

Other heads of government, it is true, have powers of appointment that are nearly as broad. What distinguishes a Canadian prime minister's appointments is that he makes almost all of them without independent oversight of any kind. In other countries, appointments to the executive are generally subject to independent scrutiny, whether by political or non-political officials. The United States, for example,

---

* As are all the provincial lieutenant governors.

requires all important presidential appointments, more than 1,200 in all, to be confirmed by the Senate, on the recommendation of the relevant Senate committee: one of the many checks and balances limiting the president's power.*

In Britain, an impartial Civil Service Commission[88] oversees most government appointments, and has since 1855. Australia, similarly, has the Australian Public Service Commission. Strictly speaking, these commissions do not make the appointments, but ensure a fair and open selection process based on merit. The prime minister still has the formal power to appoint, but is expected to follow their advice.

Canada has its own Public Service Commission, with a similar mandate. The difference lies in the handling of very senior government offices, such as permanent secretaries or, as we call them, deputy ministers. In Australia and Britain, it is expected that the prime minister will ordinarily follow the commissions' recommendations†; no such convention applies here. New Zealand goes further: even the most senior appointments, including department heads—known there as chief executives—are the responsibility of the Public Service Commissioner (though the prime minister can overrule the commissioner's recommendation).

The appointment power of a Canadian prime minister is particularly notable with regard to two important offices: senators and Supreme Court justices. In most countries, the issue of how to appoint members of the upper house does not arise: they are usually elected, either directly, as in the United States, Japan, Italy, and Australia, or indirectly, as in France, Ireland, and the Netherlands. Among countries with appointed upper houses, the Canadian system is unique in the degree to which it reserves the power of appointment to the prime

---

* In Canada, this would present the diverting spectacle of the prime minister's appointees passing judgment on the prime minister's appointees.

† The UK Civil Service Commission recommends a shortlist of candidates for permanent secretaries to the prime minister. The prime minister is expected, though not required, to choose from this list.

minister. In federal states like Germany or India, members of the upper house are appointed by the state (equivalent to our provinces) governments. In the United Kingdom, on whose House of Lords the Senate was modelled, the prime minister is expected to consult with opposition parties on appointments of new life peers, or to follow the recommendations of the House of Lords Appointments Commission (as we shall see in chapter 5).

As for appointments to a country's highest court, the US Constitution's requirement of Senate confirmation is again the most elaborately arm's-length, or certainly well-known, example of independent oversight of the executive. But it is hardly alone in requiring some form of outside participation on the selection process. Some examples:

France: The president appoints three of the nine members of the Constitutional Council; the presidents of the Senate and the National Assembly each also appoint three. Appointees are questioned in public hearings by their respective house's law committees (the president of the Republic's appointees must go through both); they can be blocked by a vote of three-fifths of the combined committees.

Germany: Appointments to the sixteen-member Federal Constitutional Court are made entirely by the legislature, split equally between the lower house of the German parliament (the Bundestag) and the upper (the Bundesrat); the chancellor (prime minister) plays no direct role. A two-thirds majority of the relevant house is required to ratify an appointment, ensuring judges enjoy wide political support.

Italy: The power to appoint the fifteen members of Italy's highest court, the Constitutional Court of Italy, is similarly dispersed. The president of Italy appoints five; five more are elected jointly by the two chambers of Italy's parliament (the Chamber of Deputies and the Senate). The remaining five appointments are made by the members of Italy's other high courts, the Supreme Court of Cassation, the Council of State, and the Court of Audit.

Japan: The fifteen members of the Supreme Court of Japan are appointed by the prime minister, but must be ratified in a referendum coincident with the first general election after they are appointed, and every ten years after until they retire. True, no judge has been rejected since the process was instituted in 1947, but the safeguard is there.[89]

High court appointments remain largely the preserve of the prime minister in Westminster-based systems, including Canada's, subject to the usual conventions: consult widely, appoint on merit, etc. However, since the passage of the Constitutional Reform Act (2005), Britain has moved to a more formalized process. A selection commission, made up of the president of the Supreme Court, another senior judge, and representatives of the various subnational judicial appointments commissions (England and Wales, Scotland, and Northern Ireland), makes recommendations. The lord chancellor (justice minister) can either approve or reject its choice, or ask it to reconsider.

Canada has only just begun to experiment with this sort of thing. Justin Trudeau instituted two independent panels to recommend names for appointment to the Senate and the Supreme Court.[90] But their recommendations are explicitly non-binding, and there remains room for doubt as to how independent these panels really are.* It is far from certain the panels will be retained under a different government,†

---

* Three of the eight members of the Independent Advisory Board for Supreme Court of Canada Judicial Appointments are chosen by the prime minister (officially, they are "nominated by the Minister of Justice") as are three of the five members of the Independent Advisory Board for Senate Appointments.

† There is precedent: in 2017 Trudeau dissolved the Advisory Committee on Vice-Regal Appointments established by his predecessor. Thus unencumbered, he appointed Julie Payette as governor general.

at least with their current members. Not that their removal would be likely to cause a stir. In this, as in other matters, Canadians are accustomed to one-man rule.

Israel provides a striking contrast: enormous popular protests engulfed the country in 2023, set off, in part, by a proposal that would allow the government to name five of the nine members of the Judicial Selection Committee that in turn recommends appointments to the country's Supreme Court. The government would still have had no power to appoint any of the judges themselves, you understand. It would only have had a bare majority of the committee that appoints them. Yet so great was the ensuing controversy that the proposal was shelved. How much worse would it have been had it been proposed that all the appointments should be made by one person, with or without the help of an advisory panel? We will never know. In Israel, as in most democratic countries, such a thing is unthinkable.

* * *

The prime minister also appoints the Cabinet. This is entirely fit and proper. The prime minister has a right to pick his own Cabinet (Sir John A. famously listed his occupation at the Charlottetown Conference guestbook as "cabinet maker"). That is how our system works.

Executive power under our Constitution rests with "the Governor in Council," meaning the governor general as advised by the Privy Council*, the functioning part of which, by convention, is the Cabinet. Cabinet is the point at which the executive and legislative branches meet, responsible for the former and to the latter—the "combining committee," as Walter Bagehot called it, "a hyphen which joins, a buckle which fastens."[91]

---

* The King's Privy Council for Canada "includes all past and present Cabinet ministers, as well as a number of distinguished persons. Members are appointed for life by the governor general, on the recommendation of the prime minister." https://www.gg.ca/en/governor-general/role-and-responsibilities/constitutional-duties/swearing-ceremony/swearing-privy-councillors

It is, in other words, the supreme institution of our system of government. The Cabinet, as it says on the Parliament of Canada website, is "the key decision-making forum in the federal government, responsible for its administration and the establishment of its policy." Or, as it says on the prime minister's website: "It is the body of ministerial advisors that sets the federal government's policies and priorities for the country." Or, as it says on the federal government's website: "Cabinet is the political forum where ministers reach a consensus and decide on priorities and issues. It is the setting in which they bring political and strategic considerations to bear on proposed ministerial and governmental actions."

By common consensus, it is the prime minister's sole prerogative to choose the Cabinet, for only a prime minister will know what particular mix of talents he requires, and how they should be made to fit together into a cohesive whole. The centrality of Cabinet's role puts a great premium on Cabinet solidarity. Ministers are supposed to consider questions of government as a group, come to a consensus as a group, and stand or fall as a group. At the same time, ministers are supposed to be individually responsible for their departments, both for the policies they adopt and how competently they administer them.

That, at any rate, is the classical view of the Cabinet. It may describe how things worked in the past, or how they work in other countries. It is not at all how Cabinet works in Canada today.

The Cabinet is not where most key decisions are made: that place is now the Prime Minister's Office. Ministers, likewise, no longer have much responsibility for their departments, except in the sense that they are responsible for explaining the prime minister's decisions in that area. The classical notion that ours is a system of Cabinet government, with the prime minister as merely the "primus inter pares," first among equals, is simply untrue. He is more correctly described as the "primus sine paribus," first without equal. Or perhaps better: "primus über alles."

A clue to Cabinet's diminishing importance might be found in the grotesque size to which it has grown. At nearly forty ministers, counting the prime minister, the current edition is among the largest

Prime Minister vs. Cabinet

in our history—the largest, in fact, in the developed world, and more than twice the average of other OECD countries.[92]

Somehow, the United States is able to govern its 340 million citizens with a Cabinet of twenty-seven: in addition to the president and the vice president, it includes the secretaries of the fifteen executive departments, plus ten other Cabinet-level officers. The UK's Cabinet is limited by statute to twenty-two (junior ministers sometimes "also attend" Cabinet meetings: there are currently five of these). Australia (twenty-three) and New Zealand (twenty) are in the same range. On the continent things are slimmer still. Italy's has sixteen

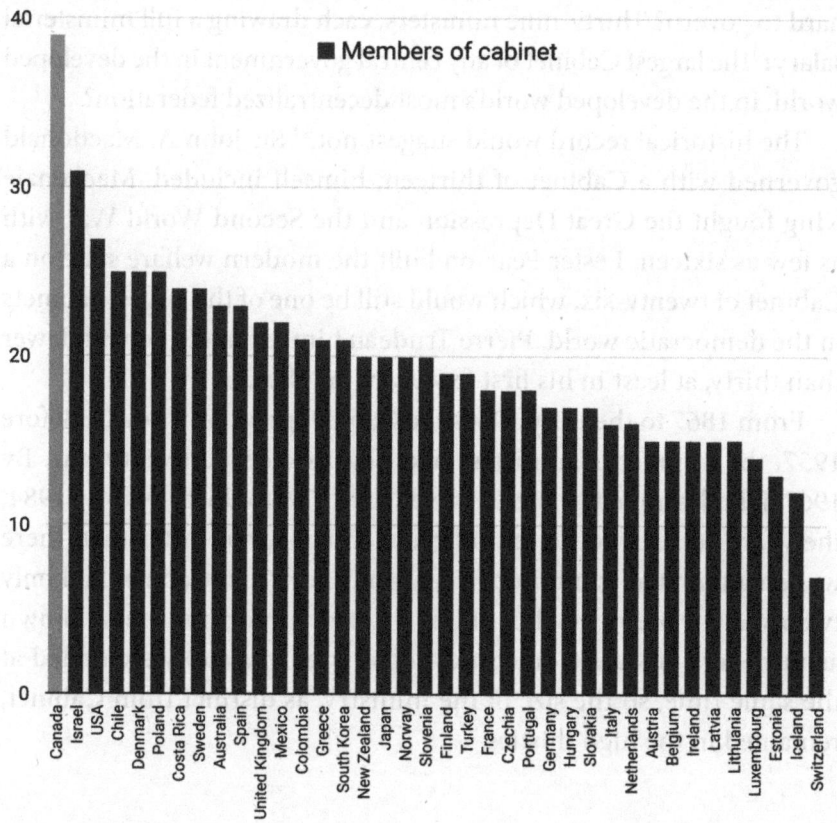

Source: National governments.

members (twenty-five, counting the nine ministers without portfolio). France has a cabinet of fifteen, as does Germany. The Scandinavian countries range from a low of nineteen (Finland) to a high of twenty-five (Denmark). And so on. Pick an OECD country. Belgium? Fifteen. Spain? Twenty-three. Japan? Twenty. Switzerland? *Seven.*

There are cabinets the size of Canada's, but they are more typically found in the Third World: the Cabinet appointed on November 17, 2005, by President Mahinda Rajapaksa of Sri Lanka, for example, included some fifty-two ministers, a world record[93]. But even in this company Canada stands out: compare the cabinets of, say, Tanzania (twenty-five ministers), Rwanda (twenty-two), and Burundi (eighteen). Is Canada, with so few problems compared to most other countries, really so hard to govern? Thirty-nine ministers, each drawing a full ministerial salary? The largest Cabinet of any central government in the developed world, in the developed world's most decentralized federation?

The historical record would suggest not.[94] Sir John A. Macdonald governed with a Cabinet of thirteen, himself included. Mackenzie King fought the Great Depression and the Second World War with as few as sixteen. Lester Pearson built the modern welfare state on a Cabinet of twenty-six, which would still be one of the largest cabinets in the democratic world. Pierre Trudeau himself made do with fewer than thirty, at least in his first few years in office.

From 1867 to the early 1960s the Cabinet grew very slowly. Before 1957, the number of ministers had never exceeded twenty-one. By 1967, it had climbed to twenty-seven; by 1977, to thirty-two; by 1984, the year Pierre Trudeau left office, to thirty-seven. After that, there was an attempt at trimming: Brian Mulroney's first Cabinet had only twenty-eight members, but about a dozen junior ministers, known as ministers of state (sometimes secretaries of state) were added at the same time, so the size of the ministry, as distinct from Cabinet, remained in the high thirties.*

---

* The ministry includes all ministers in the government, whether or not they are members of Cabinet.

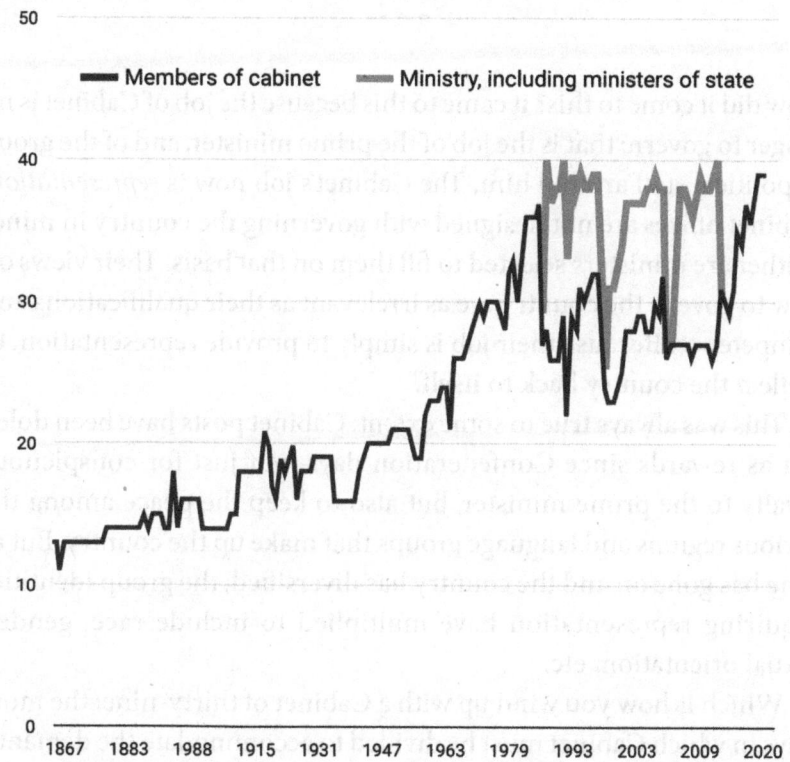

Source: Library of Parliament, ParlInfo: https://lop.parl.ca/sites/ParlInfo/default/en_CA/People/Cabinet

Even the Harper government, which began by eliminating the junior ministers, soon recanted and restored them. Under Justin Trudeau, juniors were again eliminated, but only by elevating what were previously ministers of state into full ministers, after it was pointed out that a disproportionate number of women in Trudeau's much vaunted "gender-balanced" Cabinet were to lowly ministers of state. There are no longer any ministers of state in Cabinet. But there are thirty-nine ministers.*

---

* Compare the evolution of the British Cabinet. Like the Canadian Cabinet, it grew from about a dozen in the mid-nineteenth century to about twenty by the early twentieth century, topping out at twenty-two in the 1930s. Unlike Canada's, it has stayed that size ever since. (And yes, this is comparing apples to apples: in both cases, we are counting only full ministers, not the broader "payroll vote" as it is called.)

* * *

How did it come to this? It came to this because the job of Cabinet is no longer to govern: that is the job of the prime minister, and of the group of political staff around him. The Cabinet's job now is *representation*. Cabinet offices are not designed with governing the country in mind; neither are ministers selected to fill them on that basis. Their views on how to govern the country are as irrelevant as their qualifications and competence. Because their job is simply to provide representation, to "reflect the country back to itself."

This was always true to some extent: Cabinet posts have been doled out as rewards since Confederation days, not just for conspicuous loyalty to the prime minister, but also to keep the peace among the various regions and language groups that make up the country. But as time has gone on and the country has diversified, the group identities requiring representation have multiplied to include race, gender, sexual orientation, etc.

Which is how you wind up with a Cabinet of thirty-nine: the more ways in which Cabinet must be divided to accommodate the demands of different groups for representation, the greater the total number of ministers must be, a principle familiar to students of mathematics as the lowest common denominator.

It isn't that representation is not a valid concern. Cabinet is a political body, and politics is all about representation. Other things being equal, a Cabinet that "looks like Canada" is an ideal worth striving for, for all the reasons usually advanced: to cast a broader net for talent, to draw on a wider range of life experiences, to build confidence among marginalized communities.

But a Cabinet of thirty-nine suggests maybe we've overdone it a little. Representation is a value, but it is not the only value. The more vital the task—and the Cabinet of a G7 country surely has vital tasks—the more that representation must be weighed against efficacy. The issue isn't even merit, necessarily: merit was hardly the sole or even primary consideration in the past—the heavily white-male Trump cabinet is hardly an advertisement for it in the present—and it's certainly possible to build a more diverse Cabinet while also seeking out the best and the brightest. But at some point the numbers involved become ridiculous. Thirty-nine is well past that point.

One consequence of this proliferation of offices has been a welter of overlapping responsibilities. A look at the current list of Cabinet portfolios[95] gives you some idea of the degree of superfluity involved. Every country has a minister of finance, or something similar: the minister responsible for spending, taxes, and the economy. We have a minister of finance and a minister of national revenue. And a president of the Treasury Board. And a minister of export promotion, international trade, and economic development. Also, a minister of *rural* economic development. Plus six other ministers in charge of the various regional economic development agencies. With that many ministers assigned to it, you'd think the economy would be pretty well developed by now, even without the additional efforts of the ministers of innovation and industry, energy and natural resources, fisheries and oceans, and agriculture and agri-food.

We have a minister of labour *and* a minister of employment; a minister of national defence *and* a minister of veterans' affairs (who doubles as associate minister of national defence); a minister of public safety *and* a minister of emergency preparedness; a minister of Indigenous services *and* a minister of Crown-Indigenous relations; a minister of health *and* a minister of mental health; a minister of youth *and* a minister of children; a minister of sport *and* — well, a minister of sport, for goodness sake.

Representation is something we used to think of as Parliament's role. But Parliament is not nearly so useful an instrument for this purpose. The composition of Parliament is ultimately for the benighted voting public to decide, with all of its crude whims and prejudices; an appointed Cabinet, on the other hand, is infinitely customizable. Its makeup can be tailored to the precise designs of the prime minister. And since it can, it must.

If prime ministers were not already disposed to attend to this arithmetic, an ever-vigilant public would insist upon it: the first principle any Canadian government must observe is that "all must have prizes." Each Cabinet shuffle is greeted by a chorus of complaints from every part of the country that it has been "underrepresented," not just in this province or that, but in subregions of provinces ("why are there no ministers from the Kitchener-Waterloo area?").

They are encouraged in this envious turn by the parties: at every election, leading figures in every party fan out to soberly warn each province, region, or municipality of the necessity of having "a seat at the table." Cabinet seats are thus a kind of reward for good behaviour, not only by the recipient, but by the voters, to be bestowed on those who vote the right way and withheld from those who don't.

Cabinet posts in this country are not important jobs for skilled professionals, but trinkets and baubles, made-up jobs for make-work purposes. The point is not to fulfill some urgent public responsibility but to give their recipients something to do or, more accurately, something to be.

You can see this in how the media covers a Cabinet shuffle. In other countries, a shuffle will be analyzed in terms of what shifts in government direction it might signal, or how the prime minister is balancing the differing wings of his party, or what changes in approach particular ministers will bring to their posts. An appointment might be described as an appropriate challenge for a rising talent; another, as placing a minister in over his or her head. Pundits will ask: do they have the right sort of background and experience, the judgment, character, competence, and so forth needed to do the job?

In Canada, these questions are never asked. There is no reason to ask them. Party ideologies are hazy enough, but individual MPs are not expected to have any of their own; their beliefs are assumed to be whatever the leader's are. As for the experience, talents, and character of the appointees, who cares? That's not why they were chosen, and everybody knows it.

Prime Minister vs. Cabinet

Instead, the post-shuffle analysis is restricted to counting heads: how many are from which province or subregion or city, and how many are from which gender, race, or other identity category, with percentages calculated to the second decimal point. It is a tacit admission that the individuals, like the jobs themselves, do not matter. Occasionally it will be said, after a minister has been dismissed, that he or she was not up to the job. This seems unfair. Being up to the job was not one of the job requirements.

Cabinets and Cabinet shuffles are therefore viewed entirely through the lens of symbolism and messaging. Individual ministers, so far as they are discussed at all, are rated mostly for their ability as spokespersons, selling whatever policy or talking point is cooked up for them in the Prime Minister's Office. Not for nothing are they often referred to as performers.

Yet even as performers, you can't say any of them are particularly "good" at it, at least in the sense of being able to present a case in a persuasive or sympathetic fashion. They recite their lines robotically, often get facts wrong, make no attempt to reach out to the uncommitted. It is rather for their readiness to take one for the team, to spout the same line in response to every question, to conquer, through sheer repetition, the very concept of sense—if all else fails, to run out the clock—that they have been rewarded. If there is a talent required, it is a talent for self-abasement: a willingness to say whatever is required of them, no matter how implausible.

Nevertheless, Cabinet bloat does serve one purpose: it helps to keep caucus in line. A Cabinet of thirty-nine ministers out of a caucus of one hundred fifty-three means the average Liberal MP, if he keeps his nose clean, has a roughly one in four chance of being appointed to Cabinet. But since rather more than thirty-nine MPs will be appointed to Cabinet over the life of a government, the odds, and the incentive for nose-cleaning, are better yet: more like one in three. If you are a member of a desirable demographic group or from a province or region where the governing party has few MPs, you are almost guaranteed a spot.

Add in thirty-nine parliamentary secretaries, the chief whip, the deputy whip, plus thirty or so committee chairs*, and the prime minister has more than two-thirds of the governing caucus directly beholden to him for one position or another. Why risk the government's wrath when you have a two-in-three chance of promotion?

By way of comparison, consider again the Cabinet of the United Kingdom. It includes, as mentioned, just twenty-two ministers (in Britain, they are formally known as "secretaries of state"), or twenty-six if you count the "also attends." Most of the offices are of some antiquity; their titles do not change from Cabinet to Cabinet, as they do in Canada. The chancellor of the exchequer, one of the four great offices of state (the others are the prime minister, the home secretary, and the foreign secretary), dates back to the thirteenth century.

Twenty-two ministers, out of a Labour caucus of four hundred eleven, means the average Labour MP has about a one in eighteen chance of being in Cabinet at any given time. To be sure, there are dozens of other ministers of state, parliamentary secretaries, and the like. Still, hundreds of MPs on the Labour benches know they will never be appointed to anything. They must search for other ways to distinguish themselves: by chairing a parliamentary select committee (in Britain these are elected by MPs, on a secret ballot, rather than being chosen by the party leaders), or by mastering a particular brief, or simply by representing their constituencies with distinction, asking tough questions in the House, and so forth. The incentives for sycophancy are far less powerful than they are here.

We should not underestimate the importance of this point. We saw in an earlier chapter the tedium of the MPs' lives: how little real power they have, how much of their lives are under the control of the leader's office. They suffer constant daily reminders of their irrelevance with but one thought in mind: "If I tough it out, if I endure this humiliation with a smile, if I never waver in my devotion to the leader and his team, I might one day end up in Cabinet."

---

* Including standing committees, special committees, joint committees etc.

Prime Minister vs. Cabinet

That's the truly pathetic part. All that cringing, all that bowing and scraping, and for what?* To be exposed to still further humiliation as a member of Cabinet. MPs may be nobodies, but that does not make ministers into somebodies. Mostly they are nobodies with a car and driver. Power may have passed from Parliament to Cabinet, but power has passed even more from Cabinet to the prime minister.

Ministers are not the prime minister's principal advisers: his senior staff are, with an assist from the civil servants in the Privy Council Office. Ministers have less and less control even over their own portfolios, finding themselves increasingly answering to the prime minister's advisers, without direct access to the prime minister himself. That's when policy is not imposed upon them from above, often without warning.

Prime ministers have always had a great deal of influence over Cabinet, of course. It is the nature of the job. The prime minister appoints every minister, and can fire them at any time, for any reason; they, like he, serve "at His Majesty's pleasure."† Even so, it is widely observed that the powers and relevance of Cabinet are greatly diminished versus decades past; the last time Cabinet played a role resembling the official description was under Lester Pearson. The decline is usually said to have begun during the government of Pierre Trudeau, who preferred to rely on the advice of officials in the Prime Minister's Office and the Privy Council Office. By the time of Jean Chrétien, the imperial prime ministership was already well documented, in Savoie's work but also in Jeffrey Simpson's *The Friendly Dictatorship* (and, in a more positive vein, *The Way It Works: Inside Ottawa*, by Chrétien's chief policy adviser and later chief of staff, Eddie Goldenberg.[96]) Yet Chrétien's time in office is now looked back upon as the last hurrah of Cabinet government, so far has it fallen under Stephen Harper and Justin Trudeau.

---

* "For Wales? Why Richard, it profits a man nothing to give his soul for the whole world. But for Wales?" — Sir Thomas More, to his former servant Richard Rich, now attorney general for Wales, in *A Man for All Seasons*.
† The same is true of some prisoners.

Part of this is reflected, again, in the absurd size of present cabinets. Cabinet inflation works much like inflation generally: the larger the Cabinet, the smaller the minister. The more ministers there are crowded around the Cabinet table, the less, inevitably, is the influence of each individual minister. In a Cabinet of twelve, every minister is a player. As you pass twenty, they start to blur together. By the time you near forty, they look like ants. A few portfolios matter; fewer ministers do. The rest are placeholders.

To maintain a Cabinet of such size and complexity requires constant tinkering. Accordingly, ministers tend not to stay long in their posts: an average of about twenty-four months in recent decades[97] (versus more than three years in the decades after Confederation). As it usually takes several months to get up to speed in the job, that means the most ambitious and independent-minded minister has about a year and a half to make his mark. Most leave without a trace.

It wasn't always thus. The political history of Canada is filled with giants, ministers of talent with real power to affect the course of events. Macdonald's cabinets contained ministers of the calibre of Sir George-Étienne Cartier, Sir Alexander Galt, Sir Hector-Louis Langevin, and Sir Charles Tupper. Laurier's were nearly a match, including the likes of Sir Richard Cartwright, Sir Clifford Sifton, William Fielding, and William Mulock. Borden could call upon the services of Arthur Meighen, Sir George Foster, and Sir Thomas White, among others, while the cabinets of King, St. Laurent, and Pearson presented something of a Murderers' Row of political heavy hitters: among them Ernest Lapointe, C. D. Howe, Paul Martin Sr., Robert Winters, Walter Gordon, Mitchell Sharp, and Allan MacEachen, in addition to the trio of future prime ministers: Trudeau, John Turner, and Chrétien.*

---

* It will be noted that this list contains only white men. The first woman to serve in Cabinet was Ellen Fairclough, in 1957. The second was Judy LaMarsh in 1963. The first Indigenous minister was Len Marchand, in 1976; the first Black, Lincoln Alexander in 1979; the first Chinese Canadian, Raymond Chan, *in 1993*. Unfortunately, by the time women and racial minorities began to arrive at the table, Cabinet government was already on the wane.

Which of the current crop of ministers could take their place among them? The stature of most ministers has shrunk so far that few Canadians could name them unprompted. Or even prompted: in a recent poll, Canadians were shown pictures of several members of Cabinet and asked to name them.[98] Ninety-eight percent could name the prime minister. Only 39 percent could name the (since departed) deputy prime minister and minister of finance, Chrystia Freeland—after nine years as one of the government's most senior ministers. Roughly one in five could name the foreign minister, Mélanie Joly. After that, the level of recognition falls off sharply. Just 4 percent could name the then public safety minister, Dominic LeBlanc, or the then housing minister, Sean Fraser, at the time two of the most prominent ministers in the Trudeau government. It's a fair bet the rest of Cabinet would fare worse.

The vast majority of Canadians, in other words, could not pick senior Cabinet ministers out of a police lineup. What accounts for this? Is the ministers' shrinking profile a function of their talents, or their predicament? Has the quality of ministers declined over the years, compared to their larger-than-life predecessors, or is it just their responsibilities? It may be that, like Norma Desmond, the ministers are as big as ever—it's just that "the pictures got smaller." Or it may be that it has become harder to attract serious people to such unserious positions.

Indeed, it is often difficult to say what their responsibilities are. Sometimes several ministers are assigned to the same department—the Department of Canadian Heritage currently has six ministers attached to it, for example, while the Department of Employment and Social Development has five[99]—while other ministers are obliged to hold down several portfolios at once. In some cases, it is a puzzle why the positions were created, or what they do. Could anyone describe the job of the minister of citizens' services with any precision (it sounds disturbingly like the minister of administrative affairs[100]), or the (now defunct) minister of middle-class prosperity? When you mint Cabinet posts like Argentine pesos, it's easy to lose track.

Sir Keir Starmer's Labour Cabinet in session. Search in vain for photos of their Canadian equivalent.

What is true of individual ministers is also true of Cabinet as a whole: as its numbers have grown, so its influence has declined. A Cabinet of thirty-nine is simply not a serious decision-making body. Have a look at a picture of a British Cabinet meeting, with twenty-odd ministers seated around the table. It looks chaotic, but manageable. Now imagine nearly twice as many.

(Well, you'll have to imagine it. There are no publicly available pictures of recent Canadian Cabinet meetings. There are group photos of ministers after Cabinet has been appointed, or standing around outside a Cabinet retreat, but none of them actually in session. You can find photographs online of virtually every other country's Cabinet in session: Britain, France, Germany, Italy, the US. And you can find photographs of Canadian Cabinet meetings from decades past, when Cabinets were half the size. But not lately. Possibly their officials are conscious of how ridiculous it looks.)

Cabinet meets less frequently than it did in the past. Under King, St. Laurent and Diefenbaker, Cabinet met three times a week.[101]

Prime Minister vs. Cabinet

That fell to once a week, a schedule still maintained officially, if not uniformly. This is not out of any lessening of the pace of government, but of the declining relevance of Cabinet. Meetings of Cabinet are not so much where decisions get made, as where the prime minister sounds out ministers on decisions he has already taken, or is thinking of taking: in Savoie's famous phrase, Cabinet has become a "focus group for the prime minister."[102]

The prime minister chairs the meetings, he sets the agenda, he dictates who shall speak and for how long, and, in the end, he decides: there are no formal votes of Cabinet, or none that a prime minister is obliged to follow. Though he may wish to respect the consensus of his colleagues, if it is against him, nothing prevents him from revisiting the subject when he feels the time is right. And in any debate, he can draw upon a vast staff of advisers, unmatched by any other minister.

The particular styles and approaches of prime ministers as meeting chairs will vary. Pierre Trudeau was supposed to favour a formal, academic style. Brian Mulroney was more collegial, more indulgent of ministers' personalities. Jean Chrétien was all business, and brusque in his dismissal of opinions he did not like. Stephen Harper was detail oriented. Justin Trudeau was not. But what is unchanging is the reality that the most important decisions are not made, except in the most formal sense, at Cabinet or by Cabinet, but by the prime minister and his advisers.

This need not be overstated. Like any manager, prime ministers will need to retain the trust and support of their subordinates; if their advice is not heeded, they need at least to feel that their concerns have been heard. A smart prime minister will pick his battles, coaxing and cajoling rather than laying down the law. But, in the end, there can be no doubt whose opinion carries the day. The prime minister declares "consensus"—or reserves judgment until he has consulted his staff and/or the finance minister—and that is that.

Even as a discussion forum, Cabinet meetings have limited ability to delve into an issue in any great depth or detail. There are too many ministers and too little time*. In their place has emerged a byzantine system of committees and subcommittees,[103] currently numbering fourteen (fifteen, counting the rarely convened Incident Response Group. As prime minister, Trudeau attended just two of them: the Committee on Agenda, Results and Communications, sometimes described as the real Cabinet (what the old Priorities and Planning Committee was to prime ministers past), and the new National Security Council.

Operations is perhaps the only other committee worth noting (besides the Treasury Board—the only committee mandated by statute). It is the tactical counterpart to the Committee on Agenda, Results and Communications' focus on strategy. The rest have names like the Sub-Committee on Intergovernmental Coordination and the Sub-Committee on Litigation Management. Two of the committees have identical names. They are called the Cabinet Committee on Economy, Inclusion and Climate "A" and the Cabinet Committee on Economy, Inclusion and Climate "B." I am reasonably confident this is a world first. It may even have been an oversight.[104]

Ostensibly the point of all these multiple and overlapping committees is supposed to be to bring proposals forward to the larger Cabinet for consideration. Do they? Do ministers have the sort of meaningful input in committee they do not have in meetings of the full Cabinet? Were the Trudeau Cabinet's fourteen committees more productive than the Chrétien Cabinet's four?[105] Or have committees become just another of Ottawa's many machines for official busywork, hamster wheels for ministers with too much time on their hands? One can't be sure—Cabinet confidence and all that—but if the withering assessments of the work of Cabinet committees by their British counterparts is anything to go by ("a waste of time . . . a box-ticking exercise . . . There were very few Cabinet committees [where] decisions that haven't essentially been prepared in advance were taken"), there is room for doubt on this score.[106]

---

* There is literally a timer. "You have 30 seconds."

Prime Minister vs. Cabinet

The purpose of all these meetings, one suspects, is rather to preserve the illusion of Cabinet government, mostly for the benefit of ministers themselves, allowing them to live in the pretense that they have a real say in how the country is governed. As often as not, however, the pretense is abandoned, and the prime minister will simply make a decision on an important matter, without consulting either the minister with responsibility for the file or Cabinet as a whole.

Instances of this are legion. Pierre Trudeau bypassed Cabinet on a number of critical matters, notably his decision, announced on his return from discussions with German chancellor Helmut Schmidt at the 1978 Bonn Economic Summit, to slash $2 billion from federal spending. Mulroney unilaterally committed Canada to support US policies under Presidents Reagan and Bush on NORAD renewal and other cooperative defence arrangements, as well as funding for the Hibernia energy project after Gulf Canada, a key investor, withdrew.

Chrétien's approach to Cabinet decision-making had perhaps the roundest sense of droit du seigneur to it, on matters ranging from his decision, apparently made on impulse, to invite Quebecers Stéphane Dion and Pierre Pettigrew to join as ministers, to the decision, in the course of a golf game with New Brunswick premier Frank McKenna, to share the costs of twinning the Trans-Canada Highway in the province. Rather than put the project, and the billions of dollars in spending it entailed, through Cabinet, Chrétien directed his staff to make the necessary arrangements with Treasury Board.[107]

And so on. Paul Martin initially considered, then rejected, participation in the US ballistic missile defence without so much as a how's-your-father with Cabinet. Stephen Harper committed Canadian troops to the US-led military mission in Afghanistan in similar fashion, while Justin Trudeau and Chrystia Freeland, then the minister of foreign affairs, renegotiated the North American Free Trade Agreement with the first Trump administration with limited Cabinet input.

If prime ministers have often treated their cabinets with disdain, they have been no less high-handed with individual ministers. The powerful senior ministers of the postwar era, supported by equally powerful deputy ministers, are mostly a memory. Pierre Trudeau's expansion of the committee system was expressly designed to tie the hands of individual ministers, making it difficult for them to take decisions on their own, while his expansion of the Prime Minister's Office and the Privy Council Office greatly improved his ability to survey and control what ministers were up to. Subsequent prime ministers have maintained and enhanced these changes.

At the same time, prime ministers have increasingly felt free to substitute their own decisions for those of their ministers, taking control of a file whenever the mood strikes them. During the program-review exercise in the mid-1990s, Prime Minister Jean Chrétien unilaterally imposed significant spending cuts on ministers, although that responsibility had been specifically assigned to a Cabinet committee; ministers who resisted were punished with steeper cuts.* Stephen Harper summarily overruled his environment minister, Rona Ambrose, when she expressed tentative support for international climate initiatives; he ultimately withdrew Canada from the Kyoto Protocol. Policy on such important files as the Afghanistan mission, foreign affairs (notably Canada's stance on Israel), anti-terror legislation, and the post–financial crisis stimulus package were similarly shaped and directed out of the Harper PMO. The responsible ministers in each case were left with little to do but sell decisions they had no part in making.

Justin Trudeau came to power promising that "government by Cabinet is back."[108] It soon became clear he had no more commitment to this idea than to any of his other promised democratic reforms. Indeed, it is commonly observed that power was more centralized in the PMO under Trudeau than even his predecessors. Poignant evidence is found in the published memoirs of several prominent former ministers, all of whom were bewildered to find how little agency or input they had.

---

* But then, Chrétien would have his own memories of being similarly mistreated: he was finance minister at the time of the Bonn Summit.

Prime Minister vs. Cabinet

In *Where To from Here: A Path to Canadian Prosperity*, Justin Trudeau's former finance minister, Bill Morneau, writes of his growing frustration at being left out of key decisions. Not only was his advice ignored or overruled, but he was not consulted or, in some cases, informed about policies that were squarely within his bailiwick. It became difficult to get so much as get a meeting with the prime minister, even to discuss an upcoming budget: he was told to send his suggestions to PMO staff, who would brief the prime minister on them. Morneau describes his role as having been "something between a figurehead and a rubber stamp."

Marc Garneau's memoir, *A Most Extraordinary Ride: Space, Politics, and the Pursuit of a Canadian Dream*, is only partially devoted to his career in politics, which seems to have been less happy than his career as an astronaut. Like Morneau, there is the same frustration, the same sense of decisions being taken without him, the same inability to speak directly with the prime minister. Garneau writes he was called upon only once, in his time as foreign affairs minister, to advise the prime minister. "The prime minister's aloofness led me to conclude that he did not consider my advice useful enough to want to hear from me directly, relying instead on his staff... The expectation was that communication between him and me would be via the [Prime Minister's Office], and so consequently I never knew what information, if any, reached him."

In *"Indian" in the Cabinet: Speaking Truth to Power*, former justice minister Jody Wilson-Raybould recounts how officials from the prime minister on down improperly pressured her, as justice minister and attorney general, to intervene in the prosecution of SNC-Lavalin. Here, the minister's autonomy is not ideal or theoretical: it is settled constitutional law. An attorney general *may not* be subjected to pressure, by the prime minister or anyone else, on a criminal law matter, just as she may not, except in extraordinary circumstances, intervene in prosecutors' decisions. Yet this did not stop either the prime minister or his officials from pressuring her to do precisely that, repeatedly, for months. Force of habit, one assumes.

And these were senior ministers!* If that is how little a role is left to a minister of finance, foreign affairs, or justice, imagine what molecules the other ministers have become. Certainly, ministers have no serious role in the management of the departments to which their names are attached—that is entirely devolved to their deputy ministers.† But neither do they have a great deal to say about the policies their departments pursue, whether as individuals or in concert with their Cabinet colleagues. Their jobs are to take instructions from the Prime Minister's Office and speak the lines they have been given to read, much like ordinary MPs, but at a slightly higher pay grade.

One way of gauging the relative significance of different departments in the scheme of things is by how quickly their ministers are replaced. Since 2004, the government of Canada has employed a total of six finance ministers, through seven parliaments. In the same interval, it has had seven justice ministers, eight ministers of the environment, nine ministers of public safety, ten ministers of health, and fully twelve ministers of foreign affairs.[109]

The ascendance of prime ministers over ministers has been enhanced by the recent practice of issuing, and releasing to the public, lengthy "mandate letters" to ministers from the prime minister, describing, in minute detail, the numerous policy objectives he expects them to achieve. Ministers had before been afforded considerable latitude to come up with their own policy proposals and to exercise discretion in dealing with the inevitable crises and conflicts that afflict any government. But the increasing prominence of party platforms has left less room for ministerial initiative—which might be a good thing, from a democratic accountability perspective, if platforms themselves were not so transparently the work of a handful of officials around the leader (and routinely ignored after elections).

---

* Doubtless Chrystia Freeland's memoirs will also have something to say on this. See chapter 8.
† Deputy ministers, for their part, complain of being kept out of the loop on major policy decisions, having been largely supplanted in their role as adviser to the minister by the minister's chief of staff.

Prime Minister vs. Cabinet

Of course, with very little power comes almost no responsibility. Ministers were once expected to take responsibility for the more spectacular fiascos within their departments, if not by resigning their posts—that has always been rare—then at least by accepting the usual ritual beatings in Parliament: day after day of standing before baying opposition members in Parliament, answering questions that begin or end with "when will the minister do the right thing and resign?" Ministers in disgrace had opportunities to redeem themselves by the fortitude with which they endured their punishment. But even this, the dignity of the whipping boy, has been taken from them. No one credits ministers with enough agency to blame them any more. They are no longer summarily sacked, but are quietly moved into lesser roles at the next Cabinet reshuffle, long after the reason for their demotion has been forgotten.

What must be particularly galling for ministers is that it is not the prime minister, these days, from whom they are obliged to take instructions, and to whom they are obliged to address their every request. It is the prime minister's officials, the "kids in short pants," as they are often called. It is one thing to be big-footed by the prime minister, who is, after all, elected. But who elected the kids? The problem became particularly acute under the Trudeau government. Harper, it is well-known, was a control freak, but he was a relatively informed one, with a remarkable capacity to master a brief. The control freaks under Justin Trudeau, the ones barking orders to elected ministers, were his underlings.

The power and reach of the Prime Minister's Office is unique in democratic politics. From humble beginnings, it has grown to employ more than 120, ten times the size of the average minister's office. A 2011 report by the Institute for Government in Britain found it was the third-largest among six countries studied, behind the UK and Sweden (Australia, New Zealand, and Germany were the others).[110] It was by far the largest, however, in terms of *political* staff, as opposed to civil servants, in its employ.

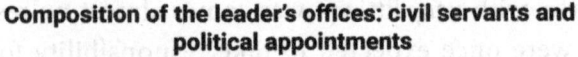

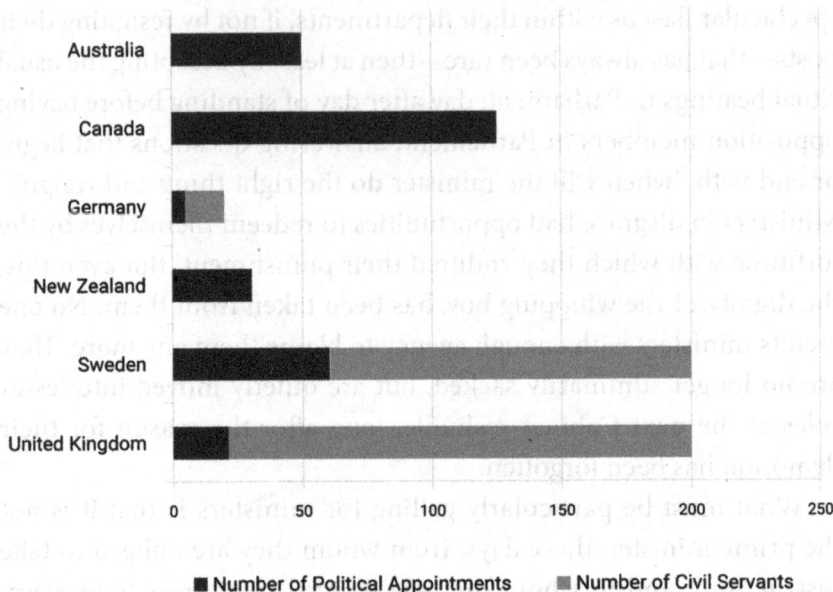

Institute for Government: *Supporting Heads of Government: A comparison across six countries, 2011* https://www.instituteforgovernment.org.uk/publication/report/supporting-heads-government

The same applies to the Privy Council Office: the number of civil servants reporting directly to a Canadian prime minister dwarfs the numbers available to other prime ministers. Combined, the number of staff either in the Prime Minister's Office or in his "department" is 80 percent larger than that of second-place Germany, a country with twice the population.

That's not the most striking indicator of how powerful the PMO has become. That, surely, is the practice that has emerged under recent prime ministers[111] of the PMO appointing ministers' chiefs of staff for them.[112] You read that right: ministers of the Crown in Canada are no longer allowed to choose their own chief of staff, the person with whom they must work more closely more than any other, and on

Prime Minister vs. Cabinet

Relative size of leaders' offices and departments

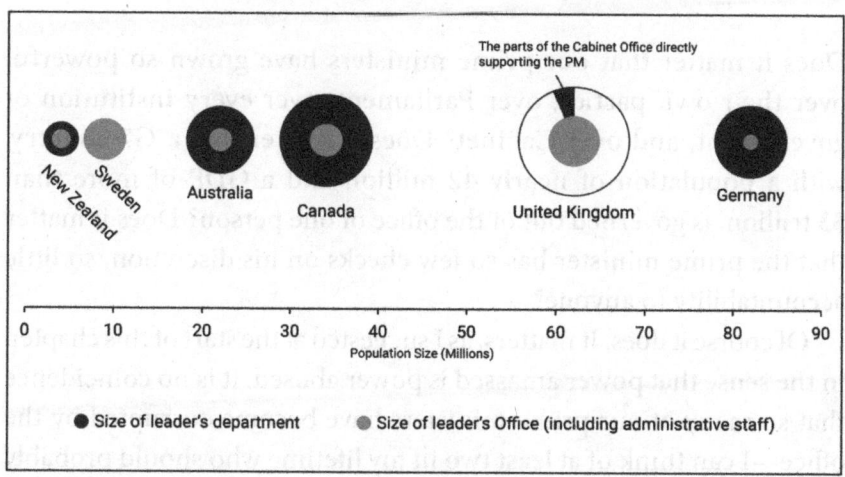

Institute for Government: *Supporting Heads of Government: A comparison across six countries, 2011* https://www.instituteforgovernment.org.uk/publication/report/supporting-heads-government

whose advice—and loyalty—they must rely. In Canada, that person answers not to the minister, but to the Prime Minister's Office. In effect, the PMO has an agent planted in every minister's office, acting as its eyes and ears.

Prime ministers since Pierre Trudeau might have taken an increasingly hands-on approach, reviewing ministerial staffing decisions, even vetoing them on occasion. But removing the power from ministers altogether marks a new stage in the PMO's apparently insatiable desire for control. I can find no comparable practice anywhere in the democratic world. When officials under British prime minister Boris Johnson, who had clashed with his chancellor of the exchequer, Sajid Javid, demanded to appoint his advisers, the minister resigned on the spot. "I don't believe any self-respecting minister would accept those conditions," Javid declared.[113] But then, self-respect is not a quality we often associate with Canadian Cabinet ministers.

* * *

Does it matter that our prime ministers have grown so powerful over their own parties, over Parliament, over every institution of government, and over Cabinet? Does it matter that a G7 country, with a population of nearly 42 million and a GDP of more than $3 trillion, is governed out of the office of one person? Does it matter that the prime minister has so few checks on his discretion, so little accountability to anyone?

Of course it does. It matters, as I suggested at the start of this chapter, in the sense that power amassed is power abused. It is no coincidence that so many of our prime ministers have become corrupted by the office—I can think of at least two in my lifetime who should probably have ended up behind bars—because so few of them pay any price for it, political or otherwise.

But it matters also for the quality of government. It is not possible to manage any institution of this size, let alone one that has taken on so many responsibilities, with so few people. Just the attempt is bound to wear down and overwhelm the participants, causing them to make many more mistakes. At the best of times, it requires a degree of knowledge that no individual or group of individuals can possess.

It matters because centralizing power inside a tiny bubble of officials tends to cut off those within from new ideas, alternative points of view, or differing experiences. When there is no one to say no, there is very little incentive to examine assumptions, to test theories against evidence, or to learn from mistakes. Everything comes to depend on the judgment of one person, at best advised by a handful of loyalists, and the longer it goes on, the more frail that judgment inevitably becomes.

Cabinet, although it advises the prime minister, is at the same time intended to be a kind of check on him. There is a reason why a prime minister has a Cabinet to advise him, as distinct from his own personal advisers. As elected officials, people with their own standing in the community and in the party, they bring a raft of different perspectives to the table—voices, and currents of opinion, a prime minister cannot afford to ignore. They keep him in contact with reality, practical and political. Strong ministers force a prime minister to consider how his latest bright idea will play in the real world. When decisions are taken collectively, rather than solely by the prime minister, there is less chance of being blindsided. When decision-making is centralized in the Prime Minister's Office, well, we've seen the result, over and over again.

How do we restore Cabinet to its rightful place, at the heart of our system of government? One solution stands out above all others: cut it in half. Fewer ministers make stronger ministers. Not only would a smaller Cabinet make a more effective deliberative body, but it would expose the folly, not to say the futility of making representation the sole criterion of Cabinet-making. The numbers simply wouldn't be there to make it work. Possibly governments would have to make do with experience, competence, and ideas.

But that's not enough, on its own. Indeed, it's impossible, on its own. You can't have Cabinet government without a prime minister who understands and values Cabinet government. That's another reason to favour leaving the election of party leaders to caucus: you are more likely to elect people with some experience, not just in politics, but in Cabinet—people who come to the job with a sympathetic view of the role ministers can play—rather than the rank outsiders our current method of electing leaders keeps forcing on party caucuses and the public.

As for the broader objective of curbing the powers of the prime minister, the solutions are more straightforward. Some of these have been treated already, in the chapters describing the imbalances between government and parliament, and leader and caucus. As the prime minister stands at the intersection of these, the same approaches recommend themselves; subjecting more of the powers that the prime minister now exercises on his own, such as when to dissolve Parliament or what constitutes a confidence vote, to independent checks and authority; making the power to veto a candidate's nomination a power of the party, rather than just of the leader; and so on. Add to that stronger oversight of the prime minister's many powers of appointment, and you are halfway to a less top-heavy, more democratic system of government.

But that leaves us, once again, with the dilemma we have been wrestling with throughout. The only person who can institute these reforms is the person who benefits most from the status quo: the prime minister. Why on earth would he want to change anything?

5
Unelected vs. Elected

THERE ARE LEGITIMATE CHECKS on government, and there are illegitimate ones.

The first line of defence against arbitrary government in our system is supposed to be the democratically elected House of Commons, in which the executive is embedded (via Cabinet) and to which it is accountable. As we have seen, that is not how our system actually works. The government's accountability to the House has become a formality, at best. The chances of a government bill being defeated or even significantly amended by MPs, at least under majority governments, are slim.

Instead, attention has become focused on two other venues for holding governments to account, the Senate and the Supreme Court. These institutions have still less of a claim to democratic representativeness than the House of Commons, but they have the compensating virtue of power: each has, in its fashion, the power to block or overturn legislation, or to force amendments to it. The question is whether, and under what circumstances, it is legitimate for either institution to do so, given that neither is elected. Since legislation is formally Parliament's handiwork, each can be seen as acting as a check, not on government, but on the House of Commons.

The Supreme Court, through its use of the power of judicial review—the process of examining legislation in light of the Constitution, and invalidating any law that is inconsistent with it—has excited most of the controversy. But it is the Senate that may be emerging as the real threat to democratic government.

* * *

The Senate is the appendix of Confederation: a largely inert organ of uncertain purpose, it is usually harmless but on occasion can grow inflamed. At which point, it can be quite lethally dangerous.

Its powers, in theory, are nearly the equal of the Commons. Under the Constitution, no bill may become law that has not been passed by both the Commons and the Senate. The Senate's power to propose, amend, or veto legislation is theoretically without limit, save two: it may not initiate money bills, and it may not defeat amendments to the Constitution, but only delay them.

What keeps the Senate from using its powers is, or is supposed to be, that its members are not elected. They are appointed. And since this is Canada, that means they are appointed by the prime minister, until recently without oversight of any kind. Nothing better symbolizes the degraded state of democracy in Canada than the continued presence at the heart of our system of government of a legislative body composed entirely of the prime minister's hand-picked appointees. No other upper house in the democratic world works on such explicitly personalist lines. Most are elected, directly or indirectly. A handful are appointed, but none is so wholly the creature of the leader: not even the British House of Lords, on which it was modelled.

Once a mostly hereditary body, the Lords is now almost entirely (besides the ninety-two remaining hereditary peers and the twenty-six "Lords Spiritual") made up of "life peers," appointed, as in Canada, by the prime minister. There the resemblance ends. Unlike in Canada,

Unelected vs. Elected

the opposition parties in Britain are entitled to recommend a certain number of appointments, in rough proportion to their standings in the House of Commons, which the prime minister is bound by convention to accept. Others are appointed on the advice of an independent non-partisan House of Lords Appointments Commission[114] to sit as "crossbenchers." To a Canadian eye, the results look remarkably unvenal. Out of 1,610 appointments to the House of Lords since the passage of the Life Peerages Act in 1958, just 731, fewer than half, went to supporters of the governing party.[115]

Contrast the record in Canada, where senators have been chosen, historically, with a partisanship that verges on the hysteric: out of 860 appointees to the Senate from 1867 to 2015, fully 832, or 97 percent of the total, took their seats as representatives of the prime minister's party.[116] The quality of appointments has also been arguably worse. Given the power to appoint more or less whom they please,* prime ministers have appointed their friends, their fundraisers, their strategists, party organizers, party donors, defeated candidates from the governing party,[117] and MPs who had crossed the floor to join it. Not to mention the occasional crook, crank or expense-account padder. To call it a patronage house is an insult to patronage.

No law decreed that appointments to the Canadian Senate should be so shabby. It was just the custom, which is to say the culture. The Senate, in its turn, helped shape that culture. It wasn't just that the Senate was corrupt: it corrupted us. The longer we put up with it, the more insidious its influence became, a legacy that continues to this day. If you want to know why our politics are so peculiarly amoral, so entirely uninterested in principle, I suggest you start with the effects of a century and a half of bending our consciences around the existence of the Senate. It was shaming, but since people can't live with shame, we grew cynical instead.

---

* The only requirements, according to the Constitution, are that they be Canadian citizens; be between the ages of thirty and seventy-five; live in, and own property valued at more than $4,000 in, the province or territory for which they are appointed; and have a net worth of at least $4,000.

The Senate's status as the House of Ill Repute had one virtue, however: it robbed it of legitimacy. That was the point. The Fathers of Confederation intended the Senate to be weak. Otherwise, they worried, it would become a rival to the House of Commons, leading to the sort of gridlock between the two houses so often seen in the US Congress. So they deliberately sandbagged it from the start, making it a patronage body. Lacking a democratic mandate, it was thought, senators would be obliged to mind their place. "There is an infinitely greater chance of a deadlock between the two branches of the legislature, should the elective principle be adopted," Sir John A. Macdonald declared, "than with a nominated chamber—chosen by the Crown, and having no mission from the people."[118] While on paper the Senate had the power to defeat any bill, the expectation, he said, was that it would "never set itself in opposition against the deliberate and understood wishes of the people."[119]

It hasn't quite worked out that way. From 1867 to 1945, the Senate killed a total of one hundred twenty-five bills[120] sent up to it by the Commons; it sent another thirty-three back with amendments that for one reason or another were not approved by the Commons. Sixty more bills died in the Senate, having failed to come to a final vote before Parliament was dissolved or prorogued. At least some of these deaths would have been deliberate, the bills stalled just long enough to ensure they never passed—the Senate's "pocket veto," commonly used to euthanize private members' bills, but also deployed from time to time against government bills.

The number of defeated bills tended to spike each time there was a change of government. The Conservative-dominated Senate greeted the election of Alexander Mackenzie's Liberals in 1874 by defeating six of their bills. Likewise, after the election of the first Laurier government, in 1896: twenty-two bills were defeated in that Parliament. And in the 1921 Parliament, the first to be led by Mackenzie King: fifteen bills were rejected.

Only after the Second World War did the Senate settle back into the somnolent role the Fathers had arranged for it. Since 1945, a

Unelected vs. Elected

mere handful of bills passed by the Commons have been defeated in the upper house: among them, a 1961 bill declaring the office of the governor of the Bank of Canada vacant; the Kim Campbell abortion bill in 1991 (killed, infamously, by a tie vote); and a private members' bill committing Canada to the Kyoto Protocol, passed over the Harper government's objections in the minority Parliament of 2008–11. Those are some pretty weighty issues to be decided in such a flagrantly undemocratic way: not by a vote of the people's elected representatives, but by a clutch of partisan appointees of uncertain distinction.

While it has usually declined to defeat bills outright, the Senate has found other ways to get up to no good, especially after the election of the Mulroney government in 1984, following decades of near-unbroken Liberal hegemony. The Liberal majority in the Senate refused to vote on legislation enacting the GST, obliging Mulroney, via a rarely invoked prime ministerial prerogative, to add and fill another eight Senate seats to see the measure through. A similar Liberal blockade of the free trade bill was resolved only after the intervention of the 1988 election.

It was around that time, too, that the Senate began forcing amendments to legislation in greater numbers. Eighteen bills were successfully amended during the first Mulroney government, half as many as in the nine previous parliaments combined. The pocket veto, after a long period of relative disuse—from 1945 to 1984 just twelve bills met that fate—has also come back into vogue, especially after the election of the first Harper government in 2006.

Senators were briefly chastened by the series of scandals that followed, notably the Mike Duffy affair, and the broader outrage over senators' abuse of their expense accounts. But Senate adventurism was soon given new life in the form of Justin Trudeau's "independent, merit-based" system of appointment. Shortly after becoming Liberal leader, Trudeau ostentatiously kicked all the Liberal senators out of his caucus. Once elected, his government established an arm's-length advisory board to assist him in selecting senators, together with a formal process by which individuals could *apply* for the job. The final choice remains the prime minister's, but senators are supposedly no longer chosen as friends or members of the governing party.

Notwithstanding their leader's directive, many Senate Liberals continued to sit as Liberals. In time, however, as the finality of the reforms sank in, they began to drift away and sit as independents, as did many Conservatives. No sooner had the number of independents begun to multiply, than they began to coalesce again—not into parties, as such, but "groups." But for the twelve remaining members of the Conservative Senate caucus, and a handful of "non-affiliateds," senators now sit as members of either the Canadian Senators Group, the Independent Senators Group, or the Progressive Senate Group.

The short-run impact of this was unmistakable. In the aftermath of the Trudeau reforms, senators became noticeably nervier about defeating government bills, or at least threatening to. It was as if a great weight had been taken off their shoulders. Relieved of the taint of partisanship, senators felt energized, emboldened. No longer was the Senate to be seen as something venal, a reward for a lifetime of partisan service—the "taskless thanks," as the phrase had it.[*] This new generation of senators could take pride in the name, appointed as they were not on the basis of partisan loyalty, but *solely on their personal merit*. In time, even those appointed under the previous system came to believe this of themselves. They began to act as if in answer to a higher calling than partisanship, a higher calling even than democracy. They had something better than a mandate from the people: the mandate of virtue.

Accordingly, the first Trudeau government witnessed a series of near-collisions between the Senate and the Commons: over Bill C-69, revamping the approval process for natural resource projects; over Bill C-48, banning oil tankers along the coast of British Columbia; over Bill C-14, legalizing assisted suicide, and others. In the end, the Senate

---

[*] Attributed to the writer and commentator Larry Zolf.

always backed down, but not before exciting much speculation that this time it might not.

Just the threat was enough for the Senate to order amendments to government bills with historic frequency: twenty-four in just four years, a fifth of all bills sent to the Senate.[121] And those were just the bills that made it to the Senate floor. How many more were never introduced in the House for fear of Senate opposition? Word had it that even federal budgets were being rewritten in anticipation of senators' objections.[122]

At length, the rebellious fervour ceased. Why? For the same reason as in the past. The government had been in power for a few years and there had been the usual relentless tide of prime ministerial appointments. For all Trudeau's promises to appoint "thoughtful individuals representing the varied values, perspectives and identities of this great country,"[123] that was not the practice. They may not have been partisan Liberals, but they were overwhelmingly from Liberal-friendly or certainly liberal-friendly professions[124], with reliably progressive views[125]. And their numbers were, and are, overwhelming. The combination of his own long tenure and the unusual number of vacancies (twenty-two) bequeathed to him by Stephen Harper allowed Trudeau to stamp the Upper House firmly in his own image. At time of writing he had appointed seventy-six of the ninety-seven sitting senators; news reports[126] suggested he would appoint ten more before he stepped down (eight to fill vacancies, two to replace retiring senators: one appointed by Harper, the other by Trudeau.) That would leave a Senate with no fewer than eighty-five Trudeau appointees out of its full retinue of one hundred five.[127] Including the three remaining Chrétien appointees, eighty-eight senators would have been appointed by Liberal prime ministers. There has never been a Senate so completely dominated by the choices of one prime minister, or one party.[128]

So the threat that the Senate might take it upon itself to start defeating government bills, which seemed real a few years ago, has passed for the moment. That may well change when, or if, a

Conservative government is elected. Senators were feisty enough when it was a Liberal government. Imagine what they will do to a Conservative government, especially one led by so combative and norm-breaking a politician as Pierre Poilievre, who would seemingly destroy all that Liberals, and liberals, find holy. Would they not consider it, not just their right, but their duty, to rein him in?

Conservatives are right to wonder if a Trudeau-appointed Senate would allow a Conservative bill to pass that, say, abolished the CBC. Their fears are unlikely to be allayed by Liberal assurances[129] that they would *never dream* of striking down legislation passed by a democratically elected Parliament, just so long as its sponsors in the governing party had publicly and explicitly campaigned on them in the previous election. Or so long as it was not flagrantly unconstitutional. Or . . .

There is a real potential for crisis. A Senate filled with avowedly partisan Liberals and bagmen might have been bashful about using its powers; a Senate endowed with the mandate of virtue will not. A partisan Senate majority that abused its position might have caused its elected counterparts to lose seats at the next election[130]; but who is accountable when a bill has been euthanized, not by shameless Liberal partisans, but by the virtuocracy?

Part of the crisis is precisely that so many people do not see it as a crisis. Time and again, whenever the Senate threatens to defeat this or that government bill, a certain section of opinion will seek to justify it on the basis of their hostility to the legislation. Ordinarily, they might say, the Senate should defer to the Commons, but *this* bill is so bad, the Senate has to intervene.

No cause, no matter how valid, can legitimize such undemocratic methods. There can be no justification in a democratic society for fifty-three unelected senators to substitute their views on how we should be governed for those of elected MPs, and the millions of Canadians they represent. It's wrong when Liberals do it to Conservative governments, and it's wrong when Conservatives do it to Liberals. It may be legal, but it is not legitimate. The fundamental principle of democracy is: government with the consent of the governed. We consent to be governed by the people we elect for the job, and no others. The Commons has a democratic mandate. The Senate does not. It is as simple as that.

That fundamental principle is not altered just because the bill the Commons passes might be unconstitutional or in violation of Charter rights: that's what we have the Supreme Court for. Neither is it relevant whether the government had a "mandate" for the legislation in question. The notion that it does—the principle, known as the Salisbury Convention,* that the Senate may not defeat a bill if it formed part of the governing party's election platform—is often cited as a significant limitation on the discretion of the upper house. It is nothing of the kind.

The prerogative of the Commons to pass a particular piece of legislation does not depend on having promised it in the last election, but solely from its members' status as the elected representatives of the people. They are elected to pass not only the legislation they promised in the campaign, but also whatever bills they see fit to pass for the life of the Parliament. As of course they must be: situations are bound to arise that were not anticipated at the time of the election, and Parliament must be able to respond to them.

The obligation of the Senate to defer to the Commons likewise has nothing to do with what was or was not said in the last election campaign. To confine that obligation to matters that were part of the governing party's election platform is merely a crafty way of saying the Senate should be free to defy the Commons on all other matters. The truth is more straightforward. The Senate is obliged to defer at all times, without exception—because the Commons is elected and the Senate is not. The Senate has the power to defy the Commons, but it does not have the legitimacy.

---

* Named for the Marquess of Salisbury, the former Conservative leader in the House of Lords, who first enunciated it, in 1945.

We would appear to be caught in a dilemma. A Senate that merely waves through bills passed by the Commons is superfluous; a Senate that defeats them is a menace. The dilemma will persist so long as we fail to address the basic underlying contradiction between the Senate's (immense) legal powers and its (total) lack of democratic legitimacy.

There are two ways to bridge this gap. One is to increase the Senate's democratic legitimacy, by electing senators instead of appointing them. The other is to reduce its powers.

Proposals for an elected Senate have been with us almost as long as the Senate itself. The idea has never been simply to mimic the composition of the House of Commons: there would be no need for a duplicate House, and every reason to dread it, given the potential for conflict and deadlock. Rather, the proposal has been for an elected upper house based on something other than the principle of representation by population (ostensibly the basis for representation in the Commons, although see chapter 7).

The argument is that democratic legitimacy is rooted in more than raw numbers. In a liberal, as opposed to a purely majoritarian democracy, the willingness of minorities to be bound by the majority depends on the understanding that the majority will not use its power to trample over minority concerns. A federation like Canada, then, with its vast disproportions between the population of its two largest provinces and of those on the periphery, arguably needs an upper house to temper the power of the majority, much as the upper house in the US or Australia does.

The Fathers of the Confederation, as we have seen, drew back from an elected Senate, unable to agree on a formula for representation and worried about creating a too-powerful rival for the Commons. They instead sought to square the circle—an upper house that could check the Commons, but not obstruct it—by the device of appointment, limiting the Senate's powers by limiting its legitimacy. But that brought problems of its own.

So weak was the Senate, most of the time, that there was no real check on the power of the central Canadian majority. This power was routinely abused, a theme of this book, feeding resentments in the less-populous regions, notably the West, and leading to demands for power to be devolved from the federal government to the provinces, to contain the potential for majoritarian mischief. The more that power was devolved, however, the more it led to demands that power be devolved further—such is human nature—leaving us in the enervated national condition in which we presently find ourselves.

Not content with their usual mulish opposition to any and all federal measures that might conceivably tread upon an inch of provincial jurisdiction—to say nothing of their continuing defiance, 158 years after the fact, of the Constitution's directive that goods from each province be "admitted free"[131] into every other—provinces have in recent years begun to demand a say in such unambiguously federal matters as international trade, immigration, and even national defence. Many a promising federal initiative has failed in the face of provincial opposition.

This is not how the country was intended to function. The federal and provincial governments were each made largely sovereign in their own sphere, and while there was some provision for the federal government to override the provinces[*], it was never envisioned that the provinces would sit in judgment of the feds. Worse, the provinces have of late begun to assert powers they do not have, ignoring or overriding federal laws and constitutional prerogatives while claiming the right to amend or rewrite the Constitution to their liking—not multilaterally, via the appropriate constitutional amending formula, but unilaterally[†].

An elected Senate would arguably turn this around. It would give the Senate the legitimacy it needs to stand up to the Commons in the name of the less populous regions. The Senate, and not the premiers, would be seen as the tribune of the regions. By integrating the representation of regional concerns at the centre, rather than distributing it to the provinces, greater legitimacy might be lent to the federal government generally.

---

* See Constitution's provisions re disallowance; reservation; Peace, Order and Good Government . . .
† For example, Quebec's Bill 96, and Alberta's Alberta Sovereignty within a United Canada Act.

That still leaves unanswered the age-old question: how could it be made to work? If rep by pop is out, what formula replaces it? Equal numbers from each region, as at our founding? Equal numbers from each province, as in the United States? And how powerful should the Senate be? Clearly, the two are related. The further you depart from rep by pop, the less you can justify giving it a veto over the Commons. That was always the trouble with the Reform Party's "Triple-E Senate" proposal. Even if you could get agreement on the first *E—elected*— there was bound to be a trade-off between the other two: *equal* (as in equal numbers of senators from each province) and *effective* (meaning its powers to check the Commons). Perhaps this could have been finessed in some way. Perhaps not.

Alas, the Triple-E dream, or nightmare, depending on your perspective, died in 2014, with the Supreme Court's ruling in the Senate reform reference. The court held that even the mildest move in the direction of reform, such as the Harper government's proposal to require prime ministers to appoint only senators who had been elected, could not be implemented without amending the Constitution, and not by a mere vote of the House of Commons and the Senate, as are sufficient for reforms that affect only Parliament, but by the dreaded general amending formula: the House, the Senate and the legislatures of seven provinces representing 50 per cent of the population. The reasoning—that an elected-but-appointed Senate would lend the Senate a soupçon of democratic legitimacy, and as such would violate the Confederation bargain of a Senate that was appointed and weak— need not detain us here. The point is that the high bar imposed by the amending formula means Senate reform is not going to happen. You can't get seven provinces to agree on the time of day.*

---

* This is of course a more general problem. The Constitution's amending formula is so rigid, and so beholden to the interests of the provinces, that it makes amendments all but impossible. So amend the amending formula? But that is even harder: it requires the agreement of all ten provinces. As with every other problem of Canadian democracy, changing it requires the consent of those who most benefit from the status quo.

Unelected vs. Elected

That leaves the second possible remedy: trimming the Senate's powers. In the UK, the powers of the House of Lords have long been circumscribed, ever since the passage of the Parliament Act 1911. The result of an especially ugly confrontation with the Commons over a budget bill, the act limited the Lords to a suspensive, rather than an absolute, veto: two years (since reduced to a year) for most legislation; a month in the case of money bills.

That's similar to an existing provision in the Canadian Constitution, mentioned earlier, limiting the Senate to a six-month suspensive veto on constitutional amendments. The six months having passed, the Commons has only to repass an amendment for it to become law. Alas, it is no more possible to legally alter the Senate's powers than it is to change its composition or method of selection. Where Britain can reform its upper house by a mere act of Parliament, in Canada it would require a constitutional amendment, once again under the general amending formula.*

Does that make any reform impossible? No. The Senate can trim its own powers, simply by passing changes to its own Standing Orders. It might, for example, adopt the six-month suspensive veto that now applies to constitutional amendments as general practice, as suggested by former Senator Michael Kirby and the late Senator Hugh Segal in their 2016 paper[132] for the Public Policy Forum. More radically, it could take the advice of Professor Andrew Heard[133] and adopt a resolution that any bill from the Commons that has not passed the Senate in six (or perhaps twelve) months—one month for money bills, following the British example—"shall be deemed to have received third reading."

Either way, that's all that's really required to solve the Senate riddle. Once it is defanged of its power to kill government bills, all the other questions about the Senate that have so long divided us—how many

---

* Among the constitutional changes listed under Section 42.1 (b) of the 1982 Constitution as being subject to the general amending formula is "the powers of the Senate."

senators should be appointed from each province, on what basis, etc.—fade into insignificance.

The current system might even prove to be the best. A Senate filled with the great and the good is a tolerable sort of outcome, provided it has no actual legislative power of any kind. If the quality of appointments was high, if it represented a broad cross section of the community and of political opinion, and if senators behaved themselves, it might acquire a certain moral power. A Senate whose power resided, not in any formal authority to defeat a bill, but in its moral authority—a Senate that really was a repository of virtue—could make a useful contribution to the government of the country, beyond the individual capacities of its members.

As it is, however, the Senate is an accident waiting to happen: an accident with the potential to do great harm.

* * *

It is at about this point that some clever person will inevitably ask: wait, if you're so concerned about unelected officials overruling the House of Commons, why don't you apply that same logic to the Supreme Court? Shouldn't you be just as concerned about unelected judges obstructing the will of the people's elected representatives, by means of the Charter of Rights?

The two are not comparable. The Supreme Court is a specialized, highly trained body whose mandate is limited to comparing one law with another, in accordance with precedent and guided by centuries of rigorous legal thinking. The Senate can reject a law for any reason it likes. All mature democracies have some equivalent of the Supreme Court; most have some equivalent of the Charter. None has anything quite like the Canadian Senate.

Yet the Senate does not attract a tenth as much controversy as the Supreme Court does. The notion that the Supreme Court represents a unique threat to parliamentary democracy—that it has all but supplanted the House of Commons, that real power now rests with the courts, that a cadre of rogue judges have taken it upon themselves to write the laws in place of the people we elect for the purpose—has become common currency in recent years, especially on the right.

Once, Parliament was supreme, runs the lament, now it is the courts. Once, the courts knew their place; now, empowered by the Charter, they have usurped the role of the legislatures. Activist judges, accountable to no one, have subverted the sovereignty of Parliament. In place of democracy, we have "judge-made law." Some blame the judges for devising ever more fanciful interpretations of the Charter that are nowhere to be found in the text. Others blame the Charter itself. In the words of one prominent critic, the day the Charter became law, Canada "surrendered any claim to democratic self-government."

All this for a document that is not hugely different from those in place in democracies around the world. The purpose of the Charter was to codify, in written form, certain democratic and legal rights on which there was an especially broad and durable consensus, much in the style of the American Bill of Rights.

Indeed, most of the Charter's provisions can be found in the Canadian Bill of Rights, passed into law in 1960. But that was a mere act of Parliament, a law like any other: it does not bind other laws, or not in a way that the courts have been willing to enforce. Like other laws, moreover, it can be amended or overridden simply by passing another law: it is not binding on Parliament, either. Third, as a federal law it was not binding on provincial laws.

The Charter's supremacy, by contrast, is explicitly affirmed by the 1982 Constitution: all laws not consistent with it are "to the extent of the inconsistency, of no force or effect." It applies equally to federal and provincial legislation. And it cannot be changed except via the Constitution's general amending formula, seven provinces with 50 percent of the population.

The reason the Charter was made harder to change was to ensure that, like other parts of the Constitution, it would be more binding on governments and legislatures than ordinary laws: not just supreme, but permanently supreme, or as permanently supreme as the amending formula can make it. In passing the Charter, legislators committed themselves and all future legislators to abide by its constraints; the majority agreed to bind future majorities to respect the rights of individuals and minorities. Having locked themselves in, they threw away the key, or at least buried it.

That has made it the target of attacks on a number of fronts: from parliamentary supremacists, vexed at the implied abridgement of the sovereignty of the Commons; from left-wing academics, concerned that it protects the privileges of the few over the will of the many; from Quebec nationalists, who see it as the ultimate instrument of "domineering federalism"; from postmodernists, amused at the very suggestion that there are such things as universal rights of a kind one might think of enshrining in a Charter.

But by far the most common critique of the Charter is that it has become a platform for judicial activists, a blank slate for rogue judges to impose their own interpretations upon it. This is not entirely without foundation. There is such a thing as judicial activism: decisions that so distort the intent and meaning of the statutes as to effectively rewrite them to suit the judge's opinions—although whether or not a particular ruling qualifies as activist will be a matter of opinion, informed in part by differing theories of jurisprudence: should the Constitution be interpreted strictly with reference to the text or "the intent of the framers," or might it be interpreted in light of contemporary circumstances and mores?

From the tone of much of the critics' commentary, however, it is plain that they consider the courts to be guilty of judicial activism any time they strike down a law. It doesn't matter how nutty the law, or how flagrantly it violates the Constitution: it all counts as unelected judges dictating to a democratically elected legislature. Their complaint, it is clear, is not really with judicial activism, which is a perversion of the Constitution, but with judicial review, which is required by it. The emotional thrust of their argument is an impatience that any constraint should be placed upon the right of the people we elect to do what they think necessary in the public interest.

Unelected vs. Elected

Because we elected them. That is always the rallying cry: "democracy." It is undemocratic, it is often said, to give the courts the last word. It is undemocratic to let a handful of unelected justices second-guess the decisions of elected legislators. So great was this sentiment that many years after the Charter became law, some conservatives were still agitating for its abolition—when they were not demanding it be amended to include protection for property rights.*

Are they right? Is the Charter, and the limits it imposes on the discretion of the legislatures, incompatible with democratic government? Or is the Charter, and judicial review, in fact the highest expression of democratic rule?

In answer, it is perhaps worth reviewing what the Charter is and how it came to be. It is an article of faith among many conservatives that the Charter, as a written codification of rights, is an aberration, an American or possibly French import wholly alien to our British constitutional tradition. Magna Carta, the Petition of Right, the Bill of Rights 1689: these apparently were never committed to paper, but were handed down in legend and song. So, it seems, was the 1960 Bill of Rights, child of that arch-American, pro-French, flaming anti-traditionalist John Diefenbaker.

Who decided there should be a Charter of Rights, to which all other laws would be subordinate? It wasn't some secretive cabal of jurists. It was the Parliament of Canada—and not at the whim of the prime minister, forced through by a narrow party-line majority, but by a vote of two hundred forty-six to twenty-four in the House and with the support of nine of the ten provincial governments.† Few bills of such significance have passed with such broad-based support.

---

* Literally true: at the 2001 Canadian Alliance convention, delegates voted on separate resolutions urging both that the Charter be repealed *and* that it be amended to include protection for property rights. One is reminded of the old Catskills joke: "Yech, the food at this restaurant is terrible! And the portions are so small!"

† Quebec, the lone holdout, already had its own Charter of Human Rights and Freedoms.

Neither was judicial review the invention of the courts. It was Parliament, not the courts, that assigned judges their current role of examining the laws for compatibility with the Charter. It was Parliament, not the courts, that decreed that "the Constitution of Canada is the supreme law of Canada," and it was Parliament that stipulated that "anyone whose rights or freedoms . . . have been infringed or denied may apply to a court of competent jurisdiction to obtain such remedy as the court considers appropriate and just."

For that matter, judicial review did not begin with the Charter. Canada has had a written Constitution, subject to judicial interpretation, since its founding: the British North America Act, aka the Constitution Act 1867. Long before 1982, the courts were tossing out laws passed by Parliament and the provincial legislatures, only on division of powers rather than Charter grounds. If one level of government believed another had invaded its jurisdiction, as laid out in Sections 91 and 92 of the 1867 Constitution, it took it to court. If the courts agreed, the law was ruled ultra vires—beyond the authority of the offending government.

The notion that the legislative branch is supreme, and immune to judicial scrutiny, has never been part of our tradition. Parliamentary sovereignty might have been the convention in Great Britain, but so was the convention that colonial legislatures could not overwrite imperial law.[134] Judicial review was built into our legal and political structure from the start, not by appeal to Montesquieu or Locke, as in the American experience, but by dint of our status as a colony and our divisions as a federation. Somebody had to adjudicate these disputes, and that somebody was the courts.

(If you really want to see some judicial activism, have a look at the series of decisions rendered by the Judicial Committee of the Privy Council, then the country's supreme legal authority, in the decades after 1867. In effect, it redrafted the terms of Confederation, turning a highly centralizing document—the Fathers of Confederation, after all, met in the waning days of the American Civil War, and were determined not to repeat the "states' rights" mistakes of the Americans—into its opposite.")

All the Charter did was let the people in on the game. Where before the courts were confined to deciding whether one level of government had encroached upon the powers of another, now they were also called upon to draw the line between government and citizen. Seen in that context, the Charter appears less revolutionary than evolutionary. Indeed, the original conservative complaint about the Charter was precisely that it involved the legislature in defining rights, rather than entrusting them to the centuries of legal precedent that make up the common law—the original judge-made law!

Which is to say that judges have always made law. The same complaints that critics make about the Charter—that it binds the hands of elected legislators, in favour of unelected judges—may be made against the whole body of written law. All laws, not just the Charter, constrain governments to act in certain ways, and not in others. All laws, not just the Charter, are interpreted and applied by judges, and as such give judges licence to "make law." All laws, not just the Charter, bind future parliaments, until they are amended or repealed. If there were no constitutions, we would still need judges to interpret the written law, and if there were no written law, there would still be the common law. To talk of judge-made law is merely to talk of the law itself, and law, whatever else it binds, is always a check on government. We do not give our rulers unfettered discretion to rule as they wish. We grant them only such powers as they specifically request, and as we, through our representatives in Parliament, explicitly permit. "The King hath no prerogative but that which the law of the land allows him," thundered the great seventeenth-century jurist Sir Edward Coke, in the seminal Case of Proclamations (1610).

---

* It was the Committee's obdurate refusal to agree to federal initiatives to deal with the Great Depression that led to its decommissioning as Canada's highest court, in 1941.

And just to be sure, we make them put it in writing. We want governments to behave in a predictable, consistent, and understandable fashion. We want to know exactly what they plan to do, and how, and for what purpose, and whether that represents a change from what they were doing before. And we want to be able to hold them to account if they do not do what they said they would—if they do not obey the law.

The rights set out in the Charter are, in short, a kind of promise. We will pass no laws, Parliament and the provinces solemnly pledged, that defy this law or that intrude upon these rights. In all our laws and in all our acts, we will abide by these guarantees. And to show they meant it—that these were not ordinary political promises, to be abandoned when expedient—they not only passed them into law, but made them part of the Constitution.

But a promise, to be binding, must have an independent adjudicator. To make an oath meaningful, you need a court to enforce it. To leave it to governments and legislatures to decide for themselves whether their laws were in conformity with the Charter—whether they had kept their promises—would make a mockery of the whole exercise. It would amount to letting them vouch for their own credit.

If governments could be judges in their own cause, the vital check on their discretion posed by the written law would fade to nothing. Laws would mean whatever the government of the day said they meant. Inconsistencies would multiply. It would be impossible to identify what principles, if any, were guiding government action, and impossible to hold governments to their word.

The point, then, is not that the courts "know best" or are superior to Parliament, or government, but that they are *other* than them: a second set of eyes, an independent arbiter. If government is to be held to its word, someone else must do the holding. That's the courts' job: to ensure that the laws that governments draft and parliaments pass are consistent with the promises enshrined in the Constitution.

That does not mean judges have, or should have, "the last word." In our system, nobody gets the last word. Ours is a system, as it has been said, of neither parliamentary nor judicial supremacy, but *constitutional* supremacy. Ensuring legislation is in compliance with the Constitution is best thought of as a joint effort between the two branches. It is, yes, a "dialogue." This is not some academic fancy. It is an observable fact. Away from the klieg lights of political controversy, it goes on every day.

A judicial finding that a particular law is unconstitutional is not normally the end of the discussion. More often, it is the beginning. Courts do not typically pass judgment, for starters, on the purpose of a piece of legislation. Rather, they look at whether, in pursuit of its purpose, it overreached—whether the same purpose might have been, and might yet be, achieved in less draconian ways.

At that, courts usually don't find fault with the whole of a law—only particular sections of it. It is open to the legislature to redraft the offending section, to the extent of its overreach. It is almost always possible to repair the parts of a law invalidated by the Court; to redraft the law, in ways that fulfill its original purpose, but at less harm to rights.

The Charter itself is an immensely forgiving document. It contains at least four and perhaps a dozen sections exempting laws that would otherwise be unconstitutional, including laws relating to affirmative action, aboriginal peoples, and separate schools, among others. Several other clauses come with built-in qualifiers: the freedom of *peaceful* assembly; the right not to be deprived of life, liberty, and the security of the person *except* "in accordance with the principles of fundamental justice," and so on.

The whole thing, moreover, is hedged with one big rider: Section 1, subjecting Charter rights to "such reasonable limits prescribed by law as may be demonstrably justified in a free and democratic society." It is not enough for a court find that there has been a breach of the Charter, however slight. Rather, it is obliged to consider whether the breach might be justified under Section 1. It is permissible for a law to violate Charter rights: it just has to be "reasonable" about it.

Is that the rule, then: Give me liberty or give me a good excuse? No. The burden of proof is always on the state to justify any limit.

Section 1 does not say merely that rights are subject to reasonable limits: it says rights are subject "only" to such reasonable limits as can be "demonstrably justified." It's quite stringent. Compare an earlier draft[135] of the clause, which allowed such limits as were "generally accepted" in a free and democratic society; or the European Convention on Human Rights[136], which permits exceptions if they are merely "necessary."

What's reasonable? An early Charter decision, *Regina v. Oakes*, set out a four-step test. The limitation must have a "pressing and substantial" objective, to which it is "rationally connected"; it must impair rights as little as possible; and the harm to rights must be proportional to the good achieved. There are, in other words, reasonable limits on reasonable limits. The government can't just say a particular limit is reasonable. It has to persuade a court that it is. And the court can't just eyeball it. It has to put it through the Oakes test.

Oakes doesn't guarantee good decisions. But as a template for "structured compromise" it may be the best attempt at balancing individual rights and the public good yet devised. Rather than define rights as either absolute or optional, it allows rights to bend, but only to the least extent necessary, and in response to the most pressing exigencies.

* * *

That's all very well in theory, a critic might object, but is that how it works in practice? I agree (the critic might continue) that the Charter is a good idea, and I accept that it is the role of the courts to interpret it. But I can't help noting how often their decisions stray beyond its actual text, finding in it things that are not implied by any sensible reading, and that it is impossible to believe were intended by its drafters. Times change, and so do the needs of law, but the usual and legitimate way to make changes to the law is to pass a bill through Parliament, not rewrite it from the bench.

Or at any rate (another critic might interject) there is certainly the potential for judicial overreach, or judicial error of one kind or another. Judges are fallible, like anyone else. Is it really wise to hand them such power? Isn't there room for some sort of safety valve, some way to ensure that Parliament's will prevails, in cases where the courts get it wrong?

Hence the current wave of enthusiasm for Section 33 of the Charter, popularly known as the notwithstanding clause, which allows governments to pass legislation in violation of the Charter. This goes beyond Section 1, which allows governments to violate the Charter so long as they are reasonable about it. To make use of Section 33, they don't have to be reasonable; they just have to be explicit. The legislation must "expressly declare" that it applies notwithstanding any inconsistency with the Charter. The exception applies for five years—more, if the declaration is renewed.

To its defenders, this is a reasonable and pragmatic compromise, in keeping with the spirit of the Charter. (It's not the Charter they have a problem with, pragmatists will often say—it's the courts.) Suppose a court misreads the Charter, or misapplies it. In that event, the legislature would not really be overriding the Charter. It would just be overriding an errant court ruling. Now suppose the courts issue a stream of such rulings. Who is the greater friend to the Charter then? The courts that keep bending it out of shape, or the governments that step in to restore it to its original meaning?

Shouldn't the judiciary, they ask, be subject to the same checks and balances as the other branches of government? Why should the courts be the only ones to define what are "reasonable limits" on the Charter? Shouldn't Parliament have the same power? Isn't that what the notwithstanding clause does: strike a balance between the two, in that distinctively Canadian tradition of compromise that goes all the way back to Wolfe and Montcalm?

No, actually. The notwithstanding clause is in a distinctively Canadian tradition, all right. It's called trying to have it both ways. It draws on the belief that we can have all the benefits of freedom, and none of the costs: that we can brag to ourselves and the world of the liberties our citizens enjoy, but discard them at the first conflict with the state's desires.

No other democratic country's Constitution contains such a gaping loophole[137]. Everyone has these fundamental freedoms, the Charter declares, upon which the state may not trespass. Unless, of course, it does. Governor George Wallace could not long sustain Alabama's segregation laws in defiance of his country's Constitution. Had he been the premier of a Canadian province, he probably could have.

The notwithstanding clause allows governments to override the most basic human rights, including freedom of expression; freedom of assembly; the right to life, liberty, and security of the person; the right to counsel; the right to be presumed innocent; the right not to be subjected to cruel and unusual punishment; and the right to equality. Or rather, it allows governments to override *some* rights, and not others. The override does not apply to language rights, or to aboriginal rights, or to "Canada's multicultural heritage." Neither does it apply to women's rights, although it did when first drafted: after feminist groups objected, a clause was added to the Charter stipulating that, while the equality of the sexes is already guaranteed under Section 15, it should be guaranteed a second time, notwithstanding notwithstanding.*

Far from balancing the power of the legislature against that of the courts, it completely unbalances the relationship. If the courts decide that a given law unreasonably limits Charter rights under Section 1, Parliament always has the option of redrafting the law, without prejudice to its original purpose. Whereas the notwithstanding clause removes the law entirely from judicial scrutiny.

We already have a reasonable limits clause. We don't need an unreasonable limits clause. Or what is the evidence that we do? The Court issues plenty of wonky, inexplicable Charter decisions, but the

---

* At the height of the Meech Lake drama, it was proposed, to answer concerns that the distinct society clause might infringe on women's rights, that the equality of the sexes be affirmed in the Constitution yet a third time.

portrait of a runaway Supreme Court striking down laws this way and that on Charter grounds is unsupported by the evidence. Since 1982, empirical studies[138] have shown, the Court has sided with the government in Charter cases roughly two-thirds of the time, finding either that the Charter had not been violated, or that if it had, it was permissible under Section 1.

That the Court has upheld one-third of Charter challenges is not evidence of activism in itself. Doubtless, some of these were ill-judged. But all of them? Subtract the cases where the Court had good reason to throw the law out, and subtract as well those in which the legislation was simply amended to take account of the Court's objections, and you are left with few, if any, of the sorts of rogue-court scenarios that are the clause's supposed justification.

For every case of judicial overreach, moreover, there are at least as many cases of judicial *underreach*. Contrary to their reputation as constitutional vigilantes, courts are most often at pains to defer to the legislatures, sometimes to the point of ignoring or distorting the Charter—what might be called "activism by omission," declining to strike down legislation where it was the clear sense of the Charter that they should.

Much of this has taken place within the refuge afforded by Section 1. The Oakes test, once such a sturdy underpinning of legal analysis, has since been considerably elasticized. The court's willingness to uphold Charter rights has grown to depend less on the rigorous logic of Oakes than on which rights are at issue and what group is involved. The result is an emerging "hierarchy of rights": procedural rights at the top, those pitting the accused against the "singular antagonist" of the state, with which the Court seems most at ease; equality rights in the middle, which may involve competing claims between different social groups, on which the Court has tacked this way and that; and the broader spectrum of individual rights at the bottom. Its record on free speech cases is especially spotty.

Between the two extremes, of excessive activism and excessive deference, the Court ought to be able to find a middle ground, neither showing such deference to the legislatures as to ignore the Charter's express limitations on government discretion, nor reading things into the Charter that aren't there, to promote ends for which it was never intended. Such a position would ask no more of the justices than that they take the law as they find it. Alas, that seems beyond them. It's no use accusing the Court of judicial activism, or inactivism: in its aimless ad hoc fashion, it is as likely to lean one way as the other. It seems to owe allegiance to no constitutional principle whatever, upholding or rewriting laws almost at random. That ought to worry everyone.

So yes, it's true: in interpreting the Charter, the courts sometimes get it wrong—not as often as claimed, and not always in the same direction, but often enough. But so what? *Nothing in the idea of judicial review depends on judges being infallible.* Courts get all kinds of things wrong, not just Charter decisions. They convict the innocent and free the guilty with distressing frequency. That does not entitle the government to try people in their place. Neither do the frequent errors of the legislatures offer justification for the executive to rule by decree. The argument for judicial review is rooted in the separation of powers, not the divinity of the bench.

So often is the notwithstanding clause now invoked, and with such scant justification, that one might almost say it is not rogue courts we should fear most, but rogue governments. This was not what was supposed to happen. When the Charter was first adopted, supporters were adamant the clause would be used sparingly, and in situations that aroused no controversy. Some Charter advocates praised it on the grounds that it would "implicate" governments in court decisions: for a government to allow a decision to stand, though it had the power to negate it, would be tacitly to endorse it, or certainly to say that it is legitimate.

That sort of argument held sway so long as the notwithstanding clause remained a largely theoretical concern. And it did, outside of Quebec. The clause was applied to every bill passed by the province's Parti Québécois government between 1982 and 1985—a fit of petulance at the new Constitution having been passed without its agreement. Over the following twenty years, another fourteen bills were added to the list, mostly routine legislation to do with pensions or schools. But the firestorm that erupted over Robert Bourassa's use of it in defence of the province's sign laws in 1988 made it controversial, even in Quebec.

Elsewhere, it was all but dormant. From 1982 to 2017, just four attempts were made to use the clause, none of which amounted to much. Yukon's use of it in 1982 to head off challenges to its Land Planning and Development Act was rendered moot, as the bill was never proclaimed. Saskatchewan used it in 1986 to order striking public-sector employees back to work, but did not need to, as the Supreme Court later ruled. Most infamously, Alberta tried to use it twice: in 1998 to deprive a group of former residents of the province's mental institutions of the right to sue the government for having forcibly sterilized them (the bill was dropped in the face of a ferocious public outcry), and in 2000 to make same-sex marriages illegal—irrelevantly, as the province has no power to legislate in that area (marriage is a federal responsibility).

More recently, the ground has shifted. To the applause of conservative legal theorists, provincial governments have begun to use the clause with more and more regularity. Since 2017, it has been invoked eight times in four provinces. The issues involved ranged from an Ontario law banning strikes in the public sector, to Quebec's laws banning the wearing of religious symbols in the public sector and the use of English in the workplace, to a Saskatchewan law forcing schools to tell parents when their children change their pronouns.

That so many attempts should be made in the space of a few years, all by conservative governments, is not coincidental. The intent seems to be to remove any lingering taboo surrounding the clause, making what was once the exception the rule—to invoke it, not occasionally, in extreme cases, but routinely, in every case, and so to normalize it through sheer repetition. Thus are governments to be liberated altogether from the constraints of the Charter: not by abolishing it (an impossibility, given the rigours of the constitutional amending formula*) but by eviscerating it. Indeed, it is increasingly deployed, not in response to judicial rulings, but in *advance* of them: inserted into a bill preemptively, such that the courts are prevented from ever examining it. For how could anyone's rights have been violated if a court has never found that they have?

It was supposed to be an emergency safety valve. Instead, the notwithstanding clause has turned out to be an all-purpose escape hatch for governments impatient with the obligations of constitutionalism. The hypotheses invoked to support its necessity—what if the Supreme Court loses its mind? what if there is some national emergency?—bear no resemblance to the circumstances in which it has actually been used.

Come down from the mountaintop of abstraction, and the clause reveals itself in all its thuggish particulars. It's not about halting judicial activism or supporting parliamentary sovereignty. It's about denying specific rights to specific groups of people, usually unpopular minorities, sexual, religious, or linguistic. Its practitioners in government may pose as defenders of the ancient rights of Parliament, but it is their own power they are protecting. Strip away the protective layers of judiciary-bashing, and you find what they really fear: not that judges will make the wrong decisions, but that they will make the right ones.

This should have surprised no one. The notion that the clause could have been confined to emergency use, indefinitely, was always a fantasy: leave a loaded gun lying around, somebody is bound to pick it up. The clause's very existence is a standing invitation to its use, a silent rebuke to everything the Charter stands for. Whether or not it is ever invoked, it is always at work, stealthily undermining the Charter's legitimacy. The rights guaranteed by the Charter, it says, are not guaranteed at all. They are not permanent and universal, but temporary and contingent—not so much rights as permissions.

---

* In this case, it would very likely require the unanimous consent of the provinces.

Unelected vs. Elected

The notwithstanding clause is, and always has been, a light in the window for partisans of arbitrary rule. And each time it is used makes the next easier, and the next, and the next, until there is little left of the Charter but fond hopes and fine phrases.

Defenders protest that the notwithstanding clause is part of the Charter, as much as the rights whose override it permits. Without it, the Charter would never have been accepted by the provinces: it was, as they say, part of the constitutional bargain. But what was that bargain? It is nonsense to pretend the current mess was what people had in mind in 1982.[139] It takes two sides to strike a bargain: if the Charter was unacceptable to its critics without the notwithstanding clause, the notwithstanding clause was acceptable to Charter advocates only on the understanding that it would rarely be used. It makes no sense that they would accept it on any other basis. A Charter that can be overridden willy-nilly, a Charter that cannot protect people from being denied employment on the basis of their religion, is no Charter at all.

If that understanding is now broken, then so is the constitutional order. The routine use of the notwithstanding clause amounts to a unilateral amendment of the 1982 Constitution and the careful balance it struck: between majorities and minorities, and between the provinces and the federal government. The Charter, that is, was part of a larger constitutional bargain, the sole counterweight to the 1982 Constitution's broadly decentralizing thrust.* If the Charter no longer has any practical effect, then one of the few remaining ties binding the nation together—our equal entitlement, as Canadians, to a common

---

* It *was* broadly decentralizing, particularly in areas of interest to Quebec. The 1982 Constitution entrenched provincial control of natural resources, subjected future constitutional amendments to provincial consent (including, in certain matters, a veto for every province), and allowed provinces to opt out of constitutional amendments that reduced their powers (with compensation in matters of language and culture). In addition, it entrenched bilingualism at the federal level, obliged the federal government to provide equalization to the provinces in perpetuity, and guaranteed Quebec three of the nine Supreme Court justices. Finally, while all the other provinces were required to provide minority language schooling to the children of parents whose mother tongue was French, Quebec alone was spared the reciprocal obligation (except for parents educated in English in Canada), until such time as it chose to opt in.

set of rights—is gone. The federation is fatally unbalanced. This is more than an affront to liberty: it is an abdication of nationhood.

We can have a Charter of Rights, it is now clear, or we can have a notwithstanding clause. We cannot have both. If this were a functioning democracy, we'd abolish the clause. But this is Canada, so we can't. As with Senate reform, any attempt to amend the constitution to remove it would run into the near impossibility of amending anything, under the formula adopted in 1982.

Does that mean we just have to live with the notwithstanding clause? That would amount over time to abolishing the Charter. The conflict between the two can no longer be avoided. A crisis threatens on two fronts: not only the Supreme Court, but also our old friend the Senate.

We have already seen how a confrontation with the House of Commons has been brewing in the Senate, dominated as it is by Liberal appointees, should the Conservatives win the next election. The notwithstanding clause may be the flashpoint. Among the bills the Conservatives plan to introduce are several criminal justice bills of the kind passed by the previous Harper government and vetoed by the Supreme Court. To prevent his bills from meeting the same fate, the Conservative leader has vowed to invoke the notwithstanding clause. In response, some senators, led by Senator Peter Harder, who was until 2019 the Liberal government's official representative in the upper house, are threatening to veto any federal bill that includes it.

Meanwhile, the Supreme Court has agreed to hear a challenge to Quebec's Bill 21, the one banning religious garb in the public sector. A Quebec court had earlier ruled that, while the legislation was manifestly in violation of the Charter, it was comprehensively shielded from being struck down by the inclusion of the requisite "notwithstanding" declaration in its text. The Supreme Court has been asked to rule on whether this use of the clause was constitutional.* You can imagine the response in the province should the Court find it was not.[140]

---

* A previous Supreme Court ruling, in the 1988 case of *Ford v. Quebec (Attorney-General)*, suggested governments had more or less complete leeway to use the clause as they saw fit.

Neither solution is satisfactory. However high-handed and illiberal the notwithstanding clause may be, for the Senate to block a duly elected government from invoking it would be worse: the remedy for autocracy is not more autocracy. As for the Supreme Court, it would seem a stretch to suggest that a clause whose purpose is to limit the application of judicial review is itself subject to judicial review.

Fortunately, there is another solution. That is for the federal government to step in. For its own part, it can easily forswear all use of the clause, whether by a motion of Parliament or legislation. And it can prevent the provinces from using it by invoking the federal power of disallowance.[141]

This may strike some readers as novel, even extreme. But it is no more than a restoration of the role assigned to the federal government at our founding. Representative though they may have been of the provinces that sent them, the Fathers of Confederation were also Victorian liberals, as much the disciples of John Locke[142] as the American founders were, and as conscious of the need to protect individual and minority rights—for their own sake, but also as the basis of the new "political nationality" transcending local identities that many of them spoke of creating.

Responsibility for the protection of minority rights from local majorities, they were equally adamant, was to be vested in the federal government. And the instrument of this was to be the disallowance power. "Under the Confederation scheme," Sir John A. Macdonald advised delegates to the Quebec conference in 1864, "we shall . . . be able to protect the minority by having a powerful central government."[143] George Brown likewise defended disallowance as a kind of appeal court for the victims of local injustice.[144]

In the first decades after Confederation, disallowance was used repeatedly for this purpose—part of the original constitutional bargain. Since then, it is true, it has fallen into disuse. Over time, and especially after 1982, the federal government and disallowance gave way to the courts and the Charter as the guarantors of rights. A new constitutional balance was struck, in place of the old.

But if the Charter, thanks to the increasing use of the notwithstanding clause, is allowed to become a dead letter, then neither the original constitutional balance nor that of the 1982 Constitution would remain. If neither the federal government nor the courts are permitted to act as guarantors of individual and minority rights, that would leave these rights, for the first time in our history, with no protection at all.

Disallowance has not, as some have claimed, become void from disuse. The last time it was invoked, it is true, was in 1943.* But constitutional texts do not simply expire with the passage of time, particularly those that were part of the Confederation bargain. Is there, nevertheless, a convention against its use? A convention applies, according to the accepted definition, only if all the players, on all sides, agree to be bound by it.[145] But no federal government has ever acknowledged that disallowance is obsolete.

Reviving its use would be controversial, without a doubt. Disallowance is rightly viewed as the "nuclear option" in federal-provincial relations, something to be used only as a last resort. But the notwithstanding clause was also supposed to be the "nuclear option." It may be that a little constitutional deterrence is in order: a declaration by the federal government that any future provincial use of the notwithstanding clause would be met by disallowance.

Or it could say that it would do so in cases where the clause is used preemptively, without the courts having pronounced on the legislation. Or in cases where use of the clause would put us offside of our international human rights commitments[146]. The point is, there are options. What is not an option is for the federal government to stand by while fundamental rights are abrogated and the Charter is slowly, or rapidly, suffocated.

The notwithstanding clause has clearly become too dangerous to be left unguarded. If it cannot be removed, then it must at least be

---

* In defence of Alberta's Hutterites, whom provincial law would have forbidden from buying land.

returned to its cage, the taboo on its use restored. Why is that a matter for democrats? Why would a book on democratic reform devote so much space to this issue? Because ultimately the Charter, and what becomes of it, is about democracy.

The Charter is a supremely democratic document: passed, as mentioned, by a super-majority of members of Parliament, with the support of nine of the ten provinces. It was Parliament's will that there should be a Charter, as it was that judges should enforce it. To demand that judges refrain from examining acts of Parliament in light of the Charter, when it is Parliament that has said they must, is ironically to ask judges to ignore the will of Parliament.

The Charter also helps to reinforce our democracy. The rights it protects are not just an expression of democratic will, but the precondition of it. The first bulwark of democratic government is a democratic culture: a vigilant public, aware of its rights and unwilling to surrender these prerogatives to those transitory tenants of the halls of power. The more we yield unnecessarily to the demands of the state, the more we absorb the habits of deference, the more the muscles of self-government will atrophy.

The link between freedom and democracy was memorably stated by John Dixon, former president of the BC Civil Liberties Association[147]. "All of us are called," he wrote, "as citizens of a democracy, to a perpetual term of office as members of a ruling assembly—and as such we all have work to do that can never be delegated. The hands and minds of sovereign citizens must be free to do their work of ruling, and thus it is that citizens claim a range of liberties and rights, not as petitioners or subjects before governments, but as the central branch of government, the legitimate source of all political authority in the state.

"The mind of every Canadian citizen," he continued, "is an element of the thinking, deliberating and judging intelligence that is the real boss in this country. Seeing this, we must also see that those minds can never tolerate an attempt . . . to pre-empt their ruling work by controlling access to the public forum of thoughts or expressions." Or, I might add, by unjustly curtailing any of their other liberties.

The Crisis of Canadian Democracy

Freedom and democracy are mutually reinforcing. Freedom makes people more democratic in spirit; democracy gives them the tools with which to secure and protect their freedom. Together they contribute to making a self-governing people both more self-governing, and more of a people. When a people are conscious of their common freedoms, they will be more willing to make democratic decisions together, to see themselves as a people, and behave like it, minorities agreeing to be bound by the majority, majorities agreeing not to abuse the minority.

The reverse is also true. It is no coincidence that the governments most eager to use the notwithstanding clause to deprive minorities of their rights are also the ones currently taking liberties with the Constitution in other ways: passing laws in open defiance of the division of powers, or purporting to amend the constitution unilaterally. That's not just an attack on the constitutional order. It is an attack on the unity of the nation-state.

Ordinarily, one would expect the national government, as the only government answerable to all the people, to protect the nation from such attacks. And yet the federal government stands mute, paralyzed—as it has for decades, under governments of either party. It does not feel it has the legitimacy to take on the provinces. In a confrontation, it fears that the public will side with the government that is nearest to them. The more the federal government fears to act, the more brazen the provinces become, and the weaker the feds are made to look. The weaker they appear, the more they lack legitimacy. And the less their legitimacy, the more they fear to act.

This is a direct consequence of the weakness of our democratic institutions. The lack of serious checks on the powers of the prime minister has rendered the office not more effective, but less. Absent such democratic accountability, the prime minister is left without the legitimacy to defend the Constitution from provincial lawlessness, undermining not only federal authority and national unity, but the rule of law itself. The country is in danger of becoming ungovernable.

6
Campaigns

THE MODERN POLITICAL CAMPAIGN, writes the historian Jill Lepore, was born in 1933 with the founding of a company called Campaigns Inc, "the first political consulting firm in the history of the world." Run by a pair of former journalists, the firm won seventy of seventy-five elections for its clients over the next two decades, in the process writing the rules for every campaign that was to follow. As summarized by Lepore, the rules included: "Make it personal: candidates are easier to sell than issues . . . Pretend that you are the Voice of the People . . . Attack, attack, attack . . . Never explain anything . . . Say the same thing over and over again . . . Simplify, simplify, simplify . . ." And, a personal favourite: "You can put on a fight, or you can put on a show."[148]

In fact, these maxims are as old as politics. Forget Campaigns Inc. Forget Machiavelli, for that matter. Read, you budding political strategists, the *Commentariolum Petitionis*, Quintus Tullius Cicero's letter to his more famous older brother, Marcus, candidate for the office of consul in the hotly contested election of 64 BC. Its advice (published in translation by Philip Freeman[149]) would be familiar to any present-day politician: promise whatever you have to—you can always renege later ("it is better to have a few people in the Forum disappointed when you let them down than have a mob outside your home when you refuse to promise them what they want"); dig up dirt on your opponents ("Remember how [another candidate] was expelled from the Senate after a careful examination by the censors?"); suck up to special interests; "stick to vague generalities," etc.

So politics has always been rotten; that hasn't changed. It has always been low and stupid and manipulative. Now it is simply low and stupid and manipulative in new and more technologically advanced ways. What has changed is people's willingness to put up with it. To be blunt, the public isn't buying what the politicians are selling. A generation ago, voter participation in federal elections regularly exceeded 75 percent. Now it is lucky to beat 60 percent. If any normal industry were experiencing this sort of decline, they would be turning themselves inside out, trying to figure out what they were doing wrong. Only in politics is such a galloping disaster treated as business as usual.

Democratic politics in this country is in a kind of death spiral, whose terminus is not dictatorship but irrelevance. It is, it seems, incapable of changing. The behavioural norms of politics, in so many ways the opposite of those that apply in everyday life, are too ingrained, too much a part of the culture. Or are they? Cultural arguments can be self-fulfilling: things are the way they are because that's just the way things are. But cultures can change, and cultures can be changed. How people behave is conditioned by how other people behave. It is also shaped by the rules and incentives they face. Change the rules, change the incentives, and behaviour can change, in ways that then become part of the culture.*

Perhaps there are changes we could make to the rules governing election campaigns that might make them more meaningful exercises, or at least less loathsome. Let me suggest four broad areas for reform: campaign advertising, campaign promises, campaign finances, and campaign debates.

---

* Mind you, what rules are possible, and when, is in turn conditioned by the culture. Chicken, meet egg.

Campaigns

* * *

Politics has never been a contest of ideas. Certainly, election campaigns have not. Occasionally they are *about* ideas, as, for example, in the free trade election of 1988. But such debates as do arise are resolved not by argument, but by combat. There isn't time, in the frenetic sprint of a campaign, to argue a case —or so people in politics tell themselves. You can't explain your position, and you can't defend yourself against the other side. All you can do is attack. Elections, as a result, are about who can tear the most flesh off the other. There isn't a lot else. A modern campaign consists mostly in what is gently referred to as "defining" one's opponents, in a way calculated to make them unrecognizable to their own mothers. The rest is devoted to deliberately misrepresenting the other parties' positions, and for the last fifty or sixty years, the preferred instrument for this sort of ritual flaying has been the attack ad.

To be clear: there's nothing wrong with politicians criticizing one another—"going negative," in the vernacular. But it matters how you go about it: whether your aim is to engage the public, or inflame it. Those in the game offer two standard defences for attack ads. One, they (the other guys) started it. This is invariably true: whatever sin may be charged against one party always has a precedent in its opponents. Which is handy, since it means neither side need justify its actions in their own right, but only by way of the other's.

And the second? Simple: they work. This is presented not as an amusing irony, a comment on man's fallen nature, but as a moral justification. (Oh, they *work*, you say? Well, in that case . . .) So often has this been repeated that it has become accepted wisdom. The myth of the all-powerful attack ad, destroying everything in its path, serves a number of interests. Losing parties find it easier to blame the winning party's attack ads, and by implication the gullible public, for their defeat than to acknowledge their own failings. Strategists for the winning party find it more pleasing to credit victory to their own genius than their opponents' disarray. Fundraisers for both parties find it useful to cite the ads as a means of pulling more cash out of their supporters. For the media, attack ads serve as a simple explanation for events that would otherwise be tiresomely complex and uncertain. Say what you will about attack ads, my fellow pundits will observe ruefully, but they work. Really? Then why do they have to keep making new ones? Elections have losers as well as winners. Somebody's ads must not be working.

Indeed, most of the ads don't work. Every campaign features attack ads on all sides. Some work. Most fail. Sometimes they even backfire, regarded by the public as so over-the-top that they redound against their sponsors rather than their intended target. Nor is it a simple matter of who can buy the most ads: the history of politics is littered with examples to the contrary. This is the dirty little secret of the trade, forgotten in all the breathless coverage of the strategies for "moving the numbers." There's a saying in Hollywood: "Nobody knows anything." Meaning nobody knows what makes a hit picture. You just try something, and see. What no one seems to want to consider is this: maybe people in politics don't know anything, either. Maybe they keep churning out the same stale ads, with the same hackneyed scripts, not because they work, but because they can't think of anything else.

Is it possible that an entire profession could get it wrong? Happens all the time. One of the "revelations" to come out of the 2008 financial crisis is how many people on Wall Street were operating on autopilot. They made their millions doing the same thing in the same way, until they discovered that what they were doing was crazy. The same is true of doctors: studies show significant variations in the rate at which certain procedures are performed in different areas and at different times that can't be explained either by prevalence or therapeutic value. It's all just habit, custom, and fad. I suppose I need hardly mention my own profession.

There is a case to be made against attack ads, but it isn't that they inevitably tilt the field in favour of one party or another. It is rather that they pollute debate, and coarsen the culture. Some degree of criticism in politics is inevitable, even welcome. But tone matters, as does truth—truth, not merely in the sense of factual correctness, but fairness, proportion, context. What is objectionable about attack ads is not that they are "negative," but that they are corrosive. They're not trying to provoke thought, but to shut it down.

These days, the attacks are more likely to be delivered not through the mainstream or mass media, but through targeted micro-media: robocalls, email blasts, and social media. You're familiar with the phenomenon by which the electorate is sliced and diced into ever more narrowly defined demographic groups, composites of age, sex, race, class, marital status, location, and so on. What you may not be aware of is how information on individual voters is increasingly being compiled and collated into *individual* psychological profiles.[150]

All the parties now keep detailed personal files on literally millions of voters. Using data purchased from private market-research companies or harvested from their own interviews with voters—and from social media pages—the parties are able to assemble quite fantastically granular psychological portraits of the voters they are trying to reach. Chances are the parties know who you are, which party you support, and what issues you care about—as well as where you shop, what sorts of things you buy, what your hobbies are, and so on: everything that makes you "tick."

It's all perfectly legal, of course—because the law has been written in such a way as to allow it. For example, the parties all have guaranteed access to Elections Canada's voter lists, though there is no obvious reason why they should. Moreover, while federal agencies like Statistics Canada are covered by the Privacy Act and private companies come under the Personal Information Protection and Electronic Documents Act (PIPEDA), the parties have taken care to exempt themselves from federal privacy laws, as earlier they exempted their telephone solicitations from the do-not-call rules that apply to other telemarketers.*

---

* They have also exempted themselves from provincial privacy laws, in anticipation of a 2024 British Columbia court decision finding that federal parties were covered by the province's Personal Information Protection Act.

The parties thus are now free to tailor their messages specifically to each voter, without concern for how the same message might be received by other voters. What the mass media of the twentieth century took away from the parties—the ability to say one thing to one group of voters and another, sometimes contradictory thing to another—the micro-media of the twenty-first century has restored to them.

The new, bespoke media environment tends also to make the attacks nastier and more dishonest, appealing to voters' worst fears and deepest hatreds. In the age of mass media, this sort of advertising would have been out in the open, for all to see; the party that attempted it risked making itself and its tactics the issue, rather than its intended target. In the age of micro-media, it is invisible to anyone but those to whom it is directed.

To churn out this filth, and to go on churning it out, requires many talents, but above all a certain shamelessness. What do I mean? Let us suppose you and I were to run into each other in a bar. We might strike up a conversation, perhaps argue some point. We've never met, and probably won't see each other again. Still, we would each be likely to take care, even in a barroom argument with a stranger, to stay within the bounds of civilized debate. I don't mean only that we would try to avoid ad hominems and other deliberate offences. I mean that there would be some inner alarm bell that would prevent us from making a plainly asinine argument, one too obviously selective in its use of facts, or too clearly directed at a straw man, or just too idiotic. We would avoid, that is, insulting the other's intelligence—because we hoped to persuade the other, but also because we would not want to look like a jerk. In the world outside politics, people understand the value of reputation. To be persuasive to others, it helps to have a reputation as a trustworthy, sensible person. Reputation is accumulated by repeated exposures over time. So we are obliged to be conscious of how our actions, advantageous as they may seem at any given moment, will be received later.

People in politics, by contrast, appear to live in a sort of perpetual now. Like small-time crooks, the future does not exist for them; neither does the past. The rule in politics, and most especially in election campaigns, seems to be to throw every argument you can think of at the public, no matter how shallow or illogical, and see if any of it sticks. It does not matter whether the argument insults the public's intelligence, or if it makes the speaker look like a jerk. In politics, all that matters is that you make your opponent look worse. The future consequences of present actions—for reputations, for politics, for the country—do not arise. All that matters is winning today.

There is a price to pay for all these accumulated todays, however. The effect of this unceasing barrage of nastiness and stupidity, the low blow and the low brow, is not merely to damage one party or the other. The whole profession is degraded, to the point that people tune out politics altogether. The comparison has often been made: if the airlines constantly ran attack ads savaging each other's safety records, nobody would fly on any of them.

Is there a way to encourage, if not more civility in politics, then at least a modicum of decency? Maybe not. But here's one suggestion, for what it's worth. Much of the worst of modern politics depends upon maintaining a degree of separation between the candidate and the campaign. The candidate takes the high road (relatively speaking), while the strategists and the advertising professionals and the other thugs in his employ go about the dirty work of smearing his opponent. The object of any reform, then, should be to close the gap between the two, to make the candidate own what his campaign has been up to.

That is the point of that line you hear at the end of American political ads: "I'm [Candidate's Name], and I approve this message." Obviously, that hasn't done a great deal to tone down the vitriol, but that's because it doesn't go far enough: by the time the viewer reaches the end of the ad, through the usual hail of attack lines and inflammatory images, that rote disclaimer is unlikely to register. My suggestion? Make the candidate voice the whole ad. They'd still be free to say what they liked. They'd just have to take responsibility for it. It's one thing for some paid announcer to sneer at his opponent, to ask insinuating questions ("How much do we really *know* about John Smith?") or repeat those moronic, store-bought slogans ("John Smith: Wrong on Immigration. Wrong for *Canada*."). I suspect if the candidate had to say it, he'd just sound silly. Which might mean we'd see fewer of them.

* * *

I have an urgent warning for the people of Canada. Even now, diverse "bad actors" are plotting to influence the result of the next election campaign by means of stealth and deception. Posing as ordinary Canadians, they plan to use anonymous social media accounts to spread falsehoods that prey on public fears, play on public prejudices, and otherwise divide Canadians from one another. I speak, naturally, of the political parties.

There is a certain irony, not to say rank hypocrisy, in the current political campaign against the scourge of disinformation in Canadian politics. That disinformation puts our democracy at risk is not at issue: no one who has watched what has been happening in other countries, or who has followed the investigations into foreign interference in Canada, can be in any doubt of that. Nevertheless, the principal threat to the integrity of the Canadian electoral process remains the participants.

If there is something ominous about the government involving itself in deciding what is and is not false information, there is something faintly hilarious about politicians raising the alarm over the spread of falsehoods during an election campaign: a good short definition of an election campaign would be "a sustained, intense, all-party burst of falsehood, slander, and misrepresentation." The question is why we tolerate this. Who, after all, are they lying to? Not each other. They are lying to us, the voters, the people who are supposed to rule, the people they are supposed to serve. If we were serious about democracy, if we took the meaning of popular sovereignty to heart, we would not put up with being lied to so brazenly by the help.

Campaigns

A culture of lying has overtaken our politics, and every party has been caught up in it, to a greater or lesser extent. Gresham's law, in economics, is the observation that "bad money drives out good." If honest coins and debased coins are both in circulation, each purporting to be of the same value, the debased coins will in time come to predominate: honest money, being worth more, will be withdrawn and hoarded, leaving its lesser rival to serve as the medium of exchange. Something like the same has happened to Canadian politics. The currency of our debates has been so debased, through so many repeated episodes of deceit, that dishonesty has become not just the medium of exchange, but the standard of value. It isn't just our politics that has been thus discredited. It is truth itself. We no longer care if our politicians keep their word; we may even prefer that they don't. Bad politics has driven out good.

Politics has never been noted as a place for unsparing honesty. At best, it consists of telling people what they want to hear; it deals in shades of truth, selective facts, exaggeration, blarney, and spin. But in most places, at most times, the expectation has been that politicians will stay within some sort of limit. If you wish to deceive, do so by the sly omission, the evasive answer, the non-denial denial. Equivocate if you can, mislead if you must, but don't say straight up, without room for ambiguity, in a manner that is intended to be believed, something that you know is false.

Small fibs, told in haste, are one thing. But the more solemn the vow, and the more important the matter, the greater the expectation that a statement could be taken at something approaching face value: if not wholly true, we could at least have some confidence that it would not be wholly untrue.

Somewhere along the way, that taboo was broken in Canada, and nowhere more so than with regard to that most basic unit of democratic currency, the campaign promise. A promise in Canadian politics is not a bond, to be redeemed at face value on some future date. It is a token, whose value is whatever it will purchase from the next fool. Campaign dishonesty has become noticeably worse in recent years: more extreme, more brazen, less furtive. The centrepiece of many a winning campaign has been what was later revealed to have been a lie, or at best a wholly broken promise, depending on if one believes the party in question knew at the time the promise would never be kept.

Perhaps it began with Pierre Trudeau, who campaigned furiously against wage and price freezes in the 1974 election—that famous, mocking, "zap, you're frozen" line—only to introduce them shortly after. There followed Brian Mulroney, who unctuously upbraided John Turner for his patronage sins ("you had an option, sir") as if he were not himself about to take the practice to new heights, or rather depths; Jean Chrétien, who promised to abolish the GST and renegotiate NAFTA, but did neither; and Stephen Harper, who having promised he would appoint no one who was not elected to either Cabinet or the Senate, on his first day as prime minister appointed his unelected Quebec organizer Michael Fortier to both, a pattern that was to be repeated in everything from fixed election dates to the taxation of income trusts.

Then there was Trudeau *fils*. The promise to run deficits of less than $10 billion was revoked within weeks of taking power. The promise of electoral reform took a little longer, the government having first to go through the motions of consulting the country on it before tossing the whole thing overboard. In between were a host of smaller betrayals. The party, and the leader, that promised open nominations, only to impose the leader's preferred candidates, is the party and the leader that promised free votes, only to whip even previously sacrosanct matters of conscience like abortion; that promised to rein in the Harper government's use of omnibus bills and prorogation only to make use of both at least as often; that promised an open competition to replace the F-35 fighter jet that turned into a closed competition to buy the F-35.

This is hardly reserved to federal politics. The list of former Ontario premier Dalton McGuinty's broken promises would fill a scrapbook, but the most notorious was surely his pledge, in his victorious 2003 election campaign, not to raise taxes without a referendum—which was no more than a promise to abide by the previous government's Taxpayer Protection Act. Seven months after coming to power he raised taxes, avoiding the referendum requirement by simply amending the law. In Manitoba, some years later, it was the turn of former NDP premier Greg Selinger: elected on a promise not to raise the provincial sales tax, he, too, reneged.

Further examples abound, from coast to coast. The former Liberal premier of New Brunswick, Shawn Graham, elected in 2006 on a promise not to sell New Brunswick Power, proposed to do just that once safely elected. The former New Democratic premier of Nova Scotia, Darrell Dexter, came to power in 2009 promising he would neither raise taxes, cut spending, nor run a deficit. He proceeded to do all three. You may recall what happened with former British Columbia Premier Gordon Campbell's disavowal, prior to his province's 2009 election, of any intent to harmonize the province's sales tax with the federal GST.

All three parties, both levels of government, time after time after time. These were not casual slips of the lip, minor items at the bottom of each party's wish list. They were central planks in their platforms, often the major point of divergence between them and their opponents, in some cases arguably the key to their victory. The taxpayers' pledge, for example, was vital to McGuinty's efforts to shake the tax-and-spend label the Conservatives had hung on him: he would not have won without it.

Facts change, of course, and a politician has a right to change his mind, the same as anyone else. But in none of the examples cited do the explanations of unforeseen circumstances and unexpected deficits ring true. We've heard these stories too many times. The promises in most cases were of a kind that could not be kept: they were foolish, and the people who made them knew it at the time. The point is not that politicians should persist in policies they know to be disastrous, just because they've promised them. The point is that they should not make such promises in the first place.

This is not politics as usual. It's something far worse. It is not just corrosive of public trust. It makes it impossible for the public to form any sort of judgment about the people who seek to lead them. Elections are not referendums, and a platform is only one of the criteria by which we choose among the parties. But how can the public assess so much as the general direction a party or leader would take, if they can have no confidence in any particular piece of evidence to that effect? It is not an answer to say they can "throw the bums out" at the next election, when the question of who said what four years before would have to contend with forty other issues. Honest government should not be considered an optional extra, to be weighed against a party's position on health care or public safety. It should be a given.

That honest government is not a given in Canada is reflected in growing public disenchantment with our politics. Elections Canada surveys find this breakdown in trust to be the primary cause of declining voter turnout. It is the most common response when voters are asked what questions they would put to their leaders at election time: *Why should we believe you?*

The whole situation has bred such cynicism that politicians have had to go to ever greater lengths to persuade people to believe them. McGuinty went so far as to sign his name, in a splashy public ceremony, to a no-tax-hike pledge drawn up by the Canadian Taxpayers Federation, almost like a contract. Leaders have even promised to resign if they don't keep their promises. What do they do if they don't keep that promise? Kill themselves?

Again: why do we put with this? We do not, as a rule, in other areas of life. People in the private sector, God knows, are capable of deceptions. The difference is that in private life, there are penalties. If a company lies to consumers about its products—if it fails to deal with them in "good faith"—it faces stiff fines or worse. Likewise, if it tries to cheat its investors: a company will find itself in trouble with securities regulators if its prospectus makes claims that are merely misleading, let alone materially false. There are laws against perjury and obstruction of justice, laws against fraud and misrepresentation, laws against libel and slander. Only in politics is it accepted that people can tell whatever lies they like without consequence.

Or at least, they can tell some sorts of lies. They can't lie to each other in Parliament or the legislatures. And they can't lie about each other, at least under some provincial laws. But lie to the public? It's open season. Lying to the public has become an accepted stratagem in Canadian politics, all part of the game, like fighting in hockey. The greatest penalty any politician expects to pay is to be thrown from office at the next election when, he or she may hope, tempers have cooled and the facts have been forgotten.

This is not Trump-style lying, so quick and constant, not to say obvious, that the intent seems less to deceive than to eliminate truth and falsehood altogether as criteria, such that the public ends up disbelieving everyone equally. These are lies that are plainly intended to be believed. But through sheer repetition, they have had the same result. We've been burned so often, with such mounting shamelessness, that we now assume they're all lying.

This isn't a problem only for voters. The politician who truly means what he says no longer has any means of establishing his bona fides. If there is no reward for keeping promises, and no punishment for breaking them, if the honest and the dishonest are treated just the same, then politicians will stop bothering. At any rate, the nice guys really will finish last, finding themselves at a permanent electoral disadvantage versus those less burdened by scruples.

So we all have a stake in devising some means of holding politicians to minimal standards of truthfulness[151]. Certainly the profession cannot be trusted to reform itself. If we are ever to regain trust in our elected leaders, rather, there will have to be legal penalties attached to lying in the political arena, as there are in the commercial or legal worlds—a "truth in politics" law.

Obviously we need to step carefully, here. Free and feisty political debates are critical to democracy. Any proposals to police political speech, therefore, even to prevent out-and-out deception, should be viewed with a high degree of skepticism, lest it extinguish freedom of speech along with it. The only known Canadian example, British Columbia's electoral fraud law*, has avoided such stifling effect mainly by being almost impossible to enforce.†

Neither does the solution lie in some blanket ban on political lying, such as the ethics-in-government advocacy group Democracy Watch has proposed[152], enforced by a public complaints process—a recipe for abusive "lawfare" by political opponents, and anyway not something the parties are ever likely to accept. Nor should they. No one in private life would put up with teams of hostile researchers following them around everywhere they went, combing through their every public or private utterance in hopes of catching them in some fib with which to haul them in front of the Truth Commission.

So, fine, we don't want to expose our elected officials to prosecution for every little slip of the tongue. We may even, politics being what it is, want to leave room for a little calculated ambiguity. Politics is different from private life in important ways, and the same precise standards need not always apply. To separate you from your money, after all, a crooked stock issuer only has to fool you. A crooked politician has to fool a majority, or at least a substantial minority, which isn't always as easy as it sounds.

But what do we do with the honest politicians? What about the politician who is telling the truth and wants the world to know it? How does he separate himself from the liars? How can he make himself believed? This conundrum is not unknown in private life: how to prove to people you've never dealt with before that you can be

---

* Section 256 (2) of the province's Election Act, which among other provisions forbids any individual or organization to "compel, persuade or otherwise cause an individual to vote or refrain from voting for a particular candidate or for a candidate of a particular political party . . . by abduction, duress or fraudulent means." https://www.bclaws.gov.bc.ca/civix/document/id/complete/statreg/96106_00_multi

† A 1997 lawsuit alleging fraud under the act in the case of the "Fudge-it Budget" forecast by the province's NDP government just before the 1996 election (the party claimed the budget was in balance, only to reveal after the election that it was not) was ultimately dismissed. The complainants failed to prove a deliberate intent to deceive. https://www.canlii.org/en/commentary/doc/1997CanLIIDocs167

trusted. Over the centuries, a number of measures have been devised to address it, from bonded couriers to sworn affidavits to money-back guarantees. Each involves the willing assumption of certain legal or financial penalties should a specific claim or promise prove to be false.

Is it so far-fetched to imagine some similar remedy for politics? Rather than impose a legal obligation on politicians to tell the truth, what if it were left to them to opt into it? The idea would be to allow politicians to voluntarily expose themselves to legal liability if the statements they are making are untrue.

Suppose there were a provision of the Elections Act a leader or candidate could invoke at his discretion to cover particular statements or documents, with provisions for fines or other sanctions if they were found to be materially false. No need to prove damages—just falsehood. But no gotchas, either, no fear of being penalized for some stray slip of the lip. The liability would be voluntarily assumed, and only with regard to statements the candidate himself specifically designated. Most political speech would no doubt remain uncovered, and be treated with the skepticism it deserved. But when the candidate really wished to be believed, when he wanted to impress upon people "this is no ordinary campaign blarney, I really mean what I'm saying here," he'd have an option. "In releasing my platform today," he might say, "I invoke Section 19 of the Elections Act" (or whatever section it was), thereby assuming the liability. Think of it like swearing an oath in court.

Such statements would no doubt be drafted with caution, as they are in private life, with particular attention to what was covered and what was not and conditions attached to different eventualities: "We will balance the budget, *provided* the economy grows by more than 2 percent annually in real terms." Fine. Voters could decide how much weight to attach to them, as they would any declarations issued without such backing. Over time, I have a feeling opting in would be the norm, rather than the exception, for important campaign statements. The question would immediately arise why a candidate did not make all of his promises in similarly binding terms, and why all candidates did not do the same. In this way, good faith would drive out bad, like Gresham's law in reverse.

* * *

There is a tension at the heart of campaign finance law. The rules are ostensibly designed to limit the influence of money in politics. But the rules are set by politicians, who are always ravenous for money.

There have to be *some* rules. There is a purely libertarian view, laid out by the US Supreme Court in the *Citizens United* decision*, that "money is speech": to prevent people from spending money to express their point of view amounts to preventing them from expressing it. That is valid as far as it goes. But even the US has some limits on contributions to political parties†: past a certain point, these would otherwise come to resemble bribes. (Money doesn't buy elections, but it can buy the odd politician.)

But what rules? That's where the arguments start. Who should be allowed to contribute to political parties? In what amounts? How much should parties be allowed to spend on election campaigns? What about advocacy groups, sometimes called "third-party" campaigns? Should they face looser spending limits than the parties? Or tighter? Is there any reason to distinguish between "pre-writ" and "post-writ" spending in the age of the permanent campaign? At what point do attempts to protect the integrity of the election process run afoul of constitutional protections for freedom of speech?

Of late, Canadian campaign finance laws have wobbled from one extreme to another. Under Jean Chrétien, we went from almost no

---

* The 2010 decision held that laws preventing corporations, unions and other organizations from spending on independent political advertising were unconstitutional. It led to a significant increase in outside spending on elections, notably through the newly formed "super PACs" (political action committees).
† These are surprisingly strict: US$3,300 per candidate per election; $41,299 annually to national party committees. Political action committees are permitted to contribute another $5,000 per candidate.

Campaigns

federal regulations on corporate and union contributions to a total ban on both, virtually overnight, while a system of per-vote subsidies to political parties,* brought in at the same time, was later abolished by Stephen Harper. Regulations on third-party spending have likewise veered from a more or less total free-for-all to near prohibition and back again.

About the only constant has been the generous system of public funding the parties have thoughtfully arranged for themselves. The per-vote subsidy was abolished by Harper on the grounds that ordinary citizens should not be forced to underwrite the campaigns of the political parties, but donations to political parties remain eligible for a tax credit of up to 75 percent—far more than you would receive for a donation to, say, cancer research—which amounts to the same thing. The parties are further subsidized in the form of a 50 percent reimbursement on their election expenses (60 percent for candidates), provided they meet certain vote thresholds. Last, there are all those government ads, especially prevalent at election time, reminding the public, at public expense, of all the good things the government is doing for them—ads that every party rails against in opposition and every party avails itself of in government.

We are far from a sensible or coherent system of campaign finance regulation. If some provinces' regulations seem excessively open-ended, with corporations and unions not only allowed to contribute directly, but also indirectly, via third-party spending campaigns, the stricter federal rules can raise their own issues. Some blame the strident partisanship and polarization of federal politics on the parties' constant need to raise funds from small donors, rather than relying on a few large corporate and union donors, as in the past.

What is to be done? Let's start with a few broad principles: the foundations on which any sound system of campaign finance regulation

---

* In the year it was abolished it provided every party with $1.95 annually for each vote it obtained in the previous election.

should be built. The first will seem obvious: the rules should treat all individuals equally. An election, fundamentally, is a conversation among the citizens. Only citizens vote, but every citizen gets a vote, and every vote is (or should be) equal. But the conversation does not begin or end on election day. Just as everyone gets the same vote, no matter what their income—there are not more votes for the rich—the objective should be to ensure that every citizen, no matter their income, has a roughly equal ability to influence the debates preceding the election.

This simple principle, a citizen-based campaign finance system, nonetheless has a number of quite radical implications. For starters, it clearly argues for eliminating all corporate and union donations: only donations from citizens should be permitted. If an election is a conversation among citizens, it makes no sense that non-citizens should be able to contribute. Corporate executives and union leaders are citizens, of course. Fine: let them donate their own money, rather than also using their positions to donate other people's money—their shareholders' and members'—on their behalf.* Not only is that unfair to them, but it's also unfair to other citizens, with no pockets to dip into but their own. It is a violation of the principle of equality.

Another implication is the elimination of public subsidy, including the tax credit for donations and the reimbursement of party and candidate expenses. The effect of the tax credit, in particular, is to allow the donor to offload three-quarters of the cost of the donation onto the public, essentially forcing everyone else to donate to the same cause. A citizen-based system is necessarily a voluntaristic one. Everyone can contribute, but no one is forced to.

If individual citizens are the only source of funds, it follows that the individual should be the unit of regulation. If the idea is to give

---

* Corporations like to say that they contribute to political parties not in the expectation of any reward, but strictly to "support the process." Yet, remarkably, their support tends overwhelmingly to go to the party most likely to be in power after the election; the closer a party is to power, moreover, the more they are likely to give. The same is observed wherever corporate donations are allowed.

every individual roughly equal ability to influence the political debate, then it is to individuals that any regulations on contributions, and spending, should apply, not the parties. Parties are merely a vehicle for groups of like-minded citizens to influence the political process. They have no moral standing beyond that of the individuals of which they are composed. It is their contributors, really, who are spending the money: the party is just a convenient front.

Party spending limits, seen in this light, are incoherent. It is fairness between individuals that should be our concern, not fairness between the parties. To subject every party to the same limit on spending, in the name of treating parties equally, is only to treat their individual members unequally. Suppose you have two parties: one with a hundred thousand members, each contributing $100; the other with a thousand members, each giving $1,000. The first has raised $10 million from its supporters; the second, $1 million. If the same $1 million spending limit applies to each, the second party's supporters will each have ten times as much "voice" as their counterparts in the first.

Yet that is what current policy amounts to. Elections Canada sets spending limits for the parties in each election based on a complex formula including the number of candidates a party nominates, the number of voters in each riding, and the number of days in the campaign. For the 2021 campaign, this worked out to about $30 million for parties that ran candidates in every riding.[153] A similar formula limits spending by candidates: in 2021, this ranged from roughly $89,000 in the riding of Charlottetown to $153,000 in Kootenay-Columbia.[154]

Contributions, meanwhile, are limited to $1,750 per party in 2025. But you can contribute to any number of different parties. You can also contribute a maximum of $1,750 to an independent candidate. But you can contribute to any number of them as well. So rich donors could potentially contribute many multiples of $1,750. Again, this makes no sense. If the principle is to give every individual the same voice in the political conversation, the limit should apply, not to each individual contribution, but to the total of all the political contributions a donor makes in a given year: no matter how many parties you contribute to, or how many candidates. Indeed, it should apply not just to general elections, but to riding nominations and leadership races as well.

Why, after all, do we limit contributions? To prevent the rich from exercising undue political influence; to achieve a rough equality between individuals, regardless of income, in their capacity to intervene in political debate. Suppose everyone had the same income. In such a world, there would be no concern at the rich having disproportionate influence, and no need to limit donations. Capping an individual's total contribution capacity—a global annual ceiling on political contributions—is the closest practical equivalent to this.

There is some acknowledgement of this principle in the regulations. There is a separate limit of $1,750 annually that applies to the total of all donations to party riding associations, contestants in party nomination races, and party candidates in general elections. Yet another $1,750 limit applies to the total of all contributions to the contestants in a party leadership race. But again, you can multiply these contribution limits by contributing to multiple parties.

If we take seriously the idea of giving every individual roughly equal ability to contribute to the political process, we need to bring all these different contribution limits under one roof: a single global annual ceiling on all political contributions of any kind—parties, candidates, riding associations, nomination races, leadership races, the works. The ceiling is the necessary and sufficient intervention. It would be up to the individual to decide how they wished to allocate their contributions within this limit, without further interference by the state.

And if we really wanted to be fair to all, we'd bring contributions to "third-party" advocacy groups under the ceiling as well. These have proliferated in recent times, seemingly as a way of getting around party spending limits: instead of the party spending money to promote itself, an ostensibly independent advocacy group spends on its behalf, in practice operating as a supplemental campaign. Simple per-contribution limits suffer from the same defect: in addition to making contributions to multiple parties, those with means can contribute to any number of third-party groups.

Clearly this can't be left wholly unregulated. We've seen the result in the United States, post-*Citizens United*, where billionaire oligarchs now personally bankroll presidential campaigns and threaten to fund primary challenges against their political opponents. Yet the solution adopted in our election laws is scarcely better. It has been more or less to ban third-party spending altogether or, when that was ruled unconstitutional by the Supreme Court, to cap it at levels that are dwarfed by party spending limits. Where parties could spend up to $30 million in the 2021 election campaign, third-party groups were limited to just $525,700.

Again, the issue is not fairness to advocacy groups: it's fairness between citizens. The key, again, is to look through these groups to the individuals of which they are composed. Parties are one way that individuals can combine to project their voice into the political arena, but they are not the only way. Nor should they be. Advocacy groups often take up issues that voters want addressed, but that the parties, for one reason or another, refuse to touch. How you choose to participate in the national discussion, whether through a formal political party or an advocacy group, should be up to you, as should your decision about how much to donate to either.

The corollary of treating every contributor equally is to treat all recipients equally. Contributions to third-party groups should count toward each person's annual limit, the same as contributions to registered political parties do. In turn, their recipients should be limited to spending no more than they were able to raise by this route. For parties, this would apply generally; for advocacy groups, to that part of their budget that was devoted to directly intervening in election campaigns. Advocacy groups would remain free to raise and spend money for other purposes as they liked. Only spending to support or oppose a particular candidate or party would come under the regulation.

The gaming problem under such a system would resolve itself: the more an individual gave to one party or cause, the less he or she would have left to give to all the others. Ideally, the money would not be donated directly, but would be processed through Elections Canada, to be passed on to its intended recipient, anonymously. This could be done on an annual basis, perhaps via your personal income tax return. Money intended for contributions could be deposited in, and drawn from, "Registered Political Contribution Accounts," like RRSPs, without the tax-free status. These could even be topped up out of public funds, for those on low income, bringing us closer still to the ideal of "rough equality" of voice.

I can't think of a better way to balance a concern for the integrity of political campaigns with a general preference for free speech. Think of it. No more bagmen, no more $1,750-a-plate dinners. No more selling of access*, none of the mutual backscratching between private interests and public officials that so disfigures the process at present. Just a civilized annual appeal to the public, like pledge week on PBS.

Beyond that, however, there would be no limits, either on contributions or spending. If a party or group could raise $10 million in this way from individual contributors, each constrained by the same annual contribution limit, it could spend $10 million. Neither would there be any need for governments to involve themselves in deciding just who should be allowed to raise and spend funds in what amounts, whether parties or third-party groups. Just a single, undifferentiated, global contribution limit.

That leaves only the question of what level the annual ceiling should be set at. It need not be high. In fact, it could be quite low: a good deal lower than current contribution limits would imply. Because—here's a secret—we don't need to spend nearly as much on political campaigns as we do. It has never been cheaper to communicate with

---

* No, a $1,750 donation is not enough to buy a particular outcome. But if you don't think it's enough to buy access, a chance to plead your case, you haven't been paying attention. How else do you think they sell the tickets?

large numbers of people; an email blast, for example, can be sent out at approximately zero cost. The only reason any of the parties continue to raise and spend such record amounts is because the other parties do. It's like an arms race. So long as the same constraint applied equally to all, I don't think any of them would miss it.

Certainly the public wouldn't. Not only is most current campaign spending a complete waste—the parties' efforts neatly cancelling each other out—but most of it pays for things that hurt democracy: attack ads, push polls, not to mention the increasingly frantic efforts to raise still more funds. What would be lost, then, if instead of the current per-contribution limit of $1,750, with multiple contributions allowed, we set the total annual ceiling per person, all contributions combined, at, say, $1,000? I'm guessing fewer pollsters, strategists, and political consultants would be employed. But what would be the downside?

* * *

There's no disputing the importance of televised leaders' debates to the modern election campaign. They often mark the start of the "real" campaign, the point when the public starts paying attention. Over the years, the debates have proved critical to the outcome of any number of federal and provincial elections. Yet their potential remains largely unrealized.

Done right, debates can make a signal contribution to the public's ability to assess leaders and their platforms, offering a rare opportunity to see all the leaders together, at length, close up, unfiltered, unedited and mostly unscripted. What comes out in these unguarded moments can be revealing. How well does each candidate understand his or her platform? How well can he explain it? Can she think on her feet? How does he react under pressure? Is she confident, and can she inspire confidence in others?

In practice, debates often degenerate into barely comprehensible panderfests, in which a bevy of overcaffeinated candidates attempt to talk over each other in the brief time left to them by the multiple moderators and ever-shifting formats: a barrage of stale talking points and canned zingers, with the occasional preening journalist for colour. At the end, the media scores the event in terms of who "won" or "lost," as if anyone knew, or as if that were the issue.

It is absurd to be deciding democratic elections on the basis of who "won" or "lost" an all-party shouting match. An election is not a debating tournament. We are not picking the best public speaker, but the leader and party we prefer should represent us in Parliament. Neither are we choosing a boyfriend: it is interesting to note which leader came off as most "likable," but that is not actually the issue.

The debates, so full of potential to illuminate the choices confronting the voters, have instead mostly had the opposite effect. Why are we so terrible at organizing them? Other countries seem capable of mounting televised debates that are halfway dignified, vaguely informative, marginally interesting, or at least not complete debacles.

Blame for these repeated fiascos can be attached to our enduring habit of treating the debates, sixty-odd years after Nixon-Kennedy, as novelties rather than as a central part of the modern election campaign. Elections are, by definition, public events. As such, their rules and practices are generally encoded in law, in the interest of transparency, predictability, and, ideally, fairness to all. The election laws of Canada and the provinces run to hundreds of pages, covering everything from how candidates are nominated to how parties raise funds to the kind of paper used in the ballots. The debates have been the outstanding exception. Their organization in each election—frequency, format, rules, and so on—has historically been left to last-minute negotiations between the political parties and a group of mostly private television networks known as "the consortium."

For all their importance to the public interest, the debates have remained, until very recently, essentially private affairs, their terms defined by the relative bargaining positions of the various organizations involved, each with an obvious axe to grind. The party that's behind in the polls typically wants six debates. The party in the lead wants none. They saw it off at one, in each official language. The networks' contribution is to insist that, if they must sacrifice valuable airtime that could otherwise have been devoted to American sitcoms or reality shows, they should mimic as nearly as possible their hysterical tone.

Hence the "prizefight" atmosphere that attends so many debates. Knowing they have just one chance to make an impression, candidates tend to be coached within an inch of their lives: either they take no chances (the front-runner) or launch a series of wild attacks (the challengers), in search of the fabled "knock-out blow." The whole election can sometimes be decided in those two hours—not enough time to do much of anything except bark out the usual talking points, plus a couple of memorized attack lines, in hopes of producing a clip for the evening news or a meme for social media.*

Segregating the events by language means only part of the country is watching at any time. That frees the leaders of the obligation to make their case to the whole country with a single, unifying message. The French debate, in particular, tends to be obsessively focused on the interests and concerns of one province, Quebec. Rather than bridge the solitudes, the debates reinforce them.

Of late, the consortium has been pushed somewhat to one side. After the chaos of the 2015 campaign, in which the Conservative leader, Harper, boycotted the official debates in favour of a handful of hastily improvised sideshows, the Trudeau government struck an independent commission with formal responsibility for organizing the debates. The idea was a sound one. Take control of the debates away from the parties and the networks, with their obvious conflicts of interest. And set the rules well in advance of any election, before the parties know who will be ahead or behind in the polls.

Alas, no sooner had the Liberals established the federal Leaders' Debates Commission than they compromised it, appointing the

---

* As the critic Rick Salutin has observed, when newscasts report, as they do after nearly every debate, that there were "no knock-out blows," what they mean is there were "no useable clips."

former governor general, David Johnston, as commissioner without consulting the opposition, and dictating in advance two of the most important rules: how many debates would be held, and who could participate. Worse, the commission, created with the intent of taking control over the process away from the networks, immediately handed it back, by contracting the production out to them.

Since then we have had the disaster of the 2019 debates, followed by the utter, toe-curling embarrassment of the 2021 debates*. The results looked an awful lot like the debates they were supposed to replace: one in English, one in French, overrun with (mostly network) moderators, in a format tailored to create the sorts of moments TV producers think exciting—leaders pointing fingers, shouting over each other—and all wrapped up inside of two hours.

Particular confusion has surrounded the question of which party leaders should be invited, and on what basis. On the one hand, it would be impractical to include the leader of every party, no matter how small or insignificant (more than twenty ran candidates in the last election). On the other hand, it would be inappropriate to limit participation, as is sometimes suggested, to the leaders of the parties with a realistic chance of winning. Again, we elect parliaments in this country, not governments. Many voters do not vote for the party they want to form a government, but rather for the party they want to keep the government in check, or just to represent them in their riding.

There has to be some sort of rule. What should it be? Representation in Parliament? Share of the popular vote in the last election? Performance in the most recent polls? All the above? In the days when there were only three parties of any significance, the issue was largely

---

* Among other ills, the 2021 debates were plagued by too many journalists asking too many questions with too little time to answer them — forty-five, in the space of two hours, compared to eight in 2008. Add to this a confusing format and overly rigid structure, with too little opportunity for interaction between the leaders. https://www.cbc.ca/news/politics/leaders-debates-report-1.6448673

moot. By 1993 the roster had expanded to include the Reform Party and the Bloc Québécois. Since then, the Green Party leader has been invited to participate in some debates (2008, 2015, and subsequently) but not others (2006, 2011).

The Debates Commission has done nothing to improve the situation. The People's Party of Canada was ruled eligible in 2019, but ineligible in 2021, although its support had grown considerably in the interim. In the latter event, the commission ruled that participation should be reserved to the leaders of parties with at least one MP, or who had won at least four percent of the vote in the last election, or had at least 4 percent support in the polls at the start of the campaign. Thus the PPC was excluded, while the Green Party, with barely half the PPC's support in the polls, was included. So was the Bloc Québécois, although it ran candidates in only seventy-five ridings and did not pretend to be a national party.

The rules for the next election look just as arbitrary. Parties must now pass at least two of three tests: at least one MP, at least 4 percent support in the polls, and with candidates in at least 90 per cent of the ridings. Why 4 percent? Why 90 per cent? Who knows? A line has to be drawn somewhere, but the reasoning for it should be transparent, fair and understandable. This is none of those.

How to fix the debates? A starting point for reform would be a truly independent debates commission. Its first decision should be to greatly expand the number of official debates, to a half dozen or more: a debate for each week of the campaign. At a stroke, the debates would move from an arbitrary but sometimes decisive sideshow to the core of the modern campaign, the spine along which they are conducted. If nothing else, this would tone down some of the hysteria surrounding them. With more time for each question, the leaders might be able to develop a thought or two; with the chance to recover from a bad performance in a subsequent debate, they might be a little more relaxed, a little less programmed.

More debates would also leave room to experiment with different formats. Whole debates could be given over to single subjects: the economy, say, or national unity, or foreign affairs. There could be debates between the relevant frontbenchers, rather than putting all the focus on the leaders. More debates could even help solve the eligibility riddle, or at least finesse it. Why not stagger the lineups, as in the US presidential primaries — three leaders one night, the other three the next? Or maybe narrow the list by one leader after each debate.

A second reform would be to make every debate bilingual. They could be divided into hour or half-hour sessions in each official language. Or just let the leaders have at it, in whatever tongue they choose, as they do in Parliament. That's what simultaneous translation is for.

Clarity would be greatly aided—a third reform—by shutting down the cross-talk. Give the moderator the power to cut the mike of any leader who interrupts or talks over another. They'd get the message soon enough.

Finally, leave the networks out of it. Never mind letting them set the rules—why involve them at all? Debates are relatively low-budget affairs, with little requirement for high-end production values. Instead of letting the networks make their usual catastrophic mess of the debates, why not leave it to the commission produce them? Or CPAC, our federally mandated public affairs channel?

The only role for the networks in the debates should be to broadcast them. Indeed, they should be required to do so as a condition of licence. The government imposes all sorts of other conditions on them, with far less justification. A few hours of free airtime every four years seems a reasonable price to pay for the profits a licence confers upon them every night in between.

I hesitate to call for a larger role for the Debates Commission, given how it has bungled its responsibilities to date, but there is nothing institutionally preventing it from organizing better debates, especially in light of other countries' experience. Organizing a decent minimum number of election debates ought to be seen less as a journalistic or philanthropic exercise and more as a basic function of the state, like putting out poll booths or counting the votes. Elections Canada does a pretty good job at that. Why should a similar standard not be expected of the commission?

These are just the official election debates, of course. There's no reason the leaders could not also take part in other, privately sponsored debates. Neither could they be compelled to participate in the official ones. However, there would be a strong expectation of participation. Leaders are not absolutely required to answer questions in Parliament, either, but there is an expectation that they should do so. Neither is anyone legally obliged to participate in a top-rated chat show like Quebec's *Tout le monde en parle*, but woe betide the leader who ducks it. Over time, the debates, if they were fair, well run, with a compelling format, might acquire something of the same status, the sorts of events a leader could ill afford to miss.

We are not condemned to the status quo. It is not beyond our ingenuity to come up with something better: not just better debates, but better elections. Let us have campaigns organized around the debates, rather than debates organized around the campaigns.

* * *

Another salutary effect of a debate-centred campaign: it would give us in the media something better to write about. We might be less inclined to treat the debates like prizefights. The focus of coverage would shift from "who won?" to "what did we learn?" More broadly, the debates might draw coverage away from the gaffes and polls and party strategy that now fill our days.

I'd be remiss if I did not dwell on our role for a bit. As political journalists, we make an invaluable contribution to ruining virtually every election campaign that comes our way. Unlike politicians, who sometimes learn from their mistakes, we just go on repeating ours. We can't help ourselves, it seems. After every election we retire to our newsroom postmortems, and each time we wearily vow: never again. Never again will we chase after every fleeting poll, salivate over every minor "gaffe." Never again the gotcha question, the constant search for "defining moments" and "turning points," the investing of trivial campaign mishaps with symbolic import. Never again will we sit up and beg for our "Gainsburgers," the little meaningless morsels of news the parties dole out each day to shape the coverage, or troop dutifully through another contrived photo op.

And then we go out and do it all. Over. Again.

Some pressure group props up a piece of poster board with a "report card" grading the parties from A to F in big, hand-drawn letters according to their compliance with its agenda, and we unfailingly put it top of the nightly news. We know it's meaningless. We know it's not really news. But it's great visuals! And what about that party leader's bus breaking down? Could it be that singular object of journalistic desire, the hack's best friend—a metaphor?

Objectively speaking, these events are of no significance to anyone except the people on the campaign: the politicians, their handlers, and the media. They offer no fresh insight on the merits or demerits of any party. They tell us nothing about the leaders' personal capacity to govern, or the relative strengths and weaknesses of their platforms. They have nothing to do with the election, and everything to do with the campaign.

The question most voters would like answered in the course of any campaign is: who are these people, and what are they going to do to us? What, instead, do we tell them? We tell them who's ahead and who's behind. And then we tell them who's behind, and who's ahead. After a while, we tell them who's still ahead, and who's still behind. Eventually, we descend on whoever's behind, and we ask them why they're behind—over and over and over. Why won't you admit you're behind? Why are you such a loser? If you were a tree, what kind of loser tree would you be? All of it apparently in the hope that if we keep at it long enough, we might be able to get them to cry. When that gets boring, we speculate on whether the ones who are ahead can stay ahead, or whether they have peaked too soon. And whatever space we have left we devote to the strategists.

Campaigns

Because, in our secret heart of hearts, that's who we wish we were—the players, the people in the room. We write about the horse race, the polls and the strategy, not because it matters to our readers, but because it matters to the pros, the people we cover, the people we identify with. We parrot their language, as we absorb their values. We report, not on the election, but the campaign; not to explain the choice, but to call the race.* Reporters play up the latest campaign mishap mostly because they think other reporters will. The story, in a sense, is about the story, just as the campaign is increasingly about the campaign, where the criterion of election is not who is the most competent or has the best policies, but who runs the smoothest campaign.

This is not always invalid. An error-filled campaign can betray something deeper and more troubling: a lack of purpose or conviction, internal divisions, any number of things. Sometimes this is practical: If a party can't run a decent campaign, how ready is it to run a government? Sometimes it is metaphysical: if a campaign is losing, does it not in some sense deserve to? But most of the time, campaign coverage of the "gaffes and glitches" school has no such justification. We do it because we have always done it. Two-fifths of political journalism is laziness and herd instinct; the rest is a toxic mixture of sentimentality, deadlines, and spite, these days undiluted even by alcohol. Whatever else it is, horse-race coverage is familiar, safe, and comforting. Rather than take the trouble to analyze the candidates' positions or assess their worth as individuals, the reporter stays securely within the ambit of objective, what-happened-yesterday news.

Better yet, the obsessive concern with describing the game in every detail affords the journalist the opportunity to interpose himself between the players and the spectators. Why tell us about how the politicos tried to spin the story? Why not ignore the spin, and get on

---

* Jay Rosen, professor of journalism at New York University, urged reporters in the last presidential campaign to take the opposite approach: to cover "the stakes, not the odds."

with the story? Perhaps it is to remind the reader of how much he needs the journalist. Without me, it says, you are lost, helpless victims of these cunning witch doctors, with their "hot buttons" and "message tracks." Only I can decode their hidden meanings for you.

Nothing infuriates the media more than the politician who will not play the game, those so artless in the ways of politics as to blurt out exactly what they mean: a "gaffe," as Michael Kinsley famously defined it, is "when a politician tells the truth." And nothing gives us greater pleasure than to see the game played out again, exactly as before: the same game, the same players, and the same monotonous, meaningless play-by-play. Once more, we can't help ourselves.

I don't know whether it's learned behaviour, or whether it's instinctive, responding to some deeply recessed part of the journalistic brain. I only know that we are hurting democracy. We aren't just missing an opportunity to help the public make sense of things at a critical time. We're making things worse. We're actually getting in the way.

* * *

Enough self-flagellation. As awful as the media's coverage of politics may be, it should not be allowed to obscure the even worse performance of the people they are covering. They are ultimately the ones responsible for politics' present state, and they are the ones responsible for fixing it.

Bad behaviour in politics is so constant, and so universal, that we do not even notice it. We're often told that we're too hard on people in politics, that we hold them to an impossibly high standard. But the truth is we hardly hold them to any standards at all: certainly none that we expect of each other. We want to believe that "there are good people in politics." And I suppose there are, in the sense that they are people with good intentions, who want to make life better for their fellow citizens. But they are also the people who stand and applaud at every Question Period inanity, who obediently read out the talking points they have been handed, who sign off on the attack ads that "define" their opponent, and the rest. It is precisely because they are

Campaigns

such good people, full of such good intentions, that they are able to rationalize it. People do the worst things for the best reasons.

It could not be otherwise. Anyone with a distaste for politics, as I've described it, is unlikely to run; if they do, they are unlikely to win; and if they do succeed, it is usually because politics changes them. It's an adversarial system, like the law. But the law is a profession; politics is a pathology. Twenty-four-hours-a-day, three-hundred-sixty-five-days-a-year immersion in partisan propaganda—my side good, your side bad, all the time, every day, without exception—would drive anyone a little mad.

People often ask: how can we reform politics? And the answer is: we can't. I've listed a few institutional changes here, but as with others, if they were likely to do any good, they'd have no chance of being enacted. We're not going to change politics until we change the culture. And we're not going to change the culture. Only people in politics can do that.

You can't separate politics from the people in it, as if they were somehow its victims and not its enablers. It's not going to change until somebody in politics—the people who quietly tell reporters of their frustrations, but go along in the end—stands up and says it's wrong of my party to behave this way. Never mind what the other guys are doing, *my* party needs to stop.

There may be good people in politics. But the problem in politics isn't the bad guys. It's the good guys.

7
Elections

EARLIER CHAPTERS HAVE LOOKED at what's wrong with the governments and parliaments that result from elections, or the campaigns that precede elections. Here we look at elections themselves: the casting and the counting of votes. Once again, we find a wide gulf between how we think our democracy works and how it actually works. It starts with the internal party elections: the contests that decide who should represent each party in each riding and who should lead the party nationwide.

In the spring of 2024, the country's newspapers were filled with revelations of efforts by foreign powers, mostly China, but also India, Pakistan, Iran, and others, to interfere in Canadian elections. The stories, based on confidential intelligence reports, were shocking enough: whisper campaigns against MPs that Beijing considered anti-China; a clandestine network funding candidates considered friendly to the regime; a nomination meeting rigged to ensure the victory of a pro-Beijing candidate; mass purchases of memberships on behalf of candidates in recent Conservative leadership races.

What was more shocking was how easy it was—how easy we have made it—to interfere in our elections. I don't mean directly. The process by which votes are cast and counted in our elections is among the most secure in the world, and subject to stringent regulatory oversight. It's happening indirectly, via the political parties, whose internal elections are among the least secure in the world, and subject to virtually no oversight whatever.

In no other democratic country are party nomination races, in particular, such abject free-for-alls, so entirely lacking in regulatory supervision, so transparently purchasable. Couple that with the many safe ridings across much of the country and it is easy to see how a foreign power might infiltrate Parliament. Lock up the nomination for a safe seat and you're in.

Shocking? If only it were. It does not take a confidential intelligence report to know that party nomination races are a mess.[155] It has been common knowledge for decades. Consider the nomination meeting referred to above, in the safe Liberal riding of Don Valley North, in Toronto. According to intelligence sources, the nomination of Liberal candidate Han Dong, in a race described as close and at a meeting described as "chaotic," was secured by the addition of a busload or two of visiting Chinese high school students. The buses were arranged and paid for by the Chinese consulate, and the students were instructed that they or their family back home might face "consequences" if they did not show up to vote for Dong. Never mind whether China was directly involved, or who hired the buses. How was it possible for a bunch of visiting foreign high school students to participate in choosing a candidate for a Canadian political party?

To vote in a federal election, you have to be at least eighteen years of age, a citizen of Canada, and a resident of the riding in which you cast your vote. To vote in a Liberal Party nomination race, you only have to be fourteen. Until the 2025 Liberal leadership race, you did not have to be a citizen, or even a permanent resident: it was enough that you "ordinarily resided" in Canada. Other parties are scarcely better. The NDP, for example, permits children as young as twelve to vote, depending on the province. And in every party, nominations are run on the same anarchic lines, frequently decided by busloads of "instant members" recruited days or perhaps hours before the nomination meeting, their memberships paid for (it is often suspected) by party power brokers. It's called "stacking the meeting," and it's as Canadian as butter tarts.

That's when the nomination race is actually a race, and has not been decided beforehand by the party. Sometimes these decisions are overt: rather than allow the members of the local riding association to decide who should represent them in the election, a candidate, often the incumbent MP, sometimes a "parachute candidate" with no previous attachment to the riding, is simply appointed by the party leadership without a nomination vote of any kind.

According to research by the Samara Centre for Democracy[156] more than half the candidates (53 percent) in the 2019 election were selected in this way: the proportion of appointees ranged from 37 percent for the NDP to 100 percent of Bloc candidates. This is necessary, parties say, to ensure racial and other forms of "diversity." Bunk, Samara finds: candidates chosen by appointment turn out to be no more diverse than those chosen by a vote of the members.

Direct appointment is just one of the ways in which party leaders can tip the scales in favour of their chosen candidates. What is more striking, and insidious, is the number of candidates who "win" their nomination in races where they are the only contestant. According to Samara, that described two-thirds of nomination races in 2019. Doubtless, some of those were candidates of such obvious merit or unassailable popularity that no one dared run against them. But the rules governing party nomination races are so opaque, so arbitrary, and so wholly at the discretion of the party executive as to make it likely, in many cases, that the absence of competition for a particular candidate was at the behest of the leader. In addition, an unknown number of candidates are ruled out from the start by the parties' highly secretive vetting procedures. Again, in most cases, disqualifications are probably due to some genuinely problematic bit of information from an aspiring candidate's past. But given the lack of transparency surrounding the process, there is corresponding potential for abuse.

All told, Samara finds, "of the more than 6,600 election candidates chosen by Canada's major federal parties over the five general elections from 2004 to 2015, only 17 percent arrived there through a competitive nomination race." In 2019, it was 14 percent.

Even in competitive races, the party's influence can be oppressive. The rules are typically confusing, unpredictable, and subject to change. Races are often called without warning, and decided in great haste, offering little chance for those outside the circle of favour to organize. Half last less than three weeks; five days is not unusual. In 253 races, Samara found, nominations opened and closed the same day.

For that matter, the "fairly" contested races—especially those—can be the scenes of the worst excesses, thanks to the tendency of parties to treat nomination races not as an opportunity for the party's loyal members to choose who should represent them in the election, but as a chance to sell memberships en bloc. The cutoff dates for new members is often indecently close to voting day, leaving races to be decided by the "instant members" in those stacked nomination meetings.

Former members of Parliament interviewed by Samara for its 2014 study *Tragedy in the Commons*[157] reported an overwhelming sense of bewilderment about the nomination process, an eerie feeling of being manipulated by unseen forces. MPs, the study's authors write, "spent a great deal of time describing how painful and mystifying they found this particular aspect of their entry into politics." They "struggled to articulate how nominations functioned, citing a lack of clarity in timelines, sources of decision-making and the application of the rules. Procedures varied widely from riding to riding, and the process appeared subject to a host of idiosyncrasies, giving the impression that the party's, rather than the people's, favoured candidate was selected." And this was how the winners assessed it! ("We cringe to imagine what those who were less successful might say.") All this was merely an introduction to the brutalization candidates were to experience later, as elected MPs—their first taste, as the Samara authors write, of "the bullying and controlling behaviour of their parties" described in chapter 3.

* * *

Did I say nomination races are a mess? Leadership races are worse. We've seen how this method of choosing leaders affects the relationship between the leader and caucus; how the leader is, from that day forward, accountable to no one, least of all the caucus he is supposed to lead. But they are also harmful in themselves. Brute contests of organizational muscle and name recognition, with little in the way of substantive issues at stake, they are plagued by allegations of corruption. If the depleted cemeteries and busloads of elderly drunks that used to elect delegates to national leadership conventions are no longer the issue, the currently dominant system of one member, one vote is every bit as prone to being gamed.

As with nomination races, leadership races are won or lost not by the party's existing members, but by the tens or even hundreds of thousands of new members signed up in the early stages of the campaign by the candidates' organizations. There is generally a "cutoff date" after which new members are ineligible to vote. For their most recent leadership vote, the Liberals, for example, set it at 41 days before the vote. In the NDP, it is 45 days. In the last three Conservative leadership races it has ranged between two and four months.

The frantic rush by all sides to sell as many memberships as possible as fast as possible inevitably gives rise to abuses. The process is costly—often cripplingly so for the candidates—and divisive, and typically leaves a stench that lingers over the party long afterward. Indeed, some sort of scandal, whether illegal fundraising, faked memberships, or bulk purchases of memberships on others' behalf (sometimes with illegally raised funds!), happens in virtually every Canadian party leadership race. Perhaps we can agree this is not coincidental. The nature of the race invites abuse. A leadership race organized along the lines of the Louisiana state lottery will produce much the same results: brief euphoria, followed by years of whisky and regret. Even if the candidates are not themselves corrupt, the process is corrupting, producing very different candidates, and leaders, than would be the case otherwise.

Elections

Suppose none of this were happening. Suppose Canadian party leadership races were fought on the highest of ethical planes. It would still be a terrible way to choose a leader, not least because it tends to elect terrible leaders. Party members are wildly unrepresentative of the general population at the best of times—fewer than 2 percent of Canadians belong to a political party[158]—but the sudden influx of so many new members often leads to the leadership being decided by a group of people who are at best unrepresentative of the party, at worst actively hostile to it. They are not party members at all, really, but leadership tourists, with no attachment to the party or its principles. Some may be caught up in the personality cult that surrounds a particular candidate. Others, like the Quebec dairy farmers who helped elect Andrew Scheer as Conservative leader in 2017, or the teachers' union members who elected Alison Redford as Alberta Conservative leader in 2011, may be special interest or single-issue voters—entryists, as they are sometimes called, whose membership purchases are strictly tactical.

Even so, the system remains. Party officials like the leadership-race-as-membership-drive model because it makes money for the party. The sudden expansion in a party's membership numbers, sometimes to multiples of pre-campaign levels, creates excitement and the illusion of momentum, as if people across the country were beating down the doors to join the party and were not simply pressed into signing up during a visit to their local shopping centre. It is easy, amid all the hoopla, to forget the people this leaves in the shade: the party's existing members—the volunteers, the long-loyal, the folks who attend party conferences and vote on resolutions, who lick envelopes and knock on doors—outvoted by people with no history of involvement with or commitment to the party, most of whom will have no further association with it beyond the time it takes to cast their ballot.

The worst part? Most of this is perfectly legal.* Other than some recent limitations on fundraising, political parties are largely exempt

---

* Michael Kinsley's aphorism seems apt here: "The scandal's not what's illegal. The scandal's what's legal."

from government regulation. The task of regulating party elections has instead been left to the parties.

It's clear the parties have failed at this. In leadership and nomination races alike, they have neither implemented serious eligibility criteria nor policed the ones they have with any rigour. It seems equally clear they don't think this is a problem—not even now, after all the revelations of how seriously foreign interference threatens the integrity of our elections. Told of the suspicious circumstances of the Han Dong nomination, the Liberal leader, Justin Trudeau, chose to do nothing. It would have been "a very significant step," he told the public inquiry into foreign interference, straight-faced, for the leader to interfere in a local nomination race. At another point he smirked at the intelligence agencies' naïveté about the Canadian political process: nomination meetings, he told the inquiry, are stacked all the time.

This cannot continue. It was one thing when the corruption of party elections was confined to domestic players. But where once we might have worried, at worst, that dead people were voting, we now have to reckon with the possibility that foreign powers are conspiring to choose our leaders. However the parties' shenanigans may have delighted us in the past, it is intolerable that they should serve as a portal for foreign dictatorships to infiltrate our politics.

The best solution, again, would be to go back to the old system of choosing party leaders, by members of caucus. If parties insist on maintaining the membership-at-large model, on the other hand, it cannot be on such open-ended terms. And yet, left to themselves, the parties are unlikely to mend their ways. Not only are they addicted to the money these races bring in, but there is also a collective action problem: if one party cleans up its act, but the others don't, it risks being put at a competitive disadvantage. Some system of external regulation is plainly in order.

Maybe we don't want to go as far as a US-style system of voter registration. But the parties could be required to maintain their own registers, with a common set of rules. At a minimum, the right to vote in party elections should be restricted to adult citizens; ideally they would also have been party members for some minimum period of time before the vote—six months, perhaps a year within which to demonstrate some attachment to the party and its principles.* Most important, responsibility for overseeing all this should be assigned to Elections Canada.

Any such proposal is sure to raise a storm of opposition. None of the parties has shown the slightest willingness to have its internal elections vetted by independent regulators—or anything else. Wherever and whenever it is proposed to regulate party behaviour—from how they choose their leaders to how they raise their funds to how the leaders' debates are organized—the same objection is raised: political parties are private organizations. How they conduct their affairs is nobody's business but their own. The state has no place in the backrooms of the nation.

This is nonsense. Corporations are private organizations, but I don't notice the parties are in any great haste to relieve them of all state supervision. Neither do parties seem to object to regulations that serve their interests, from the tax credit for political donations to the reimbursement of campaign expenses out of public funds to the legal requirement for all candidates for a party to obtain the endorsement of the party leadership.

More to the point: parties are not wholly private organizations. They are not some chess club with no influence on public events, whose only desire is to be left alone. They are machines for winning elections. Their sole purpose is to seek and wield coercive power over the rest of us. How they go about it is therefore a matter of vital public concern, and regulation in the public interest is entirely justified.

But, once again, we are caught in the same Catch-22. Who can pass legislation regulating the parties? Only the parties. And the parties aren't likely to budge. It may be a scandal now, with foreign interference on everyone's minds. But in time, they evidently hope,

---

* Eligibility periods to vote in UK party selection contests range from three to 12 months. Similar rules apply in Australia, New Zealand, France, Italy and Japan.

the public will get bored, and the media will move on. And, in this regard, they are probably right.

* * *

Once the party leaders are chosen and the candidates nominated, it is time for the election. Or rather, elections: an election in Canada is really three hundred forty-three separate elections, one for each riding. But in each one of them the principle is supposed to be the same: representation by population. One person, one vote. Everyone gets one vote, and every vote counts equally. Only, as we will see, that is not the case: every vote does *not* count equally. It depends on which riding you live in, and it depends, incredibly, on which party you vote for.

Ridings first. Where every riding contains about the same number of voters, a vote in each riding counts for much the same as in every other. But where one riding has many more voters than another, the larger riding's votes count for less: each vote contributes proportionately less to electing an MP. By this measure, Canada has one of the most unequal franchises in the democratic world.[159] Our constituencies differ in population to a remarkable degree—more than in other democracies, more than at any time in the past.

As of the 2021 census, the smallest riding in the country, Labrador, contained fewer than 27,000 people; its largest, Edmonton-Wetaskiwin, had more than 209,000, nearly eight times as large. These may be dismissed as outliers. But the 5 percent of ridings at the top of the scale are on average three times as large as the 5 percent at the bottom. Compare that to the United Kingdom, where the largest 5 percent are only twice as large, on average, as the smallest 5 percent. Or the US House of Representatives, where the gap between largest and smallest is just 31 percent.

Barely a quarter (28 percent) of Canada's ridings are within 5 percent of the average; fewer than half (48 percent) are within 10 percent of the average. The comparable figures for the UK are 36 percent and 63 percent; the US, 76 percent and 94 percent. Overall, Canada's electoral districts have a standard deviation* equal to 22.2 percent of the average, far higher than the UK at 12.3 percent and the US at 5.8. Canada's ridings are likewise more unequal in size than Australia's (standard deviation: 9.3), France's (15.8), or New Zealand's (5.5).

	Smallest riding as % of average	Largest riding as % of average	Largest riding / smallest riding	Largest 5% of ridings / smallest 5%	% of ridings within 5% of average	% of ridings within 10% of average	Standard deviation (as % of average)
Canada	24.4%	191.4%	7.85	2.9	27.5%	47.6%	22.2
US	73.6%	134.4%	1.83	1.3	76.1%	93.6%	5.8
UK	28.8%	154.4%	5.36	2.1	36.0%	62.3%	12.3
Australia	63.0%	117.0%	1.86	1.6	53.6%	82.8%	9.3
France	57.6%	148.0%	2.56	2.3	22.1%	45.9%	15.8
New Zealand	89.2%	115.2%	1.29	1.2	60.6%	93.0%	5.5

Source: author's calculations, based on national electoral district data.

Some of this reflects the usual overrepresentation of rural ridings relative to urban, found in most democratic countries; this might even be justified, to a degree, by the need to keep the geographic size of ridings to manageable dimensions. Harder to defend are the vast gaps between the provinces. The average Alberta riding, with a population of more than 125,000, is nearly four times as large as a riding in Prince Edward Island, with just 39,000 people. Between them, the four Atlantic provinces and three northern territories have a population of less than 2.8 million. Yet they have more seats, combined, than Alberta, with a population of 4.8 million.†

---

* The square root of the average of the square of the differences with the average riding size. The standard deviation of a set of data points is a measure of how dispersed they are from the mean.
† This interprovincial disparity was set to shrink a little after the 2022 redistribution, which added five seats to the most underrepresented provinces—three in Alberta, one apiece in Ontario and British Columbia. (https://www.elections.ca/content.aspx?section=res&dir=cir/red/

This is not without partisan significance. Many of the smallest seats, as it happens, tend to vote Liberal, while those huge Alberta seats tend to vote Conservative. It took a total of 43,848 votes in the last election to elect six Liberal MPs in Newfoundland, PEI, and the northern territories. That was fewer than the number of votes it took to elect *one* MP, on average, in the six largest Conservative ridings. Again, what this really means is that the votes of people in those small, Liberal, Atlantic ridings are worth many times more than the votes of people in large, Conservative, Alberta ridings.

Why do these inequities—the phrase "rotten boroughs"* comes to mind—persist? Because, like much else in Canada, they are sewn into the Constitution. The 1867 Constitution created a country based on "the proportionate representation of the provinces," or representation by population: there would have been no Confederation had it not done so.† Accordingly, it required that the seats be redistributed between the provinces after each census, in line with movements in population. But the same founding document immediately departed from the principle, specifying that no province would lose any seats unless its share of the population had fallen by at least 5 percent.‡ The "Senate floor" followed in 1915, stipulating that no province could have fewer MPs than it had

---

allo&document=index&lang=e) However, whatever ameliorative effect the redistribution might have had has been undone by the extraordinary growth in population that has occurred since then, especially in those three provinces.

As of 2021, Ontario, British Columbia, and Alberta had a combined 63.5 percent of the country's population, but only 58.3 percent of the seats, a "representation gap" of 5.2 points. Redistribution increased their share of the House to 58.9 percent, which ought to have shrunk the gap. As of December 2024, however, their share of Canada's population stands at 64.7 percent (https://www150.statcan.gc.ca/n1/pub/71-607-x/71-607-x2018005-eng.htm), meaning the representation gap has actually *widened* (to 5.8 points). By the time of the next election, it will have widened further.

For true representation by population, based on the 2021 population figures and assuming a 343-seat House, the three provinces would properly have been allotted twenty-one more seats, rather than five, or twenty-five more using the 2024 numbers.

* Parliamentary constituencies in Britain before the Reform Act of 1832 that had very few voters— as few as seven—but still were permitted to elect members of Parliament.
† It was one of the key demands of the original Reform Party, led by George Brown, who held a majority of the seats in Canada West (present-day Ontario).
‡ Called the "one-twentieth clause," it was repealed in 1946, at the behest of Quebec, of all provinces. https://www.ourcommons.ca/marleaumontpetit/DocumentViewer.aspx?Language=E&Print=2&Sec=Ch04&Seq=1

senators, a sop to the Atlantic provinces, whose relative weight in the federation was declining rapidly with the opening of the West. That effectively froze New Brunswick and PEI's representation in the House at or near their current levels (Nova Scotia's still had some way to fall before it hit its floor) even as their share of the population continued to drop, ensuring they would be overrepresented in perpetuity—or until Senate reform, whichever comes first.

Still, outside of PEI and the Territories, Canada's ridings remained relatively uniform in size until about the 1950s. That began to change as population growth surged in Alberta and British Columbia. But

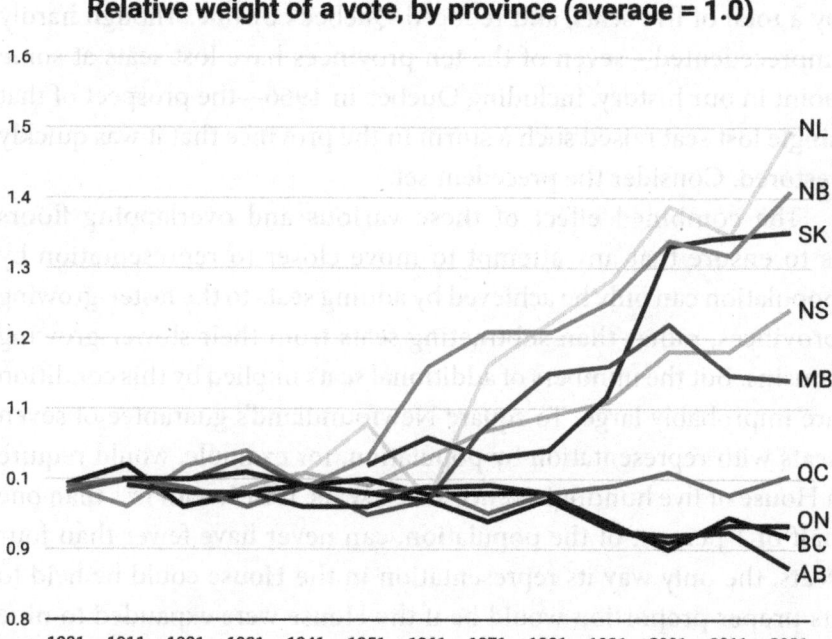

Vote weights are inversely proportional to riding size. The smaller the riding, the fewer votes it takes to elect each MP; thus each vote has greater impact. Figures shown are based on the average for all ridings in a province, relative to the national average.

Source: Andrew Sancton, *The Principle of Representation by Population in Canadian Federal Politics*, Mowat Centre, 2010, updated. PEI and Territories omitted. https://utoronto.scholaris.ca/server/api/core/bitstreams/9f9cc0f4-72d9-4327-9854-185b26cbac9d/content.

the wheels really began to fall off with the passing of the "grandfather clause" by the Mulroney government in 1985, a constitutional amendment providing that no province may have fewer seats, ever, than it had at that time.* This froze Manitoba and Saskatchewan at their current allocations. A third rule stipulates that no province that was overrepresented at the last redistribution can be underrepresented at the next[160]—a legacy of the Harper government, via the 2011 Fair Representation Act.[161]

The most recent redistricting exercise may well have added yet a fourth, informal rule: Quebec's representation can never be reduced, period. The initial proposal from the chief electoral officer would have increased Ontario, Alberta, and British Columbia's representation by a total of five seats, and reduced Quebec's by one. Though hardly unprecedented—seven of the ten provinces have lost seats at some point in our history, including Quebec in 1966—the prospect of that single lost seat raised such a storm in the province that it was quickly restored. Consider the precedent set.†

The combined effect of these various and overlapping floors is to ensure that any attempt to move closer to representation by population can only be achieved by adding seats to the faster-growing provinces, rather than subtracting seats from their slower-growing cousins. But the numbers of additional seats implied by this condition are improbably large. To square Newfoundland's guarantee of seven seats with representation by population, for example, would require a House of five hundred twenty-seven seats. If PEI, with less than one half of 1 percent of the population, can never have fewer than four seats, the only way its representation in the House could be held to its proper proportion would be if the House were expanded to nine hundred twenty-five members.

---

* Newfoundland was given a similar assurance on joining the federation in 1949. https://www.justice.gc.ca/eng/rp-pr/csj-sjc/constitution/lawreg-loireg/p1t212.html
† Prominent voices in the province continue to agitate for it to be guaranteed not just its current number of seats, but its current proportional share.

Elections

* * *

Unequal votes are not only a matter of geography. They are also baked into our electoral system.

It's easy to see how unequal riding sizes makes some votes worth more than others. What may be harder to understand is how the worth of a vote might vary depending on which party you voted for, or how such inequities persist in a system we are taught to believe is fair.

The system we use in Canada might seem straightforward enough. We elect one MP in each riding. We mark our ballots with a single x. The winner is the candidate with the most votes. Yet it produces all sorts of anomalies and absurdities—absurdities we pretend are normal.

Every election campaign begins with reporters writing long features on the so-called battleground ridings, the small number of closely fought races where, readers are told, elections are "won or lost." It has been a staple of election coverage for as long as anyone can remember— so long that it no longer occurs to anyone to ask "er, hang on: isn't *every* riding supposed to be a battleground?" What about the scores of non-battleground ridings, known as "safe seats"—a description that could be applied to more than half the seats in the House? The results in these ridings are such foregone conclusions, the same party winning them, election after election, for decades, that the parties can barely be bothered to contest them. We might as well confine the election to the battlegrounds, and save everyone a lot of time and money. Yet we pretend to find nothing unusual in this.

In the same way, we pretend that the governments we call majority governments are in fact supported by the majority—we say they have a *mandate* from *the people*. We pretend that nearly all of Western Canada votes Conservative, and nearly all of Atlantic Canada votes Liberal; that no one in our largest cities votes Conservative, or that no one in rural or small-town Canada votes Liberal; that the NDP has less popular support than the Bloc Québécois; that the Greens do not exist.

The Crisis of Canadian Democracy

We pretend all these things because that's what the election returns seem to tell us. We cite the distribution of seats as if it were representative of the distribution of opinion among the voters. And yet we know that only one "majority" government in this country has won a majority of the vote in the last sixty-five years;[162] that the last government elected with even 40 percent of the vote was in 2000, seven elections ago; that parties have frequently—seven times[*] at the federal level alone—"won" elections with fewer votes than their nearest rivals; that a majority of the vote in "Conservative" Western Canada typically goes to parties other than the Conservatives; that a majority of the vote in "Liberal" Atlantic Canada typically goes to parties other than the Liberals; that the NDP, although it usually wins fewer seats than the BQ, typically attracts usually wins nearly twice as many votes, and that the Greens, too, have nearly outpolled them on occasion.

Most extraordinary of all, we accept as normal that most voters in most elections, and some voters in all elections, will trudge to the polls knowing that their vote will make no difference whatsoever. It will elect no one, affect nothing, the same as if they had not voted at all.

Well, no, it's not normal, is it? It's distinctly abnormal. All of it. The things we accept as "part of the game," the natural consequences of democratic politics, are not integral to democracy, but only to the peculiar form of democracy practised in Canada: an electoral system known colloquially as "first past the post."

Why "first past the post"? Because the winner is the candidate who finishes first—and because only the winning candidate gets in. Each riding is represented by a single member, elected by a simple plurality of the vote: hence the system's more formal name, single-member plurality. It doesn't matter whether that plurality was obtained with 50 percent of the vote or 40 percent or 30 percent: the winning party is still awarded 100 percent of the representation. Hence perhaps the system's most accurate name: "winner take all." Summing this disproportion

---

[*] 1896, 1926, 1957, 1962, 1979, 2019, 2021.

over every riding, a party might win fewer than 40 percent of the votes and end up with 70 percent or more of the seats: a majority of the seats, with a minority of the vote.

Yet such is the system's apparent simplicity—one member, one riding*, who got the most votes, that singular x—and even more its familiarity, that it passes without question. First past the post is the only system most Canadians have ever known. It has been in exclusive use across the country for decades, not just for federal elections, but provincial, municipal, and even school board elections. This reinforces our sense of the system's naturalness.

In fact, all these things we treat as natural are choices. Instead of marking an x beside a single candidate's name, we might mark our x for several candidates, or vote for both a party and a candidate, or rank the candidates in numerical order. Instead of a simple plurality being sufficient to win a riding, we could insist on a majority, or some other threshold. And, critically, instead of electing one member per riding, we could choose to elect three, or five, or more.

Depending on how these and other elements are combined, it's possible to imagine a great number of different electoral systems. Look around the world and you find many of them in use. They fall into three broad categories.

First, there are the single-member, winner-take-all systems, like first past the post. Unlike first past the post, most of these require each Member of Parliament to be elected with a majority of the vote. This can be achieved by means of ranked or preferential voting, as in Australia, or by a two-round voting system, as in France, where the first round is used to whittle the field to two.

Second, there are the systems based on proportional representation. As the name implies, these attempt to ensure that the share of the seats a party wins is broadly in line with, or proportional to, its share of the

---

* Although this was the system at Canada's founding, inherited from the UK, it was not implemented in the UK until 1884; prior to that, MPs were elected from two-member ridings.

popular vote. The two main variants are list-based systems, as in much of Europe and South America, and the single transferable vote, as in, for example, Ireland.*

Finally, there are the hybrid systems, which elect some members in single-member districts and the rest by proportional representation. These include the mixed-member proportional model used by Germany and New Zealand, as well as the parallel voting systems in use in Japan and other countries.† (More on these later.)

Far from being the natural or normal system, first past the post is relatively uncommon: among the developed countries, only Canada, the United Kingdom, and the United States still use it; India and a scattering of African and Caribbean states account for the rest.‡

Most of the world's countries, more than one hundred in all§— including 92 percent of OECD members[163]—elect at least one chamber of their national legislatures with the help of some form of proportional representation. None of these systems are perfectly proportional, nor do they try to be. But, in all of them, there is at least a rough correlation between a party's share of the vote and its share of the seats.

In Canadian elections, on the other hand, the share of the seats a party is awarded usually bears no resemblance to its share of the vote. Every election throws up new and more bizarre examples. Take the 2021 federal election. The Liberals, with less than a third (32.6 percent) of the vote, came very close to winning a majority with 160 seats of

---

* In the first, voters elect candidates from party lists, in large electoral districts represented by a dozen or more members. In the second, voters rank candidates in order of preference, in smaller electoral districts, typically five- to seven-member.
† In mixed-member proportional systems, the number of proportional representation members varies, depending on the degree of disproportion arising from the single-member elections. In parallel voting systems, the two are wholly separate processes: the number of MPs elected in each is fixed, independent of the other.
‡ Even in these countries, there is usually some other system in use at some level of government: Canada is distinguished by the purity of its devotion to first past the post.
§ About seventy-five use proportional representation, either party-list or single transferable vote. Another thirty or so use hybrid systems incorporating elements of proportional representation. https://www.electoral-reform.org.uk/how-many-countries-around-the-world-use-proportional-representation/

the 169 required. The Conservatives, though they won a larger share of the vote than the Liberals, at 33.7 percent, received 41 seats fewer (119). The NDP, the Greens, and the People's Party, with a combined 25 percent of the vote, took 27 seats between them, or 8 percent of the total, while the Bloc, with 8 percent of the vote, won 32 seats.

The inescapable implication of this divergence between representation and population is that some votes count for more than others. Some 5.6 million people voted for the Liberals in 2021, meaning each of those 160 Liberal MPs required the support of about 34,000 voters to be elected. To elect each Bloc MP, by contrast, took more than 40,000 voters; each Conservative MP, 48,000 voters; each New Democrat, more than 121,000, while the two Green seats cost nearly 200,000 votes apiece. As for the 840,000 voters who cast their ballots for the People's Party, they were rewarded with no seats at all.

Or take the 2015 federal election. It took 38,000 votes to elect each Liberal; 57,000 for each Conservative; 79,000 for each New Democrat; 82,000 for each Bloquiste; and 603,000 for each Green—*sixteen times* as many as for each Liberal. The issue here is not fairness between the parties, but fairness between voters. A system in which some votes are worth four or six or sixteen times as much as others, depending on which party you vote for, is only approximately democratic. It is also deeply inequitable. The reason every vote is supposed to count equally, after all, is because every *person* counts equally. When we so casually dispense with the one, we should recognize that we are also dispensing with the other.

How far does Canada's system diverge from proportionality—from the principle of one person, one vote? Political scientists have a preferred measure of this. Known as the Gallagher[164] or least-squares index, it is calculated as the square root of one half the sum of the squares of the differences between each party's share of the popular vote and its share of the seats. (There are other indices, but Gallagher's is most commonly cited.) As the charts nearby show, Canadian federal elections are among the most disproportionate among the advanced democracies,[165] and have been growing more so over time.

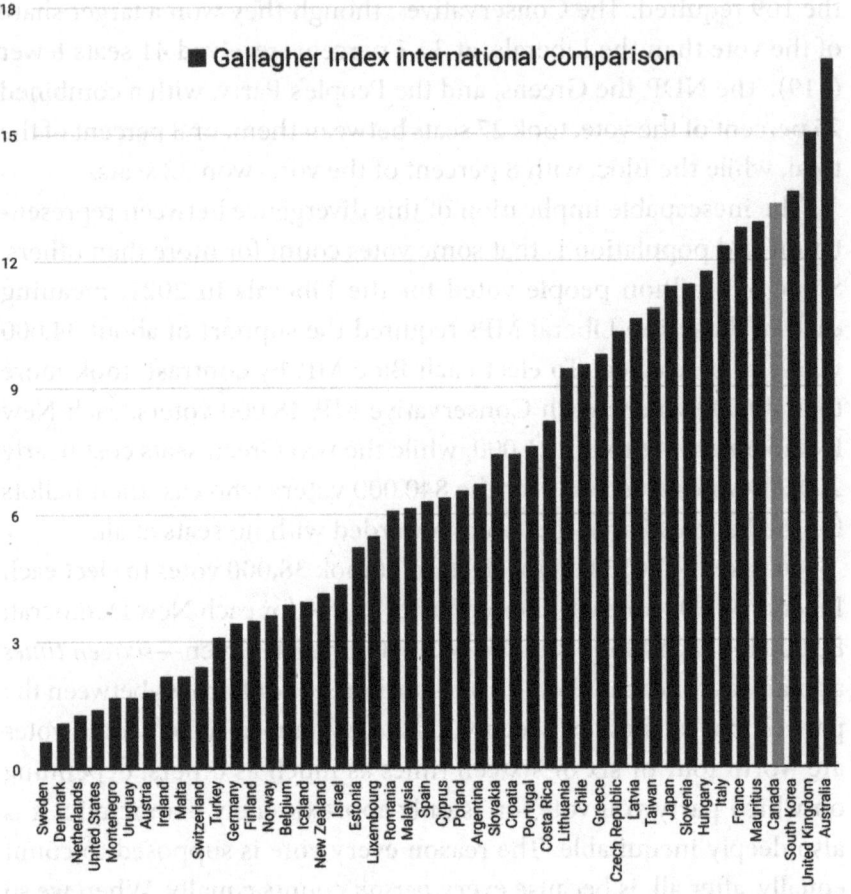

Source: https://www.tcd.ie/Political_Science/about/people/michael_gallagher/ElSystems/Docts/ElectionIndices.pdf

The charts arguably understate matters. In such a regionally diverse country as Canada, the ways in which the electoral system skews the results from proportionality will be very different in different parts of the country. They may even cancel each other out to some extent: Conservative overrepresentation in the West offsetting Liberal overrepresentation in the East. A "composite Gallagher Index," made up of the average of provincial Gallagher indices, would substantially increase our current score, to nearly nineteen.[166]

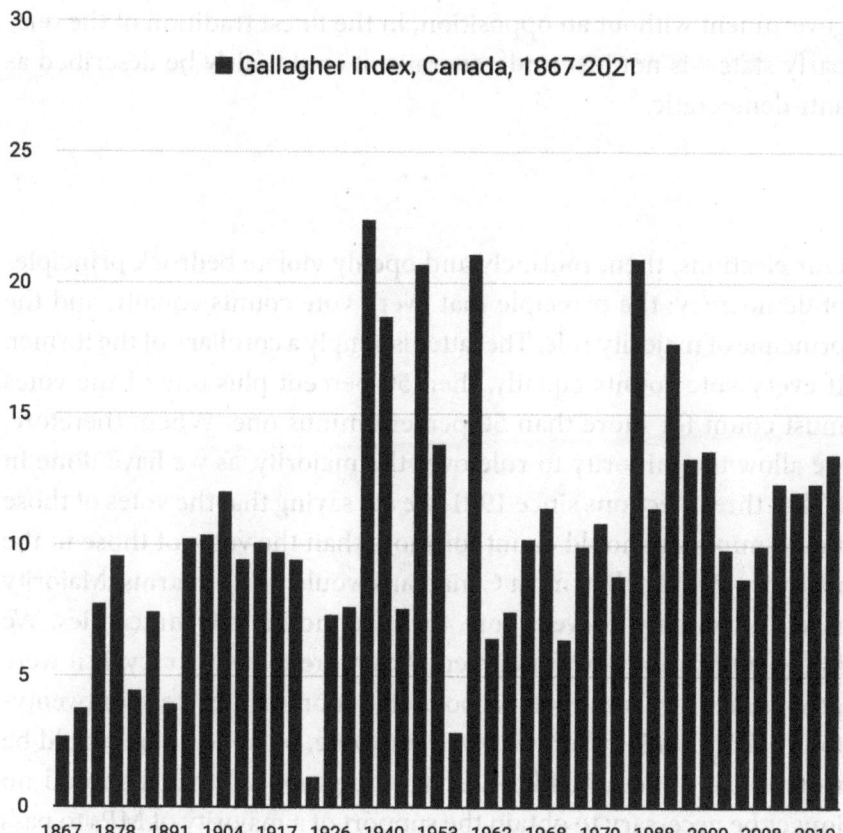

Source: https://iscanadafair.ca/gallagher-index/. Author's calculations.

The situation is worse in provincial elections, where it is common for one party to end up winning nearly all the seats. Recent examples include British Columbia in 2001 (the Liberals won seventy-seven of seventy-nine seats), PEI in 1993 (the Liberals won thirty-one of thirty-two), Alberta in 1982 (the Progressive Conservatives won seventy-five of seventy-nine), Quebec in 1973 (the Liberals won one hundred two of one hundred ten. In two elections, PEI in 1935 and New Brunswick in 1987, the winning party ran the table, taking every seat in the legislature. A system that regularly delivers a near monopoly to one party, not just on power but on *representation*—a government without an opposition, in the finest tradition of the one-party state—is not just undemocratic: it could fairly be described as anti-democratic.

* * *

Our elections, then, routinely and openly violate bedrock principles of democracy: the principle that every vote counts equally, and the principle of majority rule. The latter is simply a corollary of the former. If every vote counts equally, then 50 percent plus one of the votes must count for more than 50 percent minus one. When, therefore, we allow the minority to rule over the majority, as we have done in all but three elections since 1921, we are saying that the votes of those in the minority should count for more than the votes of those in the majority. Put like that, most Canadians would be up in arms. Majority rule, the equality of every vote, these are no mere technicalities. We know, intuitively, how fundamental they are to democracy. If it were proposed to give some voters books of four or five or sixteen or twenty-four ballots while others received only one, or none, there would be riots in the streets. If, likewise, it were proposed that it should no longer be necessary to obtain the support of a majority of MPs to pass a bill in the House, that it would be enough for 40 percent of MPs to vote in favour, the response would be the same.* Yet that is effectively how our politics is conducted.

Once again, we see the contradiction between form and substance. Because we preserve the *form* of one person, one vote, and the *form* of majority rule, we do not notice how far removed we are from the *substance* of either. Yes, we each get one ballot on election day, but if they do not have remotely the same impact, what of it?

---

* Such a system was in fact proposed for Toronto city council by the Ford government in Ontario. It was hastily withdrawn.

Elections

Similarly, that a bill passes with the support of a majority of the people who happen to be sitting in the House of Commons on that particular day is of no significance in itself. It is who those members of Parliament represent that matters. If we insist a bill have the support of a majority of MPs to pass, it must be because, somewhere at the back of our minds, we assume they represent a majority of the people.

In fairness, that used to be the case. For the first several decades of our existence, there were only two parties of any significance; they got virtually all the votes, and virtually all the seats. A two-party system will tend to be roughly proportional, a majority of the vote yielding a majority of the seats. And in virtually every election,* for a time, that is what the system delivered: majority governments in both name and fact.

That all changed in 1921, the year the Progressive Party broke the two-party stranglehold, winning 58 out of 235 seats and 21 percent of the popular vote. Elections since have seen the arrival in Parliament of first the Co-operative Commonwealth Federation (forerunners of the NDP), then the Reform Party and the Bloc Québécois, followed by the Greens.† (The People's Party has yet to elect any MPs, although its founding leader, former Conservative minister Maxime Bernier, continued to hold his seat for a time after leaving the Conservative Party.)

That's not supposed to happen. A well-known principle of political science, Duverger's law,[167] holds that first past the post is suited to two-party politics, and should tend inexorably toward it—witness the durability of the American two-party system. But once the two-party mould is well and truly cracked, it seems, it is difficult to put it back together.

---

* The exception is the election of 1896.
† Multiparty politics was slower to take root in the provinces. As late as 2006, the ten provincial legislatures combined had just twenty-nine third-party members, out of a total of six hundred eighty-seven (compared to eighty-one of the three hundred eight MPs returned in that year's federal election). By 2017 it had risen to seventy-four, though as of 2023 it had fallen back to forty-six.

First past the post works tolerably well in a two-party system. But once you add a third party, and a fourth, a fifth, and a sixth, the results start to deviate more and more from proportionality. Why is this? Recall the proper name of our system: single-member plurality. It's not the plurality part that produces these anomalies. It's the fact that we elect only one member per riding. Five or six or more parties may have the support of a substantial number of voters in a riding, but only one of those parties' supporters will end up being represented in Parliament. Winner take all.

(Yes, I know: in a legal sense every Member of Parliament represents all the voters in his or her riding. So in that sense every voter is represented and every vote counts. It's just that their *views* aren't represented. Which is surely the point of the exercise.)

This is what proportional representation advocates mean when they say that more than half the votes in any given election—the 50 percent-plus in each riding, on average, cast for candidates other than the winner—are "wasted."* Of course, these votes were counted, the same as the winner's. But they did not help to elect anyone. They were counted, but they didn't *count*.

It is this fundamental anomaly that gives rise to all the other anomalies in first past the post: the disproportion of the whole is the sum of the disproportions of the parts. Where there are only two parties, the disproportions in each riding tend to cancel each other out: what a party loses in one riding it gains in another. But where there are three or more parties, the distortions only compound with scale.

Because representation is awarded only to the party with the most votes in a riding, the system rewards parties that can "clump" their vote geographically. A party that wins a lot of votes in one part of the country, but few votes in the rest, will win more seats than a party

---

* Add in the average 21 percent winning margin in recent elections—votes in excess of the number actually needed to win—and the proportion of wasted votes arguably exceeds 70 percent.

Elections

whose votes are distributed more evenly, even if their overall share of the vote is similar. Typically, that is to the benefit of old parties, with established candidates and machines, rather than new or idea-based parties, whose appeal is likely to be more thinly spread. Most of all, it rewards regionally based parties, and the politics that go with them: a politics that emphasizes how ill-treated the people of [your region here] are by the rest of the federation—something that Canadians in every region are all too ready to believe—and the need to "fight" to get their "fair share," and so forth.

Perhaps the most vivid example of this was the 1993 federal election. The Conservatives, with 16 percent of the vote, were reduced to a humiliating two seats. Meanwhile, the Bloc surged to fifty-four seats (and official opposition status!) on the strength of 13.5 percent of the vote, while the Reform Party, with less than 19 percent of the vote, took fifty-one seats. The latter two parties had strong regional bases, in Quebec and the West respectively. They ran no candidates outside of their bases, while Conservative support was spread across the country.

But explicitly regional parties aren't the issue. The truth is that the two historic "national" parties are regional parties in all but name, dominant in one part of the country, all but non-existent in the others, for decades at a time. In the thirty-eight federal elections since 1887, the Conservatives have carried Quebec just three times: most elections they struggle to win more than a handful of seats in the province. That record of futility is mirrored by the Liberals in the West, where the party last won a majority of the seats in 1949.

Hence the term "safe" seat. In the current Parliament, 182 seats, well over half, have returned an MP from the same party in at least six of the last seven elections.[*] Voting for a particular party becomes, for a significant section of voters, a part of their regional identity; the

---

[*] In the safest of these, the 103 ridings that have voted the same way in (at least) the last seven, the average margin of victory over the last four of those elections was 30.1 percent.

region itself will commonly be described as Conservative or Liberal, though a minority of the voters in each could actually be described that way.

First past the post would seem particularly ill-suited to a country with Canada's geography: "a horizontal Chile" stretched out over thousands of kilometres, with fewer than 42 million inhabitants, divided not only by the vast distances between us but also by jurisdiction, language, and ethnicity. It exaggerates and exacerbates all of our very real regional differences, producing false or distended regional majorities in the same way as it produces false majorities overall.

On several occasions, it has come close to killing the country. In the 1980 election, the Liberals won just two seats west of Ontario, while taking seventy-four out of seventy-five seats in Quebec. (The party's Quebec delegation was large enough on its own to account for a majority of its parliamentary caucus.) These results were not an accurate reflection of their share of the vote in those two regions: 23 percent in the West and 68 percent in Quebec. But can it be doubted the results affected the Liberals' subsequent strategic calculations? Would the Trudeau government have attempted the National Energy Program if it had had more representation from the West? Would it have attempted patriation* of the Constitution if it had not been so dominant in Quebec? The Liberals won roughly a third as many votes across the West as they did in Quebec. If they had won a third as many seats in the West, the history of Canada might have been very different.

The consequences of first past the post for national unity are obvious. But it also materially contributes to one of the worst and most enduring features of our system of government: its tendency to one-party rule. The Conservative and the Liberals may each, thanks to first past the post, depend on clustering their vote on regional lines. It's just that the Liberal vote happens to have clustered in what have historically been the most populous regions, Ontario

---

* The process of severing the Constitution of Canada from British legislative supremacy.

and Quebec, while the Tory vote has clustered in the historically less populous West. Since 1896, the Liberals have won two elections for every one for the Conservatives. This wasn't because of any strong overall preference among the Canadian public for Liberal government: on average, their share of the popular vote has exceeded that of the Tories by just two percentage points, 40.5 to 38.6. Rather, it was their ability to scoop up nearly all the seats in one large province—Quebec until 1984; Ontario for several elections after that—that accounted for most of those victories.

***

This only begins to describe the ways in which first past the post warps our elections. Often these are impossible to predict. Whether a party wins a plurality in a riding will depend, for example—on how successful it has been at clustering its vote, but also on how the vote "splits" between its rivals. If the other parties are roughly level with one another, the first party will be more likely to squeeze past them than it would if one were clearly ahead of the others.

Hence the emphasis parties put on encouraging voters to cast their ballots "strategically," voting not for the party they like most, but for a party they like less, if the latter has a better chance of defeating the party they like least. This, too, is a violation of a fundamental democratic right: the right to vote for the party of your choice. We find it normal. But most other democracies would find the suggestion absurd and presumptuous—it is for voters to tell parties what to do, not the reverse.

Fortunately, voters are not cattle. Try as they might, parties find it difficult to herd them into their preferred pens. This is one of the things that makes first-past-the-post elections so hard to predict: even if the pollsters are able to call the popular vote right, an increasingly tricky task, how that translates into seats is anybody's guess.

Another wild card is the "efficiency" of a party's vote. A party's ability to cluster its vote geographically confers an electoral advantage, up to a point. Past that point, it can "overcluster," leading to a lot of wasted (i.e., surplus) votes. The Conservatives particularly suffer from this. Election after election, the party effortlessly sweeps western Canada, winning dozens of seats with 70 or 80 percent of the vote, while losing a comparable numbers of seats in Ontario, often by the thinnest of margins. Had its vote been distributed more efficiently, somewhat fewer in western Canada, somewhat more in Ontario, it might have won more seats overall with the same share of the popular vote.

The Liberal vote, by contrast, is highly efficient. Rather than aiming at attracting the largest number of votes in the largest number of seats, party strategists boast of how carefully targeted their campaigns are: how few voters they aim to persuade, in how few battleground ridings. The rest they ignore. This again is a response to the incentives in the electoral system. First past the post encourages parties to win, not as many votes as they can, but as few as they must.

For all the vaunted simplicity of first past the post, then, in one respect—the relationship between seats and votes—it is anything but simple. Rather, it is acutely unpredictable, volatile—almost random. To put it another way, first past the post is a highly "leveraged" system: a swing of just one or two percentage points in the popular vote can produce a much wider swing in seat counts, possibly spelling the difference between government and opposition. Power can oscillate wildly back and forth from one election to another, with one party after another claiming a majority of the seats, and a mandate for sweeping policy changes, on the basis of minor shifts in the popular vote—a phenomenon known as "policy lurch."

Ontario swung from the David Peterson Liberals to the Bob Rae NDP to the Mike Harris Tories within the space of five years in the early 1990s. Did Ontarians undergo a similar transformation in their attitudes to the role of government? Of course not: most of them continued voting for the same party from one election to the next. It was the swing voters, that narrow slice of voters who can be persuaded to change their allegiances between elections, that made the difference. Finding and mobilizing swing voters, accordingly, tends to absorb a vastly disproportionate share of parties' attention and energies. Policies are devised with no purpose other than to pander to a small number of voters in a few carefully targeted ridings. How small? How few? If just 15,889 voters in 21 ridings had voted Conservative rather than Liberal in the last election, it would have been the Conservatives who won the most seats and not the Liberals. They decided the election.* Again, we tend to think of this as normal, a natural part of politics. It isn't: it is a response to the particular incentives embedded in the system.

Yet the contrary strategy—turning out the base—is no less driven by the imperatives of first past the post. Rather than try to win over uncommitted voters, that is, by moderating your positions on controversial issues, you adopt a highly confrontational stance aimed at cementing the loyalties of your most passionate supporters (the base), to ensure that every one of them gets out to vote. This approach polarizes the electorate between *us* (that section of the electorate over which the party holds a monopoly) and *them* (the section it hopes to see divided among its rivals). If a party needs only a plurality of the vote to win, rather than a majority, and its opponents can be counted on to split the vote among them, it may pay that party to avoid trying to expand its base in favour of enraging it.

The choice of electoral systems doesn't just affect the results of elections, but the behaviour of the players. In a democracy, how we count the votes is how we keep score. It determines the rewards and penalties that accrue to different strategies, and the incentives for politicians to adopt one approach or the other — again, not just on election day, but every day in between. Hence the significance of first past the post's highly-leveraged, winner-take-all, beat-the-devil incentive structure. Living on a knife-edge does strange things to a person. When the range of possible outcomes in an election is not

---

* Overall, it took 1,936,211 votes in 140 ridings to assure the Liberals of a plurality: a little over 11 percent of all votes cast, or about 7 percent of those registered to vote. That was the minimum number of votes needed to defeat their nearest rival in each riding.

more seats or fewer, but the political equivalent of life or death, you will behave in ways you might not otherwise. It is surely one factor, for example, in our suffocating system of party discipline: with so much riding on the smallest shift in the polls, leaders undoubtedly feel they can't take a chance on a slip of a backbencher's lip.

In sum, first past the post allows the minority to rule over the majority, sometimes all but unopposed. It gives some voters many times the voting power of others, strands many in safe ridings, traps others in strategic voting dilemmas, and leaves most of the rest unrepresented. The parliaments it elects present a hideously distorted picture of the country, greatly inflating the support of regional parties and inflaming national divisions. And the politics it encourages is corrosive, pandering, and given to wild swings in policy. Why, then, do we persist with it?

Defenders of first past the post have an answer: the firm smack of authority. Say what you will about first past the post, they claim, at least it produces stable majority governments, capable of assuming power with a minimum of uncertainty and likely to remain there for a decent interval. Are these genuine majorities? Who cares? It is stability we want, not accuracy.

In the two-party era, as we've seen, Canada was indeed governed by a succession of majority governments that really did represent a majority of the voters. Even in the age of multiparty politics, the system continued to deliver majority governments, false and unrepresentative as they may have been. But that is no longer true: first past the post no longer delivers even the false majorities that some cite as its chief advantage. Eleven of the last twenty-two federal elections, including five of the last seven, have ended in minority governments: hung parliaments, as the British call them, with no single party in control of a majority of the seats. Provincial elections have produced as many minority governments since 2000—nine, in seven different provinces*—as in all the years before.

---

* Ontario in 2011; Quebec in 2007 and 2012; British Columbia in 2017; Nova Scotia in 2003 and 2006; New Brunswick in 2018; Newfoundland in 2019; Prince Edward Island in 2019.

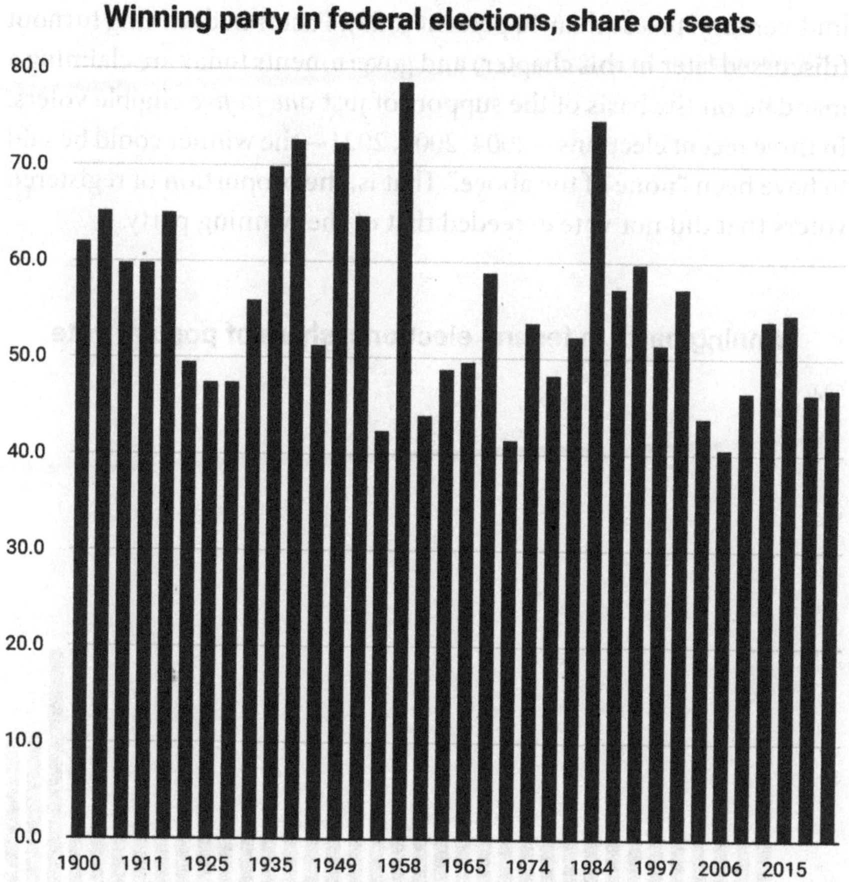

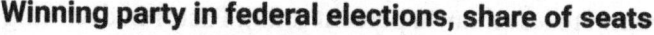

Winning party in federal elections, share of seats

Source: House of Commons Procedure and Practice, Third Edition, 2017 https://www.ourcommons.ca/procedure/procedure-and-practice-3/App10-e.html

Not only are minority governments more and more common, but they are governing with a smaller and smaller share of the popular vote. The Liberals won power in the 2021 election with fewer than 33 percent of votes cast, the weakest mandate of any Canadian government since Confederation. The previous record was set in the 2019 election. (In both, the Liberals also won fewer votes than their Conservative rivals.) The share of popular vote going to the winning party has been declining fairly steadily for more than a century: from more than 50 percent in the early twentieth century, to 40 to 45 percent mid-century, to less than 40 percent today. Factor in declining turnout (discussed later in this chapter) and governments today are claiming a mandate on the basis of the support of just *one in five* eligible voters. In three recent elections—2004, 2007, 2021—the winner could be said to have been "none of the above." That is, the proportion of registered voters that did not vote exceeded that of the winning party.

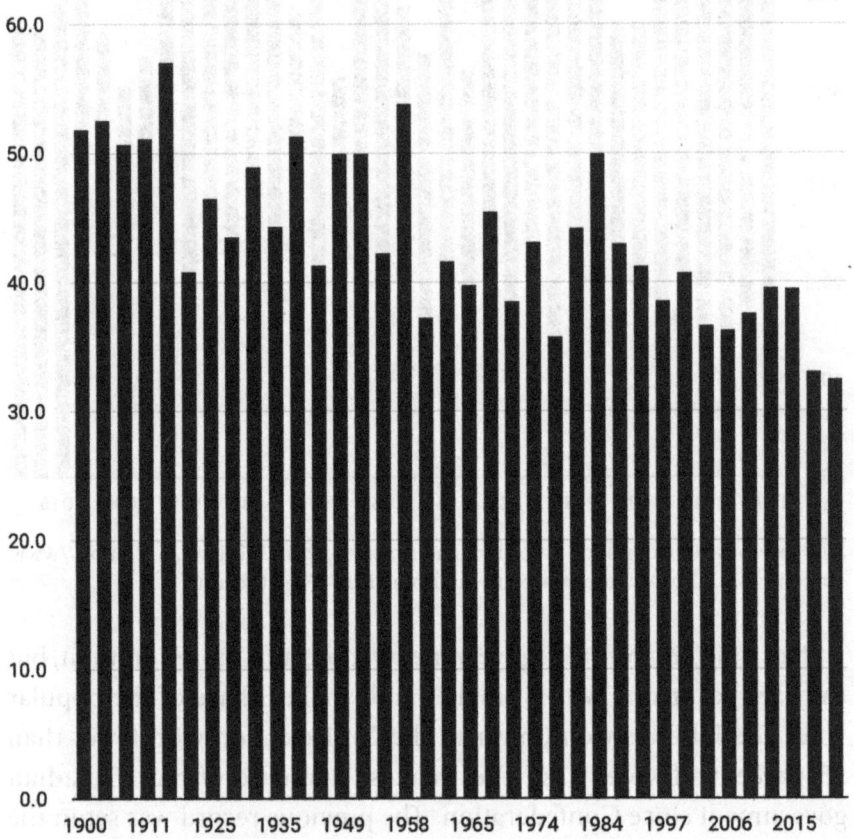

Source: https://www.sfu.ca/~aheard/elections/1867-present.html

Elections

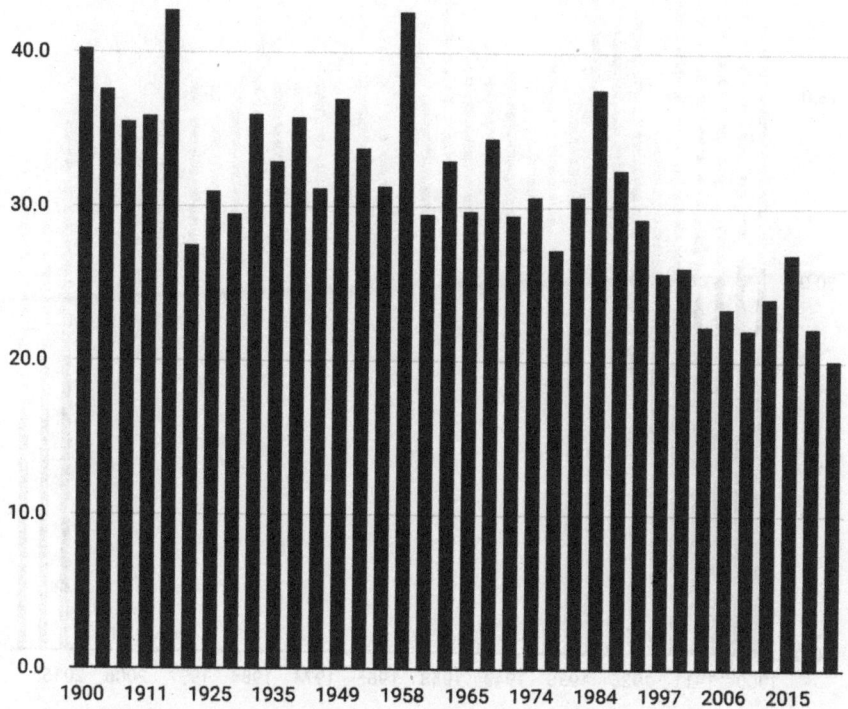

Source: https://www.sfu.ca/~aheard/elections/1867-present.html; https://www.elections.ca/content.aspx?section=ele&dir=turn&document=index&lang=e

The same decline is observable in the top two parties' share of the vote. Even after the duopoly was broken, the two main parties could still count on winning close to 80 percent of the vote between them. In the last two decades, that has been reduced to two-thirds, as the number of parties has proliferated.

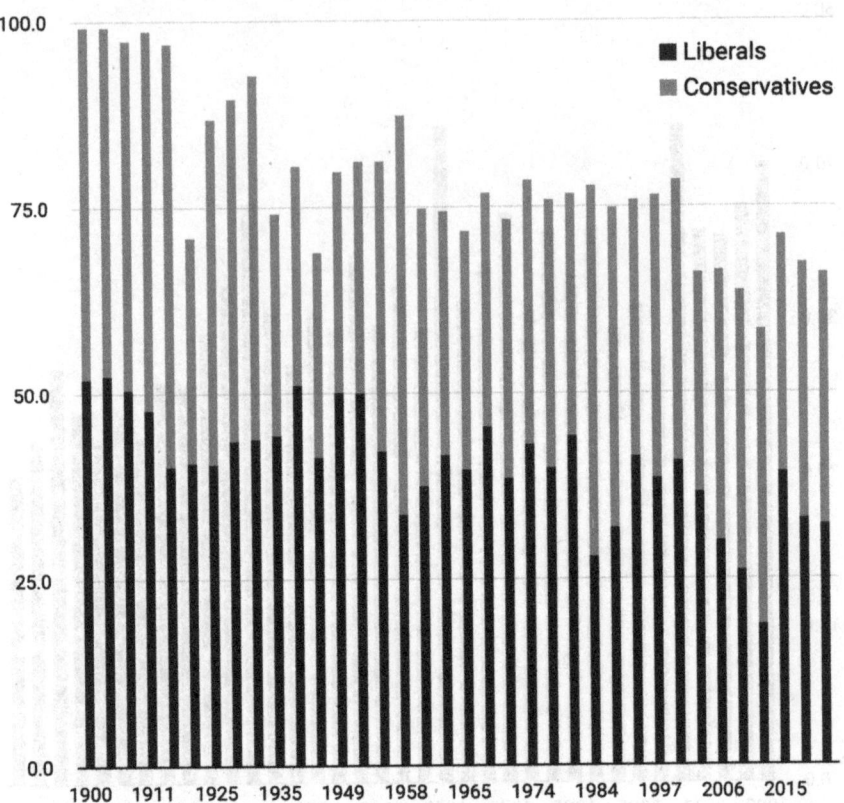

Source: https://www.sfu.ca/~aheard/elections/1867-present.html

The increasing dispersal of the vote has also lowered the bar to winning a majority, provided the vote splits in just the right way: the Conservatives in 2011 and the Liberals in 2015 were able to manage a majority with less than 40 percent of the vote, for just the second and third time ever. Neither majority, however, proved enduring.

How long can the "stable majorities" charade be maintained? At some point, the disparity will prove unbearable: not only between the proportions of votes and seats won, but also between the system as we imagine it and reality.

If that is the case—if first past the post cannot reliably deliver the majority governments that were one of its few remaining defences—if the system is delivering all the "instability" we associate with proportional representation with none of the representativeness, the question becomes: why not change it? First past the post may have been appropriate when the two-party system was in full sway. But we haven't had two-party politics since 1921. If governing from now on is increasingly going to be about assembling multiparty majorities, why not acknowledge that reality and adapt the system to the way people are actually voting, rather than pretending nothing has changed? We are trying to run six-party politics on a system built for two. As a result the only real question in each election is which unsatisfying outcome it will produce: an unstable minority or an unrepresentative majority. Maybe it's time to try something new.

By "new," I mean a proportional representation system of the sort already in use in more than a hundred countries around the world. Its virtues are mostly the inverse of first past the post's failings. Where first past the post leaves half or more of the voters unrepresented, proportional representation ensures everyone is represented, or nearly everyone. Where first past the post assigns wildly different weights to votes for different parties in different ridings, proportional representation weighs every vote equally, or nearly so.

Rather than conjure up phony majorities out of a minority of the vote, proportional representation produces genuine majority governments supported by actual majorities of the public; rather than tip policy madly back and forth in response to minor shifts in public opinion, it tends more to steady progress rooted in broad public consensus; rather than write off whole parts of the country to the dominance of one party for decades at a time, it forces all parties to compete for seats in every region, every election; rather than favour large and established parties, it give new parties with new ideas a fighting chance. And so on.

What would it look like? How would it work? More particularly, how would it differ from the system we have now? It's best to first state what is *not* being proposed: the kind of system many people have in mind when they hear the words "proportional representation." It is often described as follows: Instead of electing MPs in ridings, voters are restricted to voting for party slates. After the votes are cast, each party receives a number of seats in strict accordance with its share of the total vote. Then party brass decides which candidates on the party's list get to sit in Parliament. It's all very centralized and top-down and ... mathematical.

Never mind that nothing like that has ever been proposed for Canada—it's not even an accurate representation of how proportional representation works in other countries. Not all proportional systems use party lists, for starters. Where lists are used, candidates are not typically elected from a single national list but rather from regional, county, or municipal lists. Moreover, only a minority of list-based systems use "closed" lists, where voters select only the party and the party decides which candidates get into Parliament. More common are "open list" systems, in which voters have the option of indicating which of a party's candidates they prefer. (Closed lists themselves are usually drawn up not by the party leader, but by a vote of party members.)

Still, I get it: people in this country don't like lists. Even the hybrid model sometimes proposed,* known as mixed-member proportional, suffers from the association. The idea is to elect the bulk of the House of Commons as we do now, in single-member ridings, topped up with MPs elected in larger regional or provincial districts, perhaps twelve to twenty in each. Not only does that involve the dreaded lists, but many people find it weird to elect some MPs by one system, and the rest by a totally different system.

---

* For example, by the Law Commission of Canada, *Voting Counts: Electoral Reform for Canada*, 2004. https://publications.gc.ca/collections/Collection/J31-61-2004E.pdf. It has also been the subject of referendums in Ontario and Prince Edward Island. The proportion of constituency versus list MPs is a matter of taste: in Germany, constituency MPs are allotted at most half the total; in New Zealand, the mix is closer to 60–40 in favour of constituency MPs. The Law Commission recommended the "Scottish model," with at least two-thirds elected in single-member constituencies.

So, no lists. Instead, let me introduce you to the chief rival of list-based proportional representation, the single transferable vote. In use today in Ireland, Malta, and the Australian Senate, it was the system proposed for British Columbia in its 2005 referendum and endorsed by 58 percent of the voters. Rather than electing MPs in gargantuan regional districts, voters would elect MPs in ridings much closer in size to what they are now, with three to seven members, using ranked ballots.

That's it. That's the big scary change reform would involve. Instead of electing one member per riding, we'd elect several. And instead of marking an x beside the candidate of our choice, we'd rank them in order of preference: 1, 2, 3. And yet, those two little changes would change everything.

Of the two, the first is more fundamental. Again, the problem with single-member plurality isn't the plurality part. It's the single member. It is the winner-take-all aspect of first past the post that produces most of its distortions. Increase the number of representatives in a riding from one to several, and most of these disappear. Instead of one candidate and one party hogging all of a riding's representation, it is shared among them, in rough proportion to their support among the riding's voters. That's what makes a system proportional. It's what all proportional representation systems have in common: multi-member electoral districts.

Ranked ballots, on the other hand, do nothing to make a system more proportional, on their own. Often suggested as a "moderate" alternative to proportional representation, ranked voting will be familiar to many Canadians from party leadership races, where the second and lower choices of losing candidates are redistributed in successive rounds of counting until one candidate has over half the votes. That at least ensures the winning candidate is the choice of a majority of the voters, rather than a plurality. But it is still a single-member, winner-take-all system: as with first past the post, representation is confined to those who vote for the winner.*

---

* The same is true of two-round voting systems.

Ranked voting does have other virtues, however, especially when combined with multi-member ridings. You can rank as many or as few candidates as you like. And your choices don't all have to be from the same party: you can vote à la carte, if you wish, picking candidates from different parties. You might put a candidate from Party A first, a candidate from Party B second, another candidate from Party A third, and a candidate from Party C fourth.

Freeing voters to cross party lines in this way means candidates have to compete, not just with candidates from other parties, but also their own. And it eliminates that invidious choice so often forced on voters by first past the post: between a candidate they like running for a party they loathe, and the reverse. Ranked ballots favour MPs who can win support across party lines—mavericks, consensus-builders, independents—rather than the partisan attack dogs the current system tends to produce. (Attack your opponents too stridently and their supporters are unlikely to mark you as their second choice.) Last, ranked ballots mean no more fear of splitting the vote. If your first choice is knocked out, your vote isn't wasted: your second choice can still count.

The only complicated part is the counting. Well, it's not *that* complicated.* We've seen how ranked voting can be used in single-member ridings, where a candidate is elected once he crosses the 50 percent threshold. Obviously, that can't be the benchmark where several candidates are to be elected. But the concept is similar. Suppose a riding elects five MPs. Some quick math will tell you a candidate who wins one-sixth of the vote plus one is guaranteed to be elected, as there is no way five candidates could finish ahead of him.† For a three-MP riding, similarly, the quota would be one-quarter of the vote plus one. Above that quota, you're in. Short of it, you're out.

---

* If you *really* want to see a complicated system for allotting seats, have a look at the methods used in list-based systems: the D'Hondt method, the Sainte-Laguë formula, etc.
† This is known as the Droop quota method. It's not the only way to set the quota, but it's the most common.

Elections

Problem: what if, in a five-member riding, a candidate wins 40 percent of the first choices? He only needed 17 percent to be elected. The surplus votes in excess of the quota are effectively wasted: as with the votes for losing candidates, they do not help anyone to get elected. So in addition to redistributing the second choices of candidates who have been eliminated from contention, the single transferable vote also redistributes the surplus votes of candidates who have already clinched their seat. The result: a much larger share of the voters—in excess of 90 percent—are represented in Parliament, with fewer wasted votes.

The main knock against the single transferable vote, at least in a Canadian setting, is the size of the ridings implied—geographic size, that is. It's all right in the cities, but in some rural and northern areas we'd be talking about ridings larger than most countries.* One fix for this is to substitute single-member ridings where multi-member ridings would be impractically large, a hybrid form known as "rural-urban" proportional representation. Simulations conducted for the parliamentary committee on electoral reform in 2016 found the rural-urban model would have the lowest Gallagher score—meaning the least disproportionality—of any of the alternatives examined.[168]

Too complicated? Not the Canadian way? In fact, that *was* the system in some parts of Canada, though few are old enough to remember it. From the 1920s to the 1950s, Manitoba and Alberta used "rural-urban" single transferable vote for provincial elections: multi-member ridings in the cities, single-member ridings in rural areas.† The system was also used in several municipalities. If our grandparents could figure it out, chances are we should be able to manage.

* * *

---

* The northern ridings already are. https://en.wikipedia.org/wiki/List_of_countries_and_dependencies_by_area, https://electionsanddemocracy.ca/district-fact-sheets
† British Columbia elected part of its legislature from multi-member ridings as late as 1986, although not by single transferable vote.

There now. That wasn't so hard, was it? Even so, the very mention of electoral reform seems to cause many Canadians to break out in hives. The same people who grind their teeth in rage at the many failings of our political system at most other times become fiercely protective of it the moment anyone proposes to change it.

Why are we so attached to a system that is so manifestly inferior when there are better systems available? The short answer: because it's the system we have. Not only is it the only system most Canadians have ever known, but many Canadians seem to imagine it is the only system there is. Hence the instant and widespread predictions, whenever the subject of electoral reform arises, of the horrific consequences that must inevitably follow. The assumption appears to be that reform would involve a step into a vast and unknowable void, as if we would be adopting a system unlike any other that had ever been devised, rather than one that has worked well in dozens of other countries for decades.

So far as these countries' existence is acknowledged, the tendency is to present an account of their experience that would be unrecognizable to anyone who actually lived there, or cherry-pick horror stories of dubious relevance to Canada. The most common example of this latter kind of objection, and the surest tell of someone who has not done their homework, is some variation of "that's the system in Israel" or "that's the system in Italy." For extra emphasis, the proportional representation scaremonger may even invoke the spectre of Hitler, whose rise the listener is confidently assured was all because of Weimar Germany's use of proportional representation.

Let's get these out of the way first. Israel uses a particularly extreme form of proportional representation, discussed below, that no one has ever proposed in this country or ever would. Italy's reputation for instability derives from the first decades after the Second World War, when it, too, employed an extreme form of proportional representation*; since 1993, it has adopted a series of reforms (it now

---

* Among other peculiarities, votes in the Italian Parliament were by secret ballot.

uses a hybrid system rather like Japan's) and has become noticeably more stable. Hitler's rise to power was due a complex mix of factors—the traumas Germany had endured during and after the First World War, the polarization of Germany society, the opportunism and miscalculations of its political leaders—of which the electoral system was at worst an aggravating factor. In any case, to cite a couple of worst-case examples as if that clinched the case against proportional representation in general is a little akin to rejecting first past the post because that's the system used in Myanmar. It ignores the experience of dozens of other perfectly pleasant and well-run countries, none of them governed by Nazis.

Still, you've heard all the horror stories, amplified and distorted by proportional representation's opponents: about the "pizza parliaments" it supposedly produces, with dozens of parties in the mix, many of them of a fringe or extremist hue, none able to command a majority; about the ensuing chaos and paralysis, while the mainstream parties jockey for the support of the fringe parties; about the frequent elections and revolving-door governments, as one rickety coalition after another falls apart—and yet, the crushing sense of stasis, as the same parties end up in government, with the same leaders, election after election.

You'd be surprised how many otherwise well-informed people believe this. The following examples of press commentary are depressingly representative:

> How would you like an anti-immigrant, racist, anti-abortion or fundamentalist religious political party holding the balance of power in Canada? . . . Welcome to the proportional representation electoral system, where extreme, minority and just plain bizarre views get to rule the roost.[169]

> [Proportional representation] breaks the local bond between constituents and MPs . . . In a strict [proportional representation] system, party leaders at national headquarters select who their

candidates will be, or at least in what order they will make it into Parliament...[170]

The question naturally arises: where are these dystopian hellholes? Is that really what happens under proportional representation? Why, then, would any country adopt it—let alone a hundred countries? Or having adopted it, why would they stick with it? Surely, we should find all these proportional representation countries are in haste to abandon it. Yet such is not the case. While most first-past-the-post countries contain a flourishing proportional representation movement, there is no significant movement in any major proportional representation country in favour of first past the post.

What is the actual track record of proportional representation in policy terms? Look, first, at any list of the world's most successful countries, by whatever metric you prefer—the quality of their democracy, the freedoms they enjoy, their level of social development, or more prosaic measures like GDP per capita or government credit ratings—and you find the same names appearing near the top of every list: Norway, Sweden, Denmark, Finland, Switzerland, Belgium, the Netherlands, Luxembourg, Ireland, New Zealand, Germany, all of whose parliaments are wholly or partially elected by proportional representation. The top-rated single-member countries, Canada, Australia, France, the United Kingdom, have a hard time cracking the top ten.

There is something of an industry of academic studies showing that proportional representation yields superior outcomes in everything from the environment to income inequality to economic growth and public finance.[171] Whether or not you find these studies persuasive, there is a certain logic to the idea that a system that treats every vote equally, rather than obsessively courting a few swing voters in swing ridings, will tend to be less driven by narrow rent-seeking and more focused on policies in the broader public interest. At any rate, if the proposition is that proportional representation leads straight to rack and ruin, there is simply no evidence for this.

Elections

Very well. What about the specific charges against proportional representation: the fragmentation and division, the chaos and instability, the entrenched party elites, etc? How many parties, for starters, does one find in the typical proportional representation legislature? Are they the "pizza parliaments" of so much fevered rhetoric?

The data say no. A word on methodology first. Merely counting up all the parties with seats in a legislature, including those that have only one or two, can give a misleading picture. Accordingly, political scientists use a measure called the "*effective* number of parties," weighting them by their size. What do the data show? There's a range (see the chart overleaf). At one end, you find countries like Belgium, the Netherlands, Denmark, and Israel, with an effective number of between six and ten. At the other, countries like Malta and—surprise!—Italy, with just two and change. Most proportional representation countries are in the two to six range—the average is a little over four—slightly higher than countries in the sample that don't use proportional representation (Canada, the United States, the United Kingdom, France, and Australia), with an average score of 2.8.

The difference between the high- and low-scoring countries using proportional representation depends (in part) on the number of members elected from each electoral district: known as the system's "district magnitude." The more members you elect per district, the more finely you can slice up the electorate, and the more closely you can match the number of seats a party gets to its proportion of the vote. The reason Israel and the Netherlands, in particular, have high scores is that they treat the entire country as one electoral district.* The 120 members of the Israel Knesset, like the 150 members of the Dutch House of Representatives, are all elected at large. That's some fine slicing.

---

* Weimar Germany also suffered from this defect.

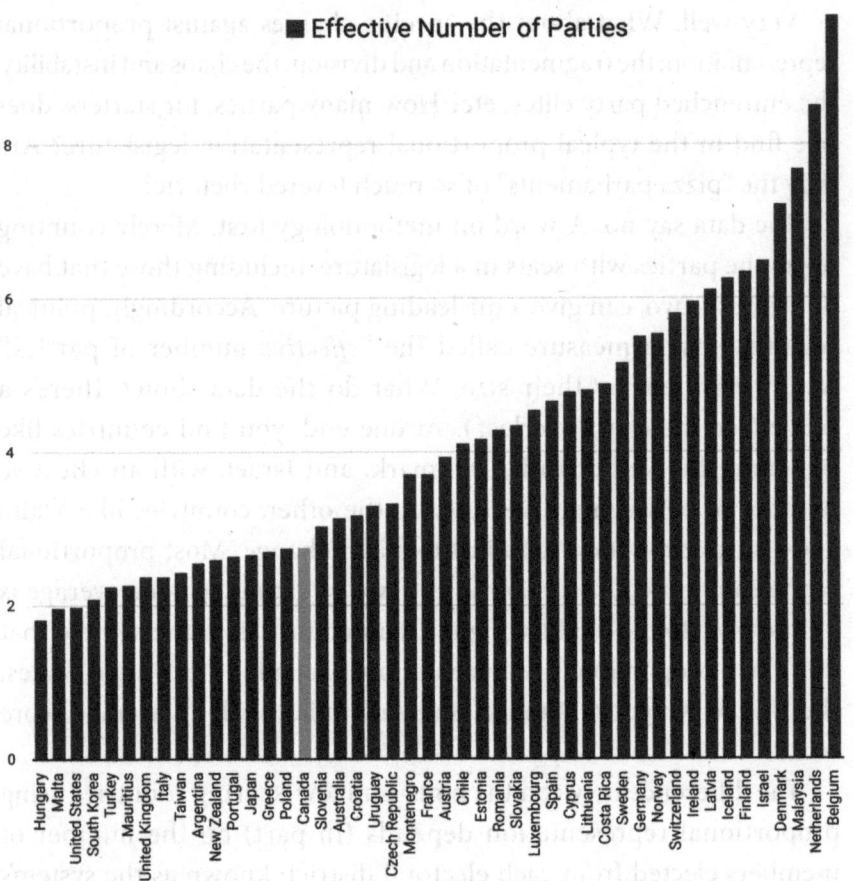

Source: www.tcd.ie/Political_Science/about/people/michael_gallagher/ElSystems/Docts/ElectionIndices.pdf

This may make sense to them: both countries are about the size of a postage stamp. But most other proportional representation countries divide themselves into several electoral districts, with much smaller district magnitudes. In fact, research shows[172] you can get most of the way to proportionality at relatively low district magnitudes—just five to seven—meaning a better trade-off with local accountability.

How unstable are these systems? The table nearby shows data for the world's twenty-three oldest continuing democracies[173]—those

Elections

that have been holding elections since at least 1945*. In that time period, Canada has held twenty-five elections. In only one of the pure proportional representation countries has there been more: Denmark, with twenty-nine. (Japan, which has a hybrid (parallel) system, has had twenty-eight. New Zealand has held twenty-seven, but for most

Country	System	Elections 1945–	Notes
Australia	Ranked ballot	30	
Austria	Open list PR	24	
Belgium	Open list PR	24	
Canada	FPTP	25	
Costa Rica	Closed list PR	18	Since 1949
Denmark	Open list PR	29	
Finland	Open list PR	22	
France	Two-round	22	
Germany	MMP	21	
Iceland	Open list PR	24	
India	FPTP	18	Since 1950
Ireland	STV	22	
Israel	Closed list PR	25	
Italy	Parallel	20	
Japan	Parallel	28	
Luxembourg	Open list PR	18	
Netherlands	Open list PR	24	
New Zealand	MMP	27	FPTP until 1993
Norway	Open list PR	20	
Sweden	Open list PR	23	
Switzerland	Openlist PR	20	
United Kingdom	FPTP	22	
United States (House of Reps)	FPTP	40	

* With two exceptions, noted in the table.

of that period used first past the post.) The average for proportional representation countries in the sample is twenty. A broader survey yields similar results: during the period 1945 to 1998, there were sixteen elections, on average, in proportional representation countries versus 16.7 in countries using first past the post.[174]

Is there the occasional post-election wrangling, while parties negotiate on the makeup of coalition governments? Yes. But the notion that this inevitably makes the large parties hostage to the fringe is contrary to both logic and fact. It's not enough that the seat-counts for each party have to precisely align so as to put the balance of power in an extremist party's hands. What happens next is far from automatic. It depends on how the players choose to behave.

The larger parties may agree to govern together, to the exclusion of the extremist party: the "cordon sanitaire" approach mainstream parties have adopted in several European countries in recent years to keep the far right out of government.* If a party's leaders do agree to a deal with an extremist party, moreover, they must be able to sell other party members on the idea: not always a sure thing. They must also be mindful of the voters' wrath at the next election. If they are judged to have made too many concessions, to a party that is too far beyond the pale, they will pay a heavy price. At any rate, at least in proportional representation it is clear who is negotiating with whom, and over what. The internal negotiations among the factions of our parties may be just as sordid, but are largely hidden from view.

It's true that coalition negotiations in other countries have occasionally stalled under proportional representation. It's rare in any individual country, but since there are so many countries that use some form of proportional representation, and therefore so many elections and subsequent negotiations, it is easy to form the impression that this is more prevalent than it is. And the same occasionally happens in our system. The 2015 federal election, a closely fought three-way

---

* Examples include Austria, Belgium, France, Germany, the Netherlands, and Sweden.

affair, was widely expected to end in a chaotic muddle. There was a great deal of speculation over whether Stephen Harper would attempt to cling to power, even if he did not win a plurality of seats, in a replay of King-Byng.* British Columbia[175] politics was "paralyzed" for weeks after the 2017 provincial election while the Liberals, the NDP, and the Greens dickered over who would form the government. Somehow, the province survived. New Brunswick[176] was similarly "paralyzed" after the 2018 election. As in BC, the province carried on. Our politics can take a little democratic uncertainty.

What of that other supposed failing of proportional representation: the inability to "throw the bums out" at regular intervals, that is, to decisively change governments, a practice so often and effusively associated with first past the post?

Since 1945, Canada has changed governments eight times (counting the Joe Clark interregnum as two). Looking at countries in the proportional representation world, you can find some that have had fewer clear changes of power: Austria (five), Germany (six†), Sweden (six). But you find as many with more. The citizens of Norway have thrown the bums out nine times in the same period; the Danes, twelve times; the Irish, fourteen.

Perhaps some governments under proportional representation have remained in power longer than would be desirable. All the same, it serves up few examples to match the Liberals' century-long dominance of Canadian federal politics, to say nothing of the uninterrupted forty-two-year reign of the Progressive Conservatives in Ontario (1943–85), or the Alberta Tories' forty-four-year dynasty (1971–2015).‡ Or, further back, the Liberals in Nova Scotia (1882–1925) or in Quebec (1897–1936). The bums aren't always for throwing.

---

* Similar speculation has occasionally surrounded the current Liberal government, and whether it might attempt to carry on governing, in concert with the NDP, should it "lose" (finish second in) the next election—assuming the Conservatives fall short of a majority.
† Or maybe seven, depending on how the February 23 election turns out.
‡ It followed the thirty-six-year-long Social Credit dynasty.

What about proportional representation's alleged tendency to propel extremists into power? That, you'll recall, was Justin Trudeau's rationale for abandoning his promise of electoral reform in 2017. Under proportional representation, he told Canadians, "a party that represents the fringe" might win "ten, fifteen, twenty seats in the House" and "end up holding the balance of power." This "would augment extremist voices," bringing on an era of "instability and uncertainty" and "putting at risk the very thing that makes us luckier than anyone else on the planet." [177]

The notion that only the electoral system stands in the way of Canadians voting neo-Nazi en masse, or Islamist, or Radical Vegan, is never far from the surface of these discussions. Like other fears of the unknown, it is easy to raise, and hard to refute so long as nobody stops to think about it for half a second. What is the evidence of this barely suppressed urge to vote for fringe or extremist parties? In a typical election, the vote for all the fringe parties *combined*— parties, that is, other than those that are or have been represented* in the House of Commons—is less than 1 percent of the vote[178]. The largest fringe party typically receives less than one-third of 1 percent.

Even at the riding level, it is the rare fringe party that manages 1 percent of the vote, and you can usually count the number who cross the 3 percent threshold on one hand. The last election was a banner outing for fringe parties, what with covid lockdowns and vaccine mandates to stir the conspiracy-minded. Yet just seventy-seven candidates from seven parties exceeded the 1 percent mark (twelve broke 3 per cent). In 2019, fifteen fringe-party candidates managed it.

Of course, if you change the voting system you also change voter behaviour. Without the formidable hurdle presented by single-member

---

* This includes the People's Party of Canada, whose leader, Maxine Bernier, was an MP at the party's founding. The PPC's support is comparable with the Greens and is many multiples of the next smallest party. Its leader has been invited to the televised leaders' debates. It is a small party, with views that are obnoxious to many, including me, but cannot meaningfully be called a fringe party.

plurality voting, perhaps it would not feel quite so futile to vote for smaller parties. Perhaps more people would. Fine. Suppose twice as many did—no, three times as many. Hell, make it four times: an eye-watering 1 or 2 percent of the vote overall, peaking at perhaps 10 or 12 percent in the odd riding. Under most forms of proportional representation—certainly under the single transferable vote*—that still wouldn't be enough to elect a single member, let alone the sizable caucus of extremists Trudeau envisaged.

The thing about fringe parties, you see, is that they're fringe. The reason so few Canadians vote for them isn't because of our electoral system, it's because few Canadians support them. That isn't likely to change just because we change electoral systems. In any case, if I think a party would be bad for Canada, it's my responsibility to get out and persuade my fellow citizens not to vote for them—not rig the system so they can't.

The world is full of people and parties with disturbing views. It's too simple to ascribe these to particular electoral systems. Just now, you'll have noticed, the gravest extremist uprising among the democracies is to be found in the United States—a first-past-the-post country. Under proportional representation, an extremist party would typically be one of eight or nine in the legislature; even if, by some misadventure, it were to become part of a governing coalition, it would have to jostle for power with several rivals. Whereas in the US, the far right only had to take over one of the two main parties. They didn't even have to win a majority.

Indeed, most of the criticisms of proportional representation could as well or better be made of first past the post. Take the "instability" canard. We've already seen how, under the current system, minority governments are increasingly the norm, rather than the exception.

---

* Recall the quota required for election in a five-member riding: one-sixth of the vote plus one. Is a far-right or far-left candidate going to get 17 percent of the vote, even with the help of second choices? Not on your life.

We associate these with instability* because under our system parties have every incentive to provoke it. A highly leveraged, winner-take-all system like first past the post encourages a gambling mindset: maybe we'll get lucky. Maybe the polls will turn up. Maybe the split votes will go our way. Maybe we'll catch a wave in the swing ridings. In consequence, all parties in a minority are in a perpetual state of alert, fingers poised over the button, ready to force an election the minute the electoral portents look right.

Under proportional representation, there is no such pay-off, and no such incentive. What's the point of putting everyone through a snap election for the gain of a few lousy seats? What's more, everyone knows that's what everyone else is thinking, so there's no reward for bluffing, either. Where parties in our system typically attempt to govern single-handedly, relying on a combination of divide-and-rule and sheer brinksmanship, under proportional representation parties typically enter into orderly, stable coalitions. *Majority* coalitions.

It is commonly said of proportional representation that it would mean the end of majority governments. In fact, it would mean the start. What we call majority governments are really minority governments; as noted earlier, ours is a system best described as institutionalized minority rule. Under proportional representation, on the other hand, to form a government, you actually have to have the support of a majority of the voters. True, that may all but rule out *single-party* majorities: it is rare these days for one party to win more than 50 percent of the vote, under any system. But multiparty majorities are a more than acceptable price to pay for *representative* majorities. If a people gets the government it deserves, it should at least get the government it voted for.

Admittedly, this requires us to undergo something of a paradigm shift. The fundamental question proportional representation confronts us with is this: Is the point of an election just to find out

---

* The average duration of a minority Parliament in Canada is a little over eighteen months. https://www.ourcommons.ca/procedure/procedure-and-practice-3/ch_02_3-e.html

who won? Or is it to find out what people want? We elect a Parliament not just to decide who will form a government, but to represent us to that government. Surely, we should wish them to represent as much of the population, in as close to its actual diversity of opinion, as is practical. The majority would still rule in the Parliament that resulted. But it would be a real, rather than a fake majority, one that represented a majority of the people, rather than an arbitrary minority of them.

That's the principle. But imagine the practical benefits that would follow. Imagine if you could go to the polls knowing that your vote mattered, that it was not more than likely to be wasted, as it is now, but would actually help elect someone. Imagine if you could vote for the party of your choice without worrying that you might be splitting the vote. Imagine if every riding, including yours, was a battleground riding, and not only the minority of ridings the parties currently bother to contest. Think of how that would change how you thought about voting.

Imagine, further, if every party could win seats in every part of the country—if every party *needed* to win seats in every party of the country. Imagine if more Liberals were elected in the West, more Conservatives in Quebec, more New Democrats than Bloquistes. Think about how that would change the national unity debate. Imagine if, instead of a politics given over almost wholly to the pursuit of swing voters and swing ridings, parties had more incentive to appeal to the broader public, offering broad-based policies in the public interest rather than bribes to narrow sectional interests. Think about how that would change how the parties behaved.

Imagine if, rather than betting the farm on a fluky majority, then using this dubious mandate to push through massive change, parties instead sought to advance their cause gradually, by the earned increments of persuasion. Imagine if parties had to work together, rather than treating each other as unimaginable aliens. Imagine . . .

Well, you can stop imagining, because it is unlikely to happen. As with virtually every other recommendation in this book, electoral reform can only happen if the people in power decide it should happen. But the reason they are in power is because they were elected under the current system. As they see it, they were elected *because* of the current system. To ask them to embrace reform is to ask them to act against their perceived self-interest.

From time to time, one party or another will discover the issue of electoral reform, recognizing its growing appeal to a frustrated public. But somehow, once elected, they always find a reason to ditch it. Sometimes the breach of promise is overt and explicit, as in Justin Trudeau's discarding of electoral reform in 2017, having promised during the 2015 election campaign that it would be "the last federal election conducted under the first-past-the-post voting system."[179] Or François Legault's comparable backflip in Quebec after the election of 2018.

Sometimes the deed is accomplished in subtler ways. The British Columbia Liberals campaigned on electoral reform in 2001. To their credit, they convened a citizens' assembly on the subject, which after lengthy deliberation recommended the adoption of the single transferable vote form of proportional representation. In the ensuing referendum, 58 percent of the public voted yes, including a majority in seventy-seven of the province's seventy-nine ridings: an impressive mandate by any standard, certainly when compared to the 46 percent of the vote the Liberals secured in the election that same day. And yet it was never enacted: the government, alas, had set the bar at 60 percent.

The government of Prince Edward Island pulled something of the same trick in 2016. In that year's referendum, the public voted 52 percent in favour of reform. That exceeded the simple majority required by the referendum legislation. Nevertheless, the premier still found reason to set it aside, on the grounds that the turnout for the vote, at 36 percent, was too low.

These events are worth bearing in mind whenever someone claims, as someone invariably does, that proportional representation has been "rejected" by the public. There have been votes in which that was true: the second and third British Columbia referendums, in 2009 and 2018, the second PEI referendum, in 2019, and Ontario's referendum in 2007. But that does not mean the issue has been settled once and for all.

Too often, the issue in these sorts of votes devolves into "do you want to live in Canada?" First past the post, rather than being presented as one option among others, is usually included on the ballot as the default: unless the voters are willing to steel themselves to vote "yes" to a system they have been told will plunge the country into chaos, "just like in Israel or Italy," the status quo remains in place.

An interesting question is why a referendum should be required to change the system when no such vote was required to install it. It's particularly interesting to see first past the post's defenders insist on it. Electoral reform, they say gravely, is far too important a matter to be decided by a mere majority government—one that may have been elected with the support of 40 percent or less of the public. For such a weighty decision, only an honest majority will do!

It's true that a decision to adopt a new electoral system should not be taken lightly. It would likely prove hard to reverse, for the same reason it is so hard to change the current system: because the fortunes of those in power would now depend on keeping the new system in place, as once they had depended on blocking it from being installed. There are ways, however, to provide against this. Electoral reform could be enacted by simple legislation, but with a proviso that the decision would be subject to a confirmatory referendum after some years. That would be a fairer fight. Instead of being asked to choose between the status quo and the unknown, the voters would be presented with a choice of two systems with which they were equally familiar: the one they have now, and the one they used to have.

Why am I talking about something that is unlikely to happen? Because it is going to happen, eventually. Probably not at the federal level. Maybe not provincial. But some level of government, somewhere in the country, is going to try *something* that isn't the status quo. It might not be true proportional representation. It might just be ranked ballots. But at that point we will have recent experience of some system somewhere on Canadian soil that isn't first past the post. It will no longer be possible to pretend that this is the only system there is, or the only system that is possible, or that any reform, of any kind, involves a frightening leap into the void. Once the monopoly of first past the post is broken, it will be easier to get a hearing for other systems.

This is a subject of some controversy among electoral reformers. Many fear the introduction of ranked ballots, for example, would forever doom efforts to bring in proportional representation: that as a country we have one shot at reform, and that's it. I think the opposite is true. Once people get a taste of change, they may be more receptive to it. Reform might be more easily digested in two bites than one. Start with ranked ballots, then add multi-member ridings: voilà, proportional representation!

* * *

As much as the current electoral system distorts our politics, there is an even larger distortion at work. For all the voters that first past the post leaves underrepresented, there are at least as many who go entirely unrepresented, and would under any system: the third to a half of eligible voters in every recent election who don't vote.

Turnout in Canadian elections has been in decline for decades: from an average of roughly 75 percent in the sixteen federal elections from 1945 to 1988, to an average of less than 65 percent in the nine elections since then.[180] In recent years, the decline has turned into a rout. The last two decades have featured six of the eight worst turnouts in federal election history, averaging just 62 percent. It is now common for turnout in provincial elections to fall below 60 percent or even 50 percent: in the 2022 Ontario election, it was 44 percent, the lowest in the province's history; in Nova Scotia, in 2024, it was 45 percent. Municipal elections are fortunate if they break 40 percent. In Toronto's 2022 election, turnout fell to just over 29 percent[181]; again, the lowest

Elections

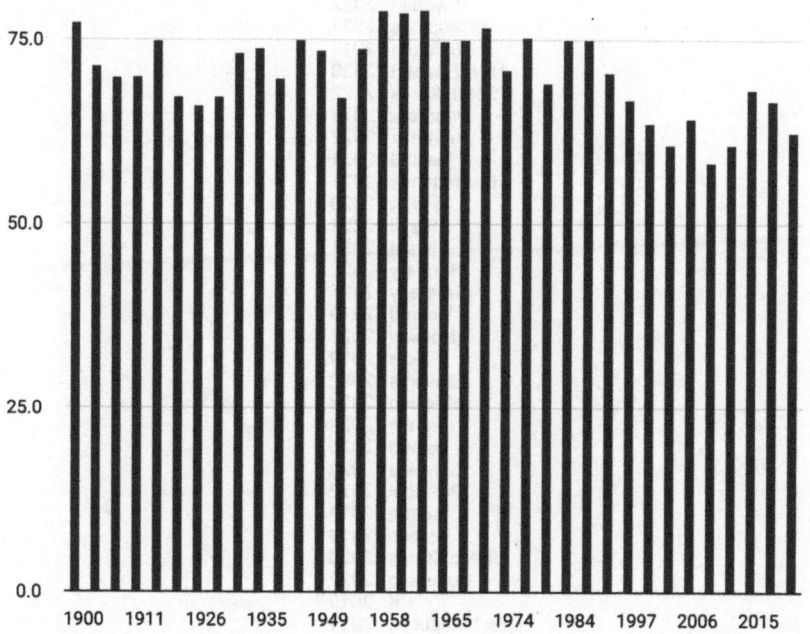

Source: Elections Canada, https://www.elections.ca/content.aspx?section=ele&dir=turn&document=index&lang=e

in the city's history. Some recent federal byelections have seen turnout rates of 15 or 16 percent.

Turnout has been declining in most countries[182], but turnout in Canada has consistently lagged behind that of other democracies: in recent elections it has been among the worst in the OECD.

There should be no need to explain why this matters. Democratic governments depend for their legitimacy on a claim to represent the people, having been chosen in free elections in which every adult citizen is eligible to vote. If half or more of those citizens are declining to do so, not only is that claim in jeopardy, so is democracy.

The Crisis of Canadian Democracy

Declining turnout in federal elections

● Voting-age popula[tion]

Uruguay	2019	
Turkey	2018	
Peru	2021	
Indonesia	2019	
Argentina	2019	
Sweden	2022	
Philippines	2022	
Belgium	2019	
New Zealand	2020	
South Korea	2022	
Denmark	2019	
Australia	2022	
Iceland	2021	
Netherlands	2021	
Taiwan	2020	
Brazil	2022	
Israel	2021	
Hungary	2022	
Germany	2021	
Finland	2019	
Norway	2021	
India	2019	
Slovenia	2022	
Mexico	2018	
France	2022	
Poland	2020	
Slovakia	2020	
Portugal	2022	
Austria	2019	
Greece	2019	
United States	2020	
Colombia	2022	
UK	2019	
Czech Republic	2021	
Latvia	2022	
Spain	2019	
Chile	2021	
Italy	2022	
Ireland	2020	
Romania	2019	
Estonia	2019	
Japan	2021	
Canada	2021	
Lithuania	2020	
Costa Rica	2022	
Croatia	2020	
Luxembourg	2018	
South Africa	2019	
Bulgaria	2022	
Switzerland*	2019	36.

0%   25%

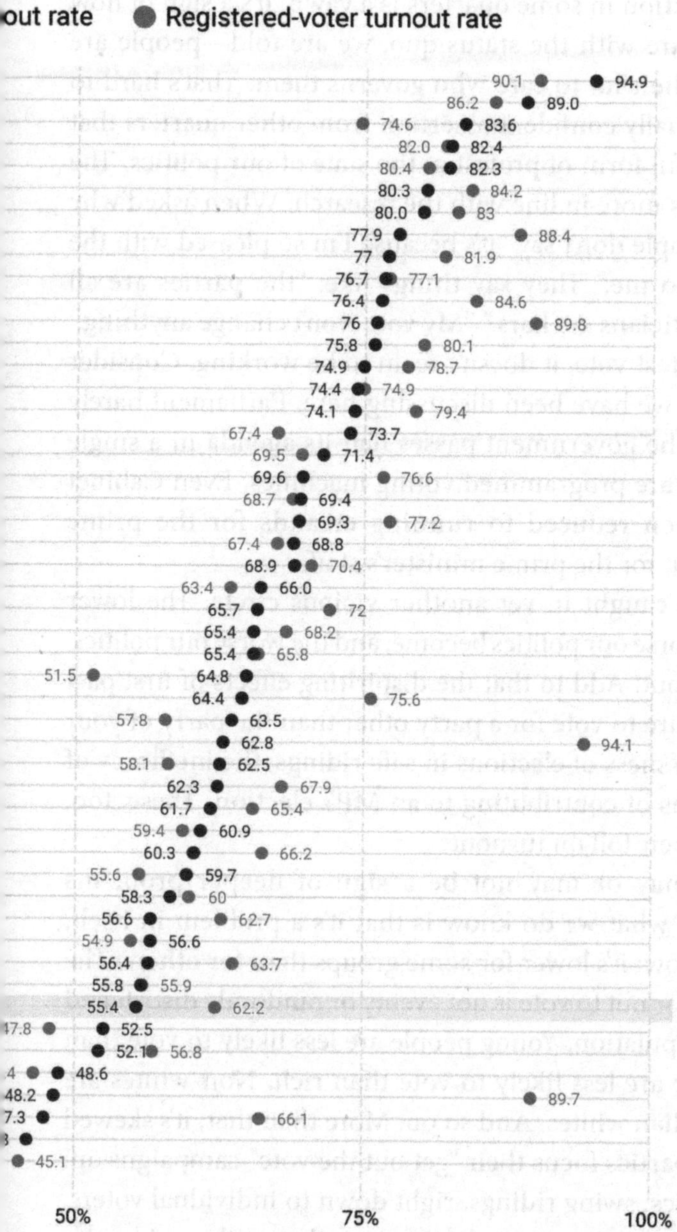

Elections

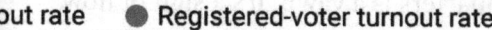

Source: Pew Research Center, https://www.pewresearch.org/short-reads/2022/11/01/turnout-in-u-s-has-soared-in-recent-elections-but-by-some-measures-still-trails-that-of-many-other-countries/

And yet the reaction in some quarters is a yawn. It's a sign of how contented people are with the status quo, we are told—people are too satisfied with their lot to care who governs them. That's hard to square with the equally confident assertion from other quarters that not voting is a useful form of protest at the state of our politics. The latter explanation is more in line with the research. When asked why they don't vote, people don't say "it's because I'm so pleased with the choices available to me." They say things like: "the parties are all the same." "All politicians are liars." "My vote won't change anything."

But if it is a protest vote, it doesn't seem to be working. Consider some of the issues we have been discussing here. Parliament barely meets any more. The government passes half its agenda in a single omnibus bill. MPs are programmed voting machines. Even Cabinet ministers have been reduced to running errands for the prime minister—or rather, for the prime minister's staff.

We seem to be caught in yet another vicious circle. The lower turnout falls, the worse our politics become; and the worse our politics, the lower the turnout. Add to that the dispiriting effects of first past the post: the pressure to vote for a party other than the party of your choice; the pointlessness of elections in safe ridings; the inefficacy of most votes in terms of contributing to an MP's election. These, too, must surely take their toll on turnout.

Low turnout may or may not be a sign of deeper problems in the system, but what we do know is that it's a problem in itself. Turnout isn't just low: it's lower for some groups than for others. The propensity to vote or not to vote is not evenly or randomly distributed throughout the population. Young people are less likely to vote than older. Poor people are less likely to vote than rich. Non-whites are less likely to vote than whites. And so on. More than that, it's skewed to the people the parties focus their "get out the vote" campaigns on: target demographics, swing ridings, right down to individual voters. Voters don't choose parties so much as parties choose them: identify them, advertise to them, motivate them, and, if necessary, drive them to the polls.

Elections

A lot of what is wrong with our politics, the relentless animus and bile, is rooted in turnout-based strategies, in which parties seek to motivate their base with tales of the terrible crimes the other side will commit should they ever get into power, while simultaneously depressing their opponents' motivation in hopes of inducing them to stay home. The result is to make elections an unrepresentative sample of public opinion. It's a bit like when the long-form census was made voluntary.* Participation became a matter of self-selection, and a self-selected sample is by definition a skewed sample. One way of making a sample representative is to pick the participants at random: that's what pollsters do. The other, even better way is to make the whole population the sample. That's what the census is supposed to do. It's also what elections are supposed to do.

Which suggests a remedy: make participation in elections, like participation in the census, compulsory. There's no doubt that it raises turnout. Have a look at the top of the international turnout standings. You'll find the same countries, election after election: Australia, Belgium., Luxembourg, Singapore, Uruguay (also the Netherlands, until 1970). All of them have mandatory voting laws, and enforce them strictly. On average, they have consistently maintained turnouts of close to 90 percent, for decades. About twenty other countries, mostly in South and Central America—Argentina, Bolivia, Peru, etc—have mandatory voting laws on the books that are loosely enforced.[183] Nevertheless, research suggests mandatory voting laws raise turnout by between 10 and 15 percentage points.[184]

Australia is a particularly striking example, given its many similarities to Canada. Before it adopted mandatory voting in 1924, voter turnout in Australia was roughly similar to ours: averaging just over 60 percent.[185] In the first election after the law was passed, it shot up to over 90 percent, where it has stayed ever since: an average turnout, over a hundred years and thirty-eight elections, of 95 percent.

---

* By the Conservatives, in 2011. It was made mandatory again under the Liberals.

Mandatory voting would eliminate the bias in our democratic sample, giving due weight to the kinds of voters who are now underrepresented. Moreover, it would eliminate turnout as a factor in our politics. When voting is universal, turnout-based strategies cease to be relevant. Rather than simply riling up the base, parties must focus on expanding it, by converting others to their cause.

Faced with a mandatory-voting law, many people suddenly discover a fervent belief in the ancient and inviolable right not to vote, that sacred liberty for which our ancestors fought and died. And you can see why. Think of the dark night of tyranny that would descend upon us, if people were forced to trot round to their local school or community centre every four years or so and spend five minutes marking a ballot. Because that's all it means. Mandatory voting does not mean you have to vote for a particular party, or for any party at all. You can spoil your ballot or decline it or vote none of the above, if you wish. The only thing you can't do is sit on your duff.

How does it work in Australia? The fines are minor at $20 (Aus.),[186] or about $18 (Can.). There are common-sense exceptions for those who are sick, or travelling, or have some other legitimate excuse. It's more a "nudge" than a penalty, but it has succeeded in creating a climate in which voting is the norm.

Okay, you may say, the cost to liberty may be slight, but still, what about the principle: isn't it my right not to vote? Maybe that means I go unrepresented, but isn't that my affair? But voting in an election isn't just about you. You're not deciding on a purely individual matter, like whether to drink Coke or Pepsi. You're contributing to an important collective discussion, arguably the most important of them all: who should govern us? When you vote, you are not just deciding how you will be governed, but how everybody will be governed. When you fail to vote, you harm not just yourself, but society. Voting is, in this light, not only a right, it is an obligation.

The best analogies are jury duty, or that other great civic obligation, paying your taxes. Left to themselves, some will choose not to serve or pay, precisely because they know that others will. It's called "free riding," and there's ample precedent for a mild, limited degree of compulsion to correct it. In short, you owe your fellow citizens your counsel. We ask few things of citizens in a free society. We accept the obligation to pay our taxes or serve on juries. Why would we balk at something far less onerous, like showing up to vote once in a while?

The other common objection is that mandatory voting will only bring out a lot of ignorant, uninformed people, by which we are meant to understand the people who don't vote now. There are two answers to this. One is that the current participants in the democratic process are not exactly Einsteins. Those who choose to exercise their franchise are not necessarily the best informed, but the best *groomed*: the ones the parties target, the ones most susceptible to their propaganda. The gullible, the partisan, the fanatic are all heavily overrepresented. Voting is objectively irrational: even the small amount of time it takes is hardly worth the infinitesimal impact a single vote is likely to have on the result. If it's rational not to vote, it follows that the most rational people are the ones not voting; by compelling them to vote, we're arguably improving the quality of the voting pool.

The second, better answer to those who worry that mandatory voting would let the riffraff in is: *listen to yourself*. Democracy is not something reserved for the well-educated and the well-informed. If it were, we'd have literacy tests. Democracy is for everybody. For people on the margins, the ones with less education or access to media, the ones who've been told all their lives their opinions don't matter, it's the one day, every four years, when people have to listen to them. That so many of them don't take advantage of that opportunity is a tragedy—for them, and for all of us. Because we benefit as a society when they do: when their experiences are brought to the table, our collective judgments are broader, fairer, and better informed.*

---

* Whether compelling people to vote makes *them* better-informed is another matter. The research is mixed. On the one hand, there is some evidence that making voting mandatory encourages voters to bone up on the issues; research also suggests the experience of voting itself can be educational. Set against that, voters are more likely to spoil their ballots or rely on party messaging under mandatory voting.

Mandatory voting won't fix all the ills that afflict our politics. But it is guaranteed to fix one: turnout. No other single reform would have as immediate, as large, as certain, as lasting, and as beneficial an influence on our democracy, and at so little relative cost. Yes, of course, we should also do everything we can to give people more positive reasons to vote: that's very much the point of this book. Research shows that proportional representation, for example, also boosts turnout,[187] by between five and eight percentage points. Imagine if we did both: mandatory voting *and* proportional representation. Suppose, therefore, that 90 percent of the adult population voted, and 90 percent of those votes helped to elect someone. That would give us a Parliament representing the votes of at least 80 percent of the adult population, versus the third or less typical of current parliaments.

Mandatory voting is a natural counterpart to proportional representation. Both seek to represent as wide a cross-section of the population as possible: not just those who vote for the winning candidate, or those who show up on voting day, but everyone. If government is about the greatest good for the greatest number, this is surely elementary.

8

The Crisis

AS I WRITE THIS, Donald Trump is preparing to take the oath of office as president of the United States for a second time. The implications for American democracy are grave. Trump has never accepted the results of the 2020 election, and attempted, by a combination of force and fraud, to have it overturned. Had he lost in 2024 few doubt he would have tried to do the same again. The only question is whether he will be willing to yield power in 2028. Some fear that, notwithstanding the constitutional prohibition on presidents serving more than two terms, he will attempt to run again. Others wonder whether he and his party will dispense with elections altogether, at least of the free and fair kind.

If these sound like extravagant fears, they are no more than a reflection of what Trump and the people around him have been saying for some time. And overturning or ignoring or rigging elections is only one of the fears people have about a second Trump presidency. Trump has said he will use the powers of the presidency to "go after" his political enemies, including prosecution and jail. He has already seen to it, with the help of a friendly Supreme Court, that he cannot be prosecuted for any crimes he might commit as president, provided these are committed in his "official capacity." His vice president has mused about defying court orders. The prospect is for a level of presidential lawlessness unknown even in Trump's first term.

Surveying all this from our vantage point to the north, it is tempting to see our own problems as relatively mild. Whatever our democracy's imperfections, we are in nowhere near the difficulty Americans face. We need to reform our democracy, but no one fears we are about to lose it. Maybe not. But America's problem is about to become our problem. Well before he took office, Trump had threatened to impose a devastating 25 percent tariff on all exports from Canada (and Mexico), then escalated that into a threat to forcibly annex the country, albeit using "economic force"—a threat that, after Greenland and the Panama Canal, nobody is treating as a joke. And yet, because of the failings in our own democratic system, we are in a peculiarly weak position to respond.

The prime minister, deeply unpopular, is also a lame duck, having announced his resignation in January, to take effect once a new party leader has been chosen. As they set about electing his replacement, the governing Liberals are divided and distracted. The government's moral legitimacy is in serious doubt, all three major opposition parties having announced they will vote no confidence at the first opportunity. They cannot do so, however, because the House isn't sitting: on the day he announced his resignation, the prime minister prorogued—that is to say, advised the governor general to prorogue—Parliament for three months, to give his party time to pick a new leader. Indeed, this Parliament may never return. Rather than wait for the government to fall on a confidence vote, the new prime minister may dissolve Parliament and call an election.

Meaning we may not have either a sitting Parliament or a legitimate government until June. At the very moment when the country is most in need of leadership, at a time of maximum national crisis, we are rudderless and adrift.

The temptation is to blame the whole mess on Justin Trudeau. If only he had not stayed so long. If only he had simply resigned. If only he had not prorogued. While Trudeau should certainly be answerable for his decisions, it seems to me this misses the bigger picture. How was it possible for one man to cause such havoc? What are the institutional flaws that permitted him such latitude?

The Crisis

How was he able to hang on as party leader, despite having lost the support of not only the country but much of his own caucus? Because the caucus did not choose him: thousands of temporary enthusiasts who signed up to vote more than a decade before did. And because the Liberal Party constitution contains no mechanism for removing a leader—not, at any rate, until after an election defeat.

True, the caucus was eventually able to persuade him to leave, but why did it take so long? Because, unlike the Conservatives, the Liberal caucus did not vote to assume the powers available to it under the Reform Act, including the power to remove the leader. In the absence of the rules of procedure set out in the Act—no triggering mechanism, no secret ballot, no agreed-upon threshold for forcing the leader's resignation—MPs were left to stumble about, as it were, in the dark, unsure of who was friend and who was foe, holding clandestine meetings and swearing each other to silence.

Why couldn't they just declare their opposition openly? Because of the immense power of a party leader, to say nothing of a prime minister—power that could snuff out their careers. To the very end, long after it was clear the prime minister could not possibly carry on, very few members of caucus dared to put their names to anything. We were told that this section of caucus or that had held a vote, but not who voted which way. There was even a letter, supposedly signed by two dozen members, none of whose signatures were ever disclosed.

Why did caucus finally turn on Trudeau? Because of the callous and high-handed way he treated his finance minister, Chrystia Freeland: first announcing $6 billion in new spending for two initiatives, a partial GST "holiday" and a near-universal $250 Working Canadians Rebate, that had not been approved by Cabinet, caucus or her; then telling her she was fired as finance minister, but insisting she stay on long enough to deliver the fall economic statement, with its embarrassing $62 billion deficit. Why did the prime minister think he could get away with treating his finance minister this way? Because he always had. Because prime ministers are free to treat their Cabinet ministers any way they like, and generally do.

Why did it take the Liberals so long, notwithstanding the accelerated schedule adopted for this occasion—only two months!—to choose a new leader? Because, the party insisted on putting the matter to a vote of the instant members, non-citizens and children who decide such matters in Canada, even in the middle of a national crisis, even in the face of warnings from the commissioner of the public inquiry into foreign interference and others that the lax rules governing parties' internal elections make them vulnerable to manipulation by foreign powers. The party had the option of letting the caucus choose. Nevertheless it decided to stick with the process that had created the problem in the first place.

Why was a prime minister who had plainly lost the confidence of the House allowed to prorogue for three months, rather than face Parliament and the music? Because, in the absence of an explicit vote of no confidence, the governor general is obliged to follow her prime minister's advice—but more because it is the prime minister who has sole authority to decide the matter.*

So Parliament will remain dark, the government will carry on in defiance of its wishes, the prime minister will cling to a job no one wants him to have, while his party spends precious weeks choosing a new leader, all in the middle of one of the gravest political crises of our lifetimes. And yet to complain about this state of affairs, to demand Parliament's immediate recall, was to invite quizzical stares, even hostility. Parliament! What do you expect *Parliament* to do? Oh, I don't know: debate? Give voice to people's fears? Buck up their nerve? Build consensus on how to proceed? Provide government with the money and the lawful authority it needs to deal with the crisis? Isn't that what we expect of our Parliament, in such times?† Apparently not.

---

* After a recent ruling of the Supreme Court of the United Kingdom (https://www.bailii.org/uk/cases/UKSC/2019/41.html) this is no longer certain. A challenge of the prorogation decision is now making its way through the Canadian court system.

† At the time of the fall of Neville Chamberlain, in 1940, Lord Halifax was the favourite to succeed him as leader of the Conservative Party and prime minister. As it happened, he declined the King's invitation. How could he lead the nation, he reasoned, if, as a peer, he could not take his seat in the House of Commons "the cockpit of democracy?"

The Crisis

This is one of the central dilemmas identified in this book. We have allowed Parliament and other institutions of our democracy to decay to such an extent that people no longer attach any importance to them or their doings. Lacking any notion of what these institutions once did, or might, they cannot conceive of what they are missing.

It's not that they're altogether wrong. Parliament is mostly a waste of time in its present form. It's the suggestion, implicit in such sneers, that Parliament is a waste of time in principle that galls. All through this book, after describing each of the many and profound failings of our democracy, I have tried to explain why it matters—why it matters that our democracy does not work as it should, and why it would be better if we fixed it. I realized after a while that I was not just making the case for this or that democratic reform. I was making the case for democracy. Because it needs making.

What the current crisis ought to have demonstrated is that democratic reform is not some nicety, a matter of tidiness or aesthetics. It is an urgent practical necessity. The inadequacies of our democratic processes are not merely of academic interest. They have serious real-world consequences. When we cannot hold government to account, because the prerogatives of the House have withered in favour of the comfort of the executive, egregious errors and serious wrongdoing are what ensue.

When members of Parliament are reduced to mere footmen for the party leaders, Parliament ceases to represent the people. Important issues and interests get overlooked, resentment builds, interest in Parliament wanes. When even Cabinet fades into irrelevance beside the prime minister and his all-powerful officials, decision-making gets more out of touch, the people in charge get more overworked, and error multiplies.

When our electoral system consistently produces such wildly unrepresentative results, it further erodes public confidence. When some voters in some ridings count for everything and others count for nothing, the latter group soon stops paying attention. When whole regions of the country are monopolized by one party, election after election, it leaves voters in those regions feeling taken for granted. Conversely, when a party wins power with only a handful of seats in one part of the country or another, it breeds a sense in *those* regions that the federal government is not really "our" government, but "theirs," greatly impeding its ability to make policy in the national interest.

One reason the degraded state of our democracy has not given rise to more discontent than it has is because, on the whole, Canada has done pretty well. And it's true: we remain one of the richest, freest, fairest, most blessed places on earth. It is hard to imagine how we could have turned out otherwise, given the advantages we started with: laden with natural resources; protected by oceans on three sides and by the United States on our fourth; able to pick and choose which immigrants we admit; and with the world's richest export market next door. Still, democracy is more likely to be an afterthought when things are ticking over relatively smoothly.

But the world is about to become a more difficult and dangerous place. The territory to which we lay claim, so vast that we cannot begin to defend it, is no longer something we can assume that others will respect. Russia is eyeing our north hungrily, as is China. Once, we might have counted on the United States to come to our defence; now we cannot be sure it would not join in the plunder. As it is, we will have to make huge increases in military spending just to meet our current NATO obligations, with the prospect of more increases to come. Spending on health care, meanwhile, will continue to soar, in line with an aging population. Revenues, given our anemic economic growth rates, are unlikely to keep pace. To the existential crisis, then, add a potential fiscal crisis. Now factor in the likelihood of the Parti Quebecois winning the next election in Quebec. And the possibility of NATO becoming involved in a war in Europe. And the probability of another pandemic. And climate change. And the social media-driven "post-truth" society, with all that it portends for democratic government. Plus whatever future artificial intelligence has in store for us.

The Crisis

Welcome to the age of crisis. We've had a lovely run of things these past one hundred and fifty-odd years, but our luck may be about to run out. The world that seemed so far away is now at our door. The stability we thought was our birthright is no longer guaranteed. The services we took for granted are suddenly no longer easily affordable. The neighbour we thought was our friend has turned on us. In this dangerous new world, the old model, where power was held close to the centre and orders were dispensed from on high, will no longer suffice. The challenges that confront us will require our citizens to make real sacrifices for the greater good, in a way they have not had to do for decades.

Persuading them to do so will not be easy. People are all too ready to suspect that some groups, or some parts of the country, are being let off easy while others are being forced to carry the greater part of the load. This country is given to division at the best of times. Under the strains to which it is likely to be put, it may well fall apart. Consider the fears, already being heard, that Trump's real game plan might not be annexation, as such, but luring Alberta into leaving the federation and joining the United States.

To meet these challenges, to summon the popular will in defence of Canada, will require those in power to take the people into their confidence. To mobilize the population, they will have to engage it. Parliament can be that rallying point, but only if all of our people, no matter what part of the country they live in, feel it is *their* Parliament—that when Parliament is debating a matter, the whole nation is. They will need to believe that their members of Parliament truly represent them, that the government truly answers to Parliament, that elections are truly reflective of public opinion. They will need to see that the political parties, in a moment of crisis, are capable of working together in the national interest, rather than always and everywhere pursuing their narrowest partisan interests.

In other words, we will need a system radically different from the one we have now.

* * *

The Crisis of Canadian Democracy

Until I began research for this book, I don't think I fully appreciated how badly things had deteriorated. I've tried to show throughout that the usual complacent answers—it's always been this way; other countries have their own problems—no longer apply. But I had no idea how much worse our system had become: worse than in the past, worse, by a number of measures, than almost any other democratic country. As mentioned:

- We have the largest Cabinet in the democratic world
- We have the most unequal riding sizes (by population) among countries with comparable legislatures
- We have one of the most disproportionate electoral systems of any democracy
- We have the most rigid system of party discipline in the democratic world
- We have one of the lowest rates of turnout in the democratic world
- A Canadian prime minister has more powers, with fewer constraints, than any other democratic head of government
- In no other democratic parliament is debate cut short so abruptly, so often
- In no other democratic parliament is so much legislation passed via omnibus bills of such indiscriminate breadth
- In no other democratic country are party nominations and leadership races such unrestricted free-for-alls.

How has this happened? Why have we let things slide to such an extent? As I suggested in chapter 2, a lot of it owes to the historic dominance of one party, the Liberals. Owing largely to a series of historical accidents—Riel, the Great War conscription, and the Great Depression—the party was left in control of Quebec, and then Ontario, the most populous parts of the country, giving rise to a longer period of political dominance that in time became self-reinforcing. Liberal machine politics, the free-handed use of government patronage and pork-barreling, was useful to maintaining Liberal supremacy, especially in regions that valued that kind of thing. As the party of power, moreover, the Liberals were better placed to recruit talented individuals for Cabinet posts. The famous Liberal "flexibility" in matters of ideology—some would call it unscrupulousness—allowed the party to shift with the prevailing political winds.

A robust set of checks and balances, leaving government and opposition in some sort of rough equipoise, is most often observed in democracies where power is highly contestable. If you're uncertain whether, in any given election, you are likely to win or lose, you'll probably be more respectful of opposition rights while in government, to protect yourself against that inevitable day when the roles are reversed. If, on the other hand, you can count on winning two elections in three, and keep on doing so for over a century, it's easy to see how you might be tempted to let things slide. As for the Conservatives, their attitude, during their brief spells in government, has been to get while the getting is good: to ram through as much legislation in as short a period as possible, on the grounds that they may not see power again for a very long time. That the system is so visibly, at least to Conservative eyes, stacked in the Liberals' favour—the bureaucracy leans Liberal, the judiciary leans Liberal, the press gallery leans Liberal—reinforces the argument that the Conservatives cannot afford to be the Boy Scouts of federal politics. Again, the Liberals abuse power because they can; the Conservatives, because (as they see it) they must.

The system that results, favouring government over Parliament, party leaders over caucus, prime ministers over Cabinet, has its own self-reinforcing tendencies. Because MPs are weak, no one can imagine why they should be strong—why, say, they should choose the party leader, or why they should do anything but obey the leader's dictates. Wasn't it because of the leader, after all, that they were elected? Because Parliament is weak, because it plays so little real role in the life of the nation, no one cares if it grows weaker. Because the House of Commons is such a circus of futility, because politics is such a wretched business, because even Cabinet ministers are essentially placeholders, it becomes more and more difficult to get capable, accomplished people to run for office—which just makes the House more of a circus, politics more wretched, and Cabinet ministers more pylon-like. Because of all this, and because our electoral system leaves so many voters feeling their votes are wasted, or undervalued, fewer and fewer people bother to vote. Which just accelerates the whole spiral of decline.

There are solutions, as we've seen. We can place limits on the prime minister's unilateral powers of dissolution and prorogation; spell out the confidence convention in legislation; subject more appointments to independent oversight; end the leader's veto on candidates' nominations; give MPs the power to elect their leader; clean up party membership rules; give the Speaker power to decide who asks questions in Question Period, or when debate should be cut short; place curbs on the use of omnibus bills; ban members from reading speeches in the House; move the benches closer and rip out the desks; get rid of the cameras, or let them roam freely; cut the Cabinet in half; confine the Senate to a suspensive veto; pass a Truth in Politics law; make leaders voice their own ads; hold more debates in both languages; reform campaign finance laws; equalize riding sizes; move to a more proportional system of voting; make voting mandatory.

But here, as I've argued throughout, you run into the biggest self-reinforcing loop of all: the system can only be changed by those who were elected under the existing system. The prime minister's powers cannot be reduced without the prime minister's consent. MPs dare not bring their leader to heel so long as they are under the leader's heel. Before you can regulate the parties' chaotic internal elections, the parties would have to enact the regulations. Reform of our electoral system requires the approval of those who benefit from the status quo. And so on. We are bound, it seems, by an iron ring of self-interest, an infinite cycle of inertia.

Is there any hope of breaking out of this? Probably not. But maybe. Any system seems unreformable until it is reformed. Revolutions

The Crisis

always begin with a first step, a first breach in the unbreachable wall. Change just one thing, and you make it possible, at least, to turn one of those vicious circles into a virtuous circle. The Reform Act, for example, as limited in scope as it is, may have planted the seeds of further reform. The Conservatives were first to use it to dismiss their leader. We shall see what sort of precedent that sets. Ideally, MPs from other parties would look enviously at their newly empowered Conservative counterparts, and demand similar authority for themselves. (The Liberals must surely have learned from their disastrous experience under the cult-like leadership of Justin Trudeau.) Ideally, having once breathed the heady air of freedom in this way, MPs of all parties would start to unravel more of the leadership's apparatus of control. Ideally. Alternatively, a victorious Pierre Poilievre might order his MPs, at their first caucus meeting after the next election, to rescind the power they had claimed in 2021, and the brief candle of reform would be extinguished.

There are other possible starting points. Some parties, like the NDP and the Greens, have historically favoured electoral reform—for self-interested reasons, you might say, since they are the parties who usually suffer most under first past the post. Should the NDP, in particular, find itself holding the balance of power in some future Parliament, it might make electoral reform the price of its support. True, it never has in the past, neither at the federal nor provincial level. Nor has any provincial NDP government ever implemented such a reform. But hope springs eternal. Somewhere, someday, some government is going to bring in electoral reform of some kind and the monopoly of first past the post will be broken. Then all things will be possible.

Or maybe the system will reach a point, beset by one or more of the multiple crises I've described, where it cracks under the strain—where the crisis of Canadian democracy, long apprehended, becomes real. Deadlocked, lacking legitimacy in one part of the country or the other, fearing the Americans might take advantage of our divisions, and understanding that our survival as an independent nation depends on the strength that comes from unity and the unity that comes from self-government, some future Parliament might decide on a radical shift of strategy; some grand coalition might emerge, some hitherto unexpected alignment of the parties, left and right, government and opposition, that would make sweeping democratic reform possible. The same approach, if memory serves, was responsible for our founding.

Notes

1. Economist Intelligence Unit, *Democracy Index 2023*, https://www.eiu.com/n/campaigns/democracy-index-2023/
2. Freedom House, *Freedom in the World 2024*, https://freedomhouse.org/countries/freedom-world/scores?sort=desc&order=Total%20Score%20and%20Status
3. UK Parliament, *Hansard*, November 11, 1947 https://hansard.parliament.uk/commons/1947-11-11/debates/110a3531-22eb-4dff-9ff3-041c29e16967/OrdersOfTheDay
4. Christopher Moore, "Firing the Boss an MP's Right," *National Post*, August 14, 2002 https://www.christophermoore.ca/mooreSNarticle1.html
5. "... a presidential system without the checks and balances of Congress." Peter Russell, "The Charter and Canadian Democracy," in James Kelly, Christopher Manfredi (eds.), *Contested Constitutionalism* (Vancouver, University of British Columbia Press, 2009), p. 299. Also see Denis Smith: "We seem to have created in Canada a presidential system without its congressional advantages."
6. Environics Institute, *Support for Democracy in Canada: A Report from the 2021 Americas Barometer Survey*, September 2021. https://www.environicsinstitute.org/docs/default-source/default-document-library/americas-barometer-2021-final-sept-03.pdf?sfvrsn=d8a690d2_0. Though this poll shows some recent deterioration in public satisfaction. https://www.biv.com/news/commentary/confidence-in-government-crashes-as-canadians-feel-left-behind-survey-reveals-9167756
7. *House of Commons Procedure and Practice*, Third Edition (2017), The House of Commons and Its Members. https://www.ourcommons.ca/procedure/procedure-and-practice-3/ch_04_4-e.html
8. Chief Electoral Officer of Canada, *A History of the Vote in Canada*, 2021. https://www.elections.ca/res/his/WEB_EC%2091135%20History%20of%20the%20Vote_Third%20edition_EN.pdf
9. Library of Parliament, ParlInfo, *Women's Right to Vote in Canada*. https://lop.parl.ca/sites/ParlInfo/default/en_CA/ElectionsRidings/womenVote
10. Christopher Moore, *1867: How The Fathers Made a Deal* (Toronto, McClelland & Stewart, 1998).
11. UK Parliament, *Second Reform Act 1867*. https://www.parliament.uk/about/living-heritage/evolutionofparliament/houseofcommons/reformacts/overview/furtherreformacts/

12 By the 1880s that was nearer to two-thirds; by the 1900s, over 80 percent. Calculation based on: https://www150.statcan.gc.ca/n1/pub/98-187-x/4151287-eng.htm, https://www.elections.ca/content.aspx?section=ele&dir=turn&document=index&lang=e, https://www12.statcan.gc.ca/census-recensement/2016/dp-pd/pyramid/acc/acc-hist-eng.cfm?Type=1
13 Calculation based on: https://www.elections.ca/content.aspx?section=ele&dir=turn&document=index&lang=e#ftn2, https://www.elections.ca/res/his/WEB_EC%2091135%20History%20of%20the%20Vote_Third%20edition_EN.pdf p. 158. The current average is over 80,000.
14 David Farr, "Reconstituting the Early Debates of the Parliament of Canada," *Canadian Parliamentary Review*, Spring 1992. http://www.revparl.ca/15/1/15n1_92e_Farr.pdf. The reports by *The Globe* and *The Mail* were of such quality that they were clipped and saved by staff at the Library of Parliament. They remain the primary source for historians on Parliament's early years.
15 Thomas Poguntke (ed.), Paul Webb (ed.), *The Presidentialization of Politics: A Comparative Study of Modern Democracies*, Oxford University Press, 2005. https://academic.oup.com/book/12672/chapter-abstract/162669662
16 International Parliamentary Union, IPU Parline, *Number of days the parliament/chamber met in plenary, per year*, https://data.ipu.org/compare/?field=num_days_parl_plen&region=0&structure=any__lower_chamber&chart=bar&year_to=2025#
17 *House of Commons Procedure and Practice*, Third Edition (2017), "Parliaments Since 1867 and Number of Sitting Days." https://www.ourcommons.ca/procedure/procedure-and-practice-3/App11-e.html
18 Parliament of Australia. https://www.aph.gov.au/About_Parliament/House_of_Representatives/Powers_practice_and_procedure/Practice7/HTML/Chapter3/The_election_process. The "return of the writs" marks the official confirmation of the election result, usually two or three weeks after the election.
19 Thirty-six days, on average in Canada, versus eight days in the UK. Dave Snow, "Will Justin Trudeau prorogue Parliament in the new year? History shows there's little political cost to the practice," *The Hub*, December 2, 2024. https://thehub.ca/2024/12/02/dave-snow-will-justin-trudeau-prorogue-parliament-in-the-new-year-history-shows-theres-little-political-cost-to-the-practice/
20 Liberal Party of Canada, *A New Plan For a Strong Middle Class*, 2015. https://liberal.ca/wp-content/uploads/sites/292/2020/09/New-plan-for-a-strong-middle-class.pdf
21 Wikipedia, *List of Government Defeats in the House of Commons (UK) Since 1945*. https://en.wikipedia.org/wiki/List_of_government_defeats_in_the_House_of_Commons_since_1945
22 Paul Martin's government alone was defeated on no fewer than forty votes: Andrew Heard, "Just What is a Vote of Confidence: The Strange Case of May 10, 2005," *Canadian Journal of Political Science*, June 2007, p. 396 https://www.cambridge.org/core/journals/canadian-journal-of-political-science-revue-canadienne-de-science-

Notes

politique/article/abs/just-what-is-a-vote-of-confidence-the-curious-case-of-may-10-2005/3BF43F0879FD9BF3D82FA37739AF0CC1

23 Library of Parliament: Parlinfo, *Votes in the House of Commons which led to a call for a Federal Election*. https://lop.parl.ca/sites/ParlInfo/default/en_CA/Parliament/defeatsElection.

Donald Desserud, *The Confidence Convention under the Canadian Parliamentary System*, Canadian Study of Parliament Group. https://cspg-gcep.ca/pdf/Parliamentary_Perspectives_7_2006-e.pdf

24 Canadian Press, "Liberal Government Tottering," *Sherbrooke Daily Record*, February 20, 1968. https://numerique.banq.qc.ca/patrimoine/details/52327/2997336

25 Heard, pp. 408-413.

26 Nicholas A. MacDonald and James W.J. Bowden, "No Discretion: On Prorogation and the Governor General," *Canadian Parliamentary Review*, Spring 2011. http://www.revparl.ca/english/issue.asp?param=203&art=1417

27 Fraser Harland, "Constitutional Convention and Cabinet Manuals," *Canadian Parliamentary Review*, Winter 2011 http://www.revparl.ca/34/4/34n4_11e_Harland.pdf.

28 Janyce McGregor, "John Baird's Decade in Federal Politics: 13 Quotes to Remember," CBC News, February 3, 2015. https://www.cbc.ca/news/politics/john-baird-s-decade-in-federal-politics-13-quotes-to-remember-1.2943299

29 Andrew Blick, Peter Hennessy, *Good Chaps No More? Safeguarding the Constitution in Stressful Times*, The Constitution Society, London, 2019.

30 *House of Commons Procedure and Practice*, Third Edition (2017), The Curtailment of Debate. https://www.ourcommons.ca/procedure/procedure-and-practice-3/ch_14_2-e.html

31 Yves Y. Pelletier, "Governing by Time Allocation; The Increasing Use of Time Allocation in the House of Commons, 1971 to 2021," *Canadian Parliamentary Review*, Winter 2021, p. 4. https://www.canlii.org/en/commentary/doc/2021CanLIIDocs13569

32 Ibid., p. 5. "The Commons will no longer represent a forum for public debate but will flounder and disintegrate as an anachronistic tower of Babel, scorned by the Canadian people."

33 UK House of Commons Information Office, *Programming of Government Bills*, 2010. https://www.parliament.uk/globalassets/documents/commons-information-office/p10.pdf

34 Parliament of Australia, *Consideration of legislation by the House* https://www.aph.gov.au/About_Parliament/House_of_Representatives/Powers_practice_and_procedure/Practice7/HTML/Appendices/Appendix17

35 Phil Smith, "Parliament: Why so much urgency?", RNZ, https://www.rnz.co.nz/national/programmes/the-house/audio/2018928155/parliament-why-so-much-urgency

36 Alan Finlayson, "What is the Point of Parliamentary Debate: Deliberation, Oratory, Opposition and Spectacle in the British House of Commons," *Redescriptions: Political Thought, Conceptual History and Feminist Theory* April 2017. https://journal-redescriptions.org/articles/10.7227/R.20.1.2

37 Statutes of Canada 2012, *Bill C-38*. https://www.parl.ca/Content/Bills/411/Government/C-38/C-38_4/C-38_4.PDF
38 Statutes of Canada 2013, *Bill C-4*. https://www.parl.ca/Content/Bills/412/Government/C-4/C-4_4/C-4_4.PDF
39 Adam Dodek, "Omnibus Bills: Constitutional Constraints and Legislative Liberations," *Ottawa Law Review* 48:1, 2017, p. 19. https://commentary.canlii.org/w/canlii/2017CanLIIDocs131.pdf. "There were 12 budget bills tabled between 1994 and 2005, averaging 73.6 pages. Between 2006 and 2011, 11 budget bills were tabled, averaging 308.9 pages."
40 Statutes of Canada 2016, *Bill C-15*. https://www.parl.ca/Content/Bills/421/Government/C-15/C-15_4/C-15_4.PDF
41 Statutes of Canada 2018, *Bill C-86*. https://www.parl.ca/Content/Bills/421/Government/C-86/C-86_4/C-86_4.PDF
42 Statutes of Canada 2018, *Bill C-74*. https://www.parl.ca/Content/Bills/421/Government/C-74/C-74_4/C-74_4.PDF
43 Statutes of Canada 2019, *Bill C-19*. https://www.parl.ca/Content/Bills/441/Government/C-19/C-19_4/C-19_4.PDF
44 House of Commons of Canada 2023, *Bill C-47*. https://www.parl.ca/Content/Bills/441/Government/C-47/C-47_1/C-47_1.PDF
45 House of Commons of Canada 2024, *Bill C-69*. https://www.parl.ca/Content/Bills/441/Government/C-69/C-69_1/C-69_1.PDF
46 *Criminal Law Amendment Act, 1968-69*. https://anti-69.ca/wp-content/uploads/2019/02/1969-Omnibus-Bill.pdf
47 Statutes of Canada 1994, *Bill C-17* https://www.parl.ca/Content/Bills/351/Government/c-17/c-17_4/c-17_4.pdf
48 Dodek, p.18.
49 Liberal Party of Canada, *A New Plan For a Strong Middle Class*, 2015. https://liberal.ca/wp-content/uploads/sites/292/2020/09/New-plan-for-a-strong-middle-class.pdf
50 Dodek, p. 9.
51 Selected Decisions of Speaker Peter Milliken, 2001-2011. https://www.ourcommons.ca/procedure/speakers-decisions/peter-milliken/ch01/decision19-e.html
52 Yan Campagnolo, "Cabinet Immunity in Canada: The Legal Black Hole," *McGill Law Journal*, December 2017. https://lawjournal.mcgill.ca/article/cabinet-immunity-in-canada-the-legal-black-hole
53 Canadian Press, "Parliamentary committees are 'weak,' 'waste of time': Parliamentarians from both sides find committees too partisan and ineffective. Can they be fixed?", May 7, 2012. https://www.cbc.ca/news/politics/parliamentary-committees-are-weak-waste-of-time-1.1276540
54 Public Policy Forum, *Time for a Reboot: Nine Ways to Restore Trust in Canada's Public Institutions*, October 2015, p. 12. https://ppforum.ca/wp-content/uploads/2018/03/PPF_TimeForAReboot_ENG_v6.pdf
55 Ian Campbell, "It's difficult to 'follow the money': former MPs, bureaucrats, and PBOs

Notes

say budget and estimates process makes it tough for Parliament to hold government spending to account," *Hill Times,* March 14, 2024. https://www.hilltimes.com/story/2024/03/14/its-difficult-to-follow-the-money-former-mps-bureaucrats-and-pbos-say-budget-and-estimates-process-makes-it-tough-for-parliament-to-hold-government-spending-to-account/414949/

Neil Moss, "'The system is broken': $30.7-billion in spending estimates not reviewed by House committees," *Hill Times,* June 14, 2023. https://www.hilltimes.com/story/2023/06/14/the-system-is-broken-30-7-billion-in-spending-estimates-not-reviewed-by-house-committees/390115/

56 Peter Aucoin, Mark D. Jarvis & Lori Turnbull, *Democratizing the Constitution: Reforming Responsible Government* (Toronto, Emond Montgomery Publications, 2011).

57 Library of Parliament, *Omnibus Bills: Frequently Asked Questions.* https://lop.parl.ca/sites/PublicWebsite/default/en_CA/ResearchPublications/201279E#ftn1

58 Paul Seaward, "Applause," The History of Parliament, January 15, 2017. https://historyofparliamentblog.wordpress.com/2017/01/15/applause/

59 Gloria Galloway, "Is Canada's party discipline the strictest in the world? Experts say yes," *The Globe and Mail,* February 7, 2013. https://www.theglobeandmail.com/news/politics/is-canadas-party-discipline-the-strictest-in-the-world-experts-say-yes/article8313261/

60 Alex Marland, *Whipped: Party Discipline in Canada* (Vancouver, UBC Press, 2020), p. 4.

61 Samara Centre, "House Inspection: A Retrospective of the 42nd Parliament," January 21, 2020. https://www.samaracentre.ca/articles/house-inspection

62 "Rebel MPs–2019-2024, Westminster Parliament," The Public Whip, 2022. https://www.publicwhip.org.uk/mps.php?parliament=2019&sort=rebellions

63 Molly E. Reynolds and Naomi Maehr, "Vital Statistics on Congress," Brookings Institution, November 2024

64 Lucinda Flavelle and Philip Kaye, "Party Discipline and Legislative Voting," *Canadian Parliamentary Review,* Summer 1986. http://www.revparl.ca/9/2/09n2_86e_Flavelle.pdf

65 Jean-François Godbout, *Lost on Division: Party Unity in the Canadian Parliament* (Toronto, University of Toronto Press, 2020).

66 Conservative Party of Canada, *Stand Up For Canada,* 2006. https://www.poltext.org/sites/poltext.org/files/plateformesV2/Canada/CAN_PL_2006_PC_en.pdf

67 Library of Parliament, *Party Discipline and Free Votes,* https://publications.gc.ca/collections/collection_2019/bdp-lop/eb/YM32-5-2018-26-eng.pdf

68 Brian Platt, "Tuesday Night Massacre: Trudeau ejects Jody Wilson-Raybould, Jane Philpott from Liberal caucus," *National Post,* https://nationalpost.com/news/politics/jody-wilson-raybould-says-shes-been-kicked-out-of-the-liberal-caucus

69 Christian Noel, "Poilievre's office maintains tight control over what Conservative MPs say and do: Party staffers monitor caucus for signs of message indiscipline and

fraternization with other MPs," CBC News, November 20, 2024. https://www.cbc.ca/news/politics/poilievre-iron-fist-caucus-discipline-1.7387552

70 Marland, p. 3.
71 Parliament of Australia. https://www.aph.gov.au/About_Parliament/House_of_Representatives/Powers_practice_and_procedure/Practice7/HTML/Chapter15/Question_Time
72 Nick Thompson, "By the Numbers: Question Period," *Public Policy and Governance Review*, February 16, 2020. https://ppgreview.ca/2020/02/16/by-the-numbers-question-period/
 House of Commons Procedure and Practice, 2000 edition, Questions, Note 41. https://www.ourcommons.ca/marleaumontpetit/DocumentViewer.aspx?DocId=1001&Sec=Ch11&Seq=4&Language=E#fn41
73 *House of Commons Procedure and Practice*, Third Edition (2017), The Physical and Administrative Setting. https://www.ourcommons.ca/procedure/procedure-and-practice-3/ch_06_3-e.html
 UK House of Commons Press Office, correspondence with author, December 11, 2024.
74 James Lancaster, "The Nemon Statue and Marble Arch," *Finest Hour* 134, Spring 2007. https://winstonchurchill.org/publications/finest-hour/finest-hour-134/the-nemon-statue-and-churchill-arch/
75 UK Parliament, *Churchill and the Commons Chamber*, https://www.parliament.uk/about/living-heritage/building/palace/architecture/palacestructure/churchill/
76 Library of Parliament, *Television and the House of Commons*, 1990. https://publications.gc.ca/Collection-R/LoPBdP/BP/bp242-e.htm
77 *House of Commons Procedure and Practice*, Third Edition (2017), Private Member's Business https://www.ourcommons.ca/procedure/procedure-and-practice-3/ch_21_1-e.html
78 Library of Parliament, Parlinfo, *Private Members' Public Bills Passed by Parliament*. https://lop.parl.ca/sites/ParlInfo/default/en_CA/legislation/privateMembersBills?permalink=216
79 Allison Loat, Michael MacMillan, "Welcome to Parliament: A Job With No Description," Samara Exit Interviews: Volume 1, 2010. https://issuu.com/samaracanada/docs/welcometoparliament_eng
80 Allison Loat, Michael MacMillan, *Tragedy in the Commons: Former Members of Parliament Speak Out about Canada's Failing Democracy* (Toronto, Samara Centre, 2014), pp. 86-97.
81 Ibid., pp. 109-111.
82 James W. J. Bowden, "Party Discipline & the King Doctrine," *The Dorchester Review*, May 26, 2023. https://www.dorchesterreview.ca/blogs/news/party-discipline-the-king-doctrine
83 Michael Chong, "The increasing disconnect between Canadians and their Parliament," *Policy Options*, September 1, 2010. https://policyoptions.irpp.org/magazines/

Notes

making-parliament-work/the-increasing-disconnect-between-canadians-and-their-parliament/

84 Parliament of Australia. https://www.aph.gov.au/About_Parliament/Parliamentary_departments/Parliamentary_Library/Research/Quick_Guides/2022-23/PartyChangesChallenges.

85 Eoin O'Malley, "The Power of Prime Ministers: Results of an Expert Survey," *International Political Science Review* (2007), Vol 28, No. 1, 7–27. (A survey of 250 experts in 22 countries, covering prime ministers from 1980-2000.) https://www.researchgate.net/profile/Eoin-Omalley-3/publication/242075899_The_Power_of_Prime_Ministers_Results_of_an_Expert_Survey/links/02e7e52cd35e21f8a7000000/The-Power-of-Prime-Ministers-Results-of-an-Expert-Survey.pdf

86 Jeffrey Simpson, *The Friendly Dictatorship* (Toronto, McClelland & Stewart, 2001), p. xi.

87 Donald Savoie, *Governing from the Centre: The Concentration of Power in Canadian Politics* (Toronto, University of Toronto Press, 1999), pp. 72, 87.

88 UK Civil Service Commission. https://civilservicecommission.independent.gov.uk/

89 Judiciaries Worldwide. https://judiciariesworldwide.fjc.gov/country-profile/japan

90 These are: the Independent Advisory Board for Senate Appointments (https://www.canada.ca/en/campaign/independent-advisory-board-for-senate-appointments.html) and the Independent Advisory Board for Supreme Court of Canada Judicial Appointments (https://www.fja-cmf.gc.ca/scc-csc/2022/report-rapport-eng.html).

91 Walter Bagehot, *The English Constitution*, Second Edition (London, 1873), p. 50.

92 The figures that follow are drawn from national government websites. To avoid cluttering the page with footnotes, however, let me draw readers' attention to the remarkable WhoGov Dataset, a project of the Nuffield Politics Research Centre at the University of Oxford, which collects data on cabinets around the world. https://politicscentre.nuffield.ox.ac.uk/whogov-dataset/

93 *Most cabinet ministers appointed by a government*, Guinness World Records. https://www.guinnessworldrecords.com/world-records/most-cabinet-ministers-appointed-by-a-government

94 Library of Parliament, Parlinfo, *Size of Ministries*. https://lop.parl.ca/sites/ParlInfo/default/en_CA/People/Cabinet

95 Prime Minister of Canada, *Cabinet*. https://www.pm.gc.ca/en/cabinet

96 A contrarian view is found in *At the Centre of Government: The Prime Minister and the Limits on Political Power* (Montreal, McGill-Queen's University Press, 2018), by Harper's former chief of staff, Ian Brodie, who believes prime ministers are neither so powerful, nor backbenchers so weak, as most analysis would suggest. See also Graham White, *Cabinets and First Ministers* (Vancouver, UBC Press, 2005), and Patrice Dutil, *Prime Ministerial Power in Canada: Its Origins under Macdonald, Laurier, and Borden* (Vancouver, UBC Press, 2017).

97 Library of Parliament, Parlinfo, *Departments and Roles: 1867–Today*. https://lop.parl.ca/sites/ParlInfo/default/en_CA/Federal/areasResponsibility

98 David Coletto, "Do You Know Who This Is? The Implications of Recognizability in Canadian Politics," Abacus Data, July 15. 2024. https://abacusdata.ca/recognize-political-leaders-canada-abacus-data-poll/
99 Library of Parliament, Parlinfo, *Departments and Roles: 1867 - Today*.
100 *Yes, Minister,* episode list. https://www.imdb.com/title/tt0080306/episodes/
101 Savoie, p. 63.
102 Savoie, p. 260.
103 Prime Minister of Canada, *Cabinet Committees Mandate and Membership.* https://www.pm.gc.ca/en/cabinet-committee-mandate-and-membership
104 Paul Wells, "The Climate Committee Double-Double," *Maclean's,* December 6, 2021. https://macleans.ca/politics/ottawa/the-climate-committee-double-double/
105 David Johnson, "White Paper: Chrétien Command Mode," *Thinking Government: Public Administration and Politics in Canada.* https://www.thinkinggovernment.com/reports/4-chretien-command-mode.html
106 Institute for Government, *Cabinet Committees,* August 4, 2017. https://www.instituteforgovernment.org.uk/explainer/cabinet-committees
107 Savoie, p. 75.
108 Chris Hall, "Justin Trudeau begins his bold experiment in 'government by cabinet,'" CBC News, November 5, 2015. https://www.cbc.ca/news/politics/government-cabinet-chris-hall-1.3304812
109 Library of Parliament, Parlinfo, *Departments and Roles: 1867–Today.* https://lop.parl.ca/sites/ParlInfo/default/en_CA/Federal/areasResponsibility
110 Institute for Government, *Supporting Heads of Government: A comparison across six countries,* 2011. https://www.instituteforgovernment.org.uk/publication/report/supporting-heads-government
111 Public Policy Forum, *Time For A Reboot,* p. 15.
112 Abbas Rana, "PMO completes hiring of chiefs of staff to 26 cabinet ministers, 10 ministers still waiting to recruit their top aides," *Hill Times,* December 9, 2019.
113 Rowena Mason, Heather Stewart Peter Walker, "Sajid Javid resigns as chancellor in Boris Johnson reshuffle," *The Guardian,* February 13, 2020. https://www.theguardian.com/politics/2020/feb/13/sajid-javid-resigns-as-chancellor-amid-boris-johnson-reshuffle
114 Created in 2000. Its function is limited to nominating members to sit as crossbenchers, and vetting proposed appointments for any impropriety. The prime minister is not bound to follow its advice. https://www.mishcon.com/news/the-house-of-lords-appointments-process, https://lordsappointments.independent.gov.uk/vetting
115 UK House of Lords Library, *House of Lords data dashboard: Peerage creations,* December 23, 2024. https://lordslibrary.parliament.uk/house-of-lords-data-dashboard-peerage-creations/
116 Wikipedia, *List of Senate of Canada Appointments by Prime Minister.* https://en.wikipedia.org/wiki/List_of_Senate_of_Canada_appointments_by_prime_minister

Notes

117 Ten of Stephen Harper's fifty-nine appointees were defeated Conservative election candidates. https://www.ndp.ca/news/reality-check-stephen-harpers-patronage-appointments-failed-candidate-edition

118 Jason Robert VandenBeukel, Christopher Cochrane, Jean-Francois Godbout, "Birds of a Feather? Loyalty and Partisanship in the Reformed Canadian Senate," *Canadian Journal of Political Science*, December, 2021, p. 832. https://www.cambridge.org/core/services/aop-cambridge-core/content/view/9A69455D2090C8750DF6D1D6BE5261E2/S0008423921000548a.pdf/birds-of-a-feather-loyalty-and-partisanship-in-the-reformed-canadian-senate.pdf.

119 Joel I. Colón-Ríos and Allan C. Hutchinson, "Constitutionalizing the Senate: a Modest Proposal," *McGill Law Journal*, June 2015. https://lawjournal.mcgill.ca/article/constitutionalizing-the-senate-a-modest-democratic-proposal/

120 Library of Parliament, Parlinfo, *Bills Sent to Other House that Did not Receive Royal Assent*. https://lop.parl.ca/sites/ParlInfo/default/en_CA/legislation/otherNoRoyalAssent

121 VandenBeukel, Cochrane, Godbout, p. 844.

122 John Ivison. "Liberals altering upcoming budget to pass through empowered Senate," *National Post*, January 16, 2017.

123 CBC News, "Justin Trudeau statement: 'Senate is broken, and needs to be fixed,'" January 29, 2014. https://www.cbc.ca/news/politics/justin-trudeau-statement-senate-is-broken-and-needs-to-be-fixed-1.2515374

124 Jason Robert VandenBeukel, *Revolution in the Red Chamber? The Senate of Canada in the 21st Century*, PhD thesis (Toronto, University of Toronto, 2022), p. 100. https://utoronto.scholaris.ca/server/api/core/bitstreams/c3e2650b-b0ed-42e2-a8b2-7c7382c48c9f/content

125 Ibid., p.119. Trudeau-appointed senators were the most likely group to vote with each other, and with the government.

126 Daniel Leblanc, "Trudeau to fill Senate vacancies before retiring: source," CBC News, January 27, 2025. https://www.cbc.ca/news/politics/trudeau-senate-appointments-1.7440716

127 Senate of Canada, *Current Senators*. https://sencanada.ca/en/senators/#panel-listview

128 Library of Parliament, Parlinfo, *Senators Appointed on the advice of the Prime Minister*. https://lop.parl.ca/sites/ParlInfo/default/en_CA/People/senatorsPrimeMinisters

129 Emmett MacFarlane, "Beware of Predictions of Senate-created constitutional crisis," *Declarations of Validity*, May 14, 2024. https://emmettmacfarlane.substack.com/p/beware-predictions-of-a-senate-created

130 Howard Anglin and Ray Pennings, "Canada is careening towards a constitutional crisis in the Senate," *The Hub*, May14, 2024. https://thehub.ca/2024/05/14/howard-anglin-and-ray-pennings-canada-is-careening-towards-a-constitutional-crisis/

131 Section 121, Constitution Act 1867, https://laws-lois.justice.gc.ca/eng/const/page-4.html#docCont

132 Michael Kirby and Hugh Segal, *A House Undivided: Making Senate Independence Work*, Public Policy Forum, September 22, 2016. https://ppforum.ca/publications/a-house-undivided-making-senate-independence-work/
133 Andrew Heard, "Let the Senate reform itself," *National Post*, March 16, 2015.
134 Encoded in the *Colonial Laws Validity Act*, 1865. https://albertalawreview.com/index.php/ALR/article/download/2452/2439/2564
135 PrimaryDocuments.ca, *Report: The Notwithstanding Clause, Section 33 of the Constitution Act, 1982*. https://primarydocuments.ca/report-the-notwithstanding-clausesection-33-of-the-constitution-act-1982/
136 *European Convention on Human Rights*. https://www.echr.coe.int/documents/d/echr/convention_eng
137 Israel's Basic Laws have an override clause, but only with regard to freedom of occupation. https://en.wikipedia.org/wiki/Basic_Law:_Freedom_of_Occupation
138 Sujit Choudhry and Claire E. Hunter, "Measuring Judicial Activism on the Supreme Court of Canada: A Comment on Newfoundland (Treasury Board) v. NAPE," *McGill Law Journal*, 2003. https://lawjournal.mcgill.ca/wp-content/uploads/pdf/1267072-Choudhry___Hunter.pdf
139 Library of Parliament, *The Notwithstanding Clause of the Charter*, 2008, pp. 4-6. https://lop.parl.ca/staticfiles/PublicWebsite/Home/ResearchPublications/HillStudies/PDF/2018-17-E.pdf. The contemporaneous quotations, from the participants and from expert commentators, are quite striking on this point: it would be used only "in the unlikely event of a decision of the courts that is clearly contrary to the public interest" (Roy McMurtry); "a safety valve to correct absurd situations . . . unlikely ever to be used except in non-controversial circumstances" (Jean Chrétien); "will rarely be used" (Gérard La Forest); "the exercise of the power would normally attract such political opposition that it would rarely be invoked" (Peter Hogg).
140 Or so we are told: https://nationalpost.com/opinion/stephane-serafin-legal-activists-put-the-notwithstanding-clause-at-risk. I'm old enough to remember similarly dire prophesies in the event the Supreme Court were to rule that Quebec did not have a constitutional right to secede unilaterally from the federation. The Court so ruled, the separatist government turned purple with rage, and that was about it.
141 Under sections 56 and 90 of the 1867 Constitution, the federal Cabinet may "disallow" (annul) any provincial law within one year of its passing. https://laws-lois.justice.gc.ca/eng/const/FullText.html. Since 1867 one hundred twelve provincial laws have been disallowed.
142 Janet Ajzenstat, *The Canadian Founding: John Locke and Parliament* (Montreal, McGill-Queen's University Press, 2007).
143 Claude Bélanger, "The Constitution Act, 1867, the Confederation Debates and Provincial Autonomy," *Quebec History*, February 26, 2001. "The main reason for its inclusion in the Constitution Act, if we are to trust the opinion of most of the Fathers

Notes

of Confederation, was to protect minority rights . . . not to subjugate the provinces." http://faculty.marianopolis.edu/c.belanger/quebechistory/federal/autonomy.htm

144 Robert C. Vipond, "Alternative Pasts: Legal Liberalism and the Demise of the Disallowance Power," *University of New Brunswick Law Journal*, Vol. 39 (1990), p. 128. https://journals.lib.unb.ca/index.php/unblj/article/view/29775/1882524956

145 Russell Green, "Can the Federal Government Disallow Québec's 'Anti-Religious Symbols' Act?", Centre for Constitutional Studies, June 27, 2019. https://www.constitutionalstudies.ca/2019/06/can-the-federal-government-disallow-quebecs-anti-religious-symbols-act/

146 Amir Attaran and Gib van Ert, "The Notwithstanding Act: a proposal for reform," *Hill Times*, November 30, 2022. https://www.hilltimes.com/story/2022/11/30/the-notwithstanding-act-a-proposal-for-reform/357289/

147 John Dixon, *The Keegstra case: Freedom of speech and the prosecution of harmful ideas*, British Columbia Civil Liberties Association: Position Papers, March 20, 1986. https://bccla.org/resource/the-keegstra-case-freedom-of-speech-and-the-prosecution-of-harmful-ideas

148 Jill Lepore, "The Lie Factory", *The New Yorker*, Sept. 24, 2012. https://www.newyorker.com/magazine/2012/09/24/the-lie-factory

149 Quintus Tullius Cicero (Author), Philip Freeman (Translator), *How to Win an Election: An Ancient Guide for Modern Politicians*, Princeton University Press, 2012.

150 Elizabeth Judge, Michael Pal, "Voter Privacy and Big-Data Elections," *Osgoode Hall Law Journal*, Winter 2021. https://digitalcommons.osgoode.yorku.ca/cgi/viewcontent.cgi?article=3631&context=ohlj

151 Lori Turnbull, "Deception in Politics: An Ethical Offence," presented to the Canadian Political Science Association annual meeting, June, 2008. https://cpsa-acsp.ca/papers-2008/Turnbull.pdf. The diagnosis is correct, even if I disagree with her prescription.

152 Duff Conacher, "Honest is the best policy—and it should be required by law," *The Globe and Mail*, June 5, 2019. https://www.theglobeandmail.com/opinion/article-in-politics-honesty-is-the-best-policy-and-should-be-required-by/

153 Canadian Press, "Elections Canada announces campaign spending cap of about $30M for three big parties," September 3, 2021. https://globalnews.ca/news/8166917/elections-canada-campaign-spending-cap/

154 Elections Canada, *Understanding spending limits*. https://www.elections.ca/content.aspx?section=fin&dir=lim&document=index&lang=e

155 Catherine Lévesque, "Sabrina Maddeaux suspends Conservative nomination campaign alleging misconduct," *National Post*, May 9, 2024. https://nationalpost.com/news/politics/sabrina-maddeaux-suspends-conservative-nomination-campaign-alleging-misconduct

156 *Party Favours: How Federal Election Candidates are Chosen*, Samara Centre, July 17, 2019. https://www.samaracentre.ca/articles/party-favours

See also: Adelina Petit-Vouriot, "Modernizing election should start with party nomination processes," *Policy Options*, September 21, 2021. https://policyoptions.irpp.org/magazines/septembe-2021/modernizing-elections-should-start-with-party-nomination-processes/

157 Allison Loat, Michael MacMillan, *Tragedy in the Commons*, p. 43-45.
158 William Cross and Lisa Young, "Are Canadian Political Parties Empty Vessels? Membership, Engagement and Policy Capacity," *IRPP Choices*, 2006.
159 Matthew Mendelsohn, *Some Are More Equal Than Others*, Mowat Centre for Policy Innovation, March, 2010. https://utoronto.scholaris.ca/items/334a0db3-40ca-41ca-b252-418090287590
160 Government of Canada, *Fair Representation Act moves every province towards rep by pop*, 2011. https://www.canada.ca/en/news/archive/2011/10/fair-representation-act-moves-every-province-towards-rep-pop.html
161 Justice Laws, *Fair Representation Act, 2011*. https://laws-lois.justice.gc.ca/eng/annualstatutes/2011_26/page-1.html
162 *Canadian Election Results by Party, 1867 to 2021*. www.sfu.ca/~aheard/elections/1867-present.html
163 OECD Members and Partners https://www.oecd.org/about/document/ratification-oecd-convention.htm
164 After its inventor, the Irish political scientist Michael Gallagher, of Trinity College Dublin. https://www.tcd.ie/research/profiles/?profile=mgllgher
165 The chart shows figures for the forty-six countries that appear in the upper range of both the Economist Democracy Index and the UN Human Development Index.
166 Election-Modelling.ca, Overview of ERRE Constrained Simulations, 2016. http://election-modelling.ca/2021_static/overview/erre.html
167 Wikipedia, *Duverger's Law*. https://en.wikipedia.org/wiki/Duverger%27s_law
168 Byron Becker, *Modeling Elections: Submission to ERRE: Special Committee on Electoral Reform*, www.ourcommons.ca/Content/Committee/421/ERRE/Brief/BR8454480/br-external/BeckerByronWeber-e.pdf
169 Bill Tieleman, "Proportional Representation Empowers the Extreme and the Bizarre," *The Tyee*, August 16, 2016. https://thetyee.ca/Opinion/2016/08/16/Proportional-Representation-in-Canada/
170 Lorne Gunter, "Proportional representation breaks the community bond," *Toronto Sun*, July 29, 2016. https://torontosun.com/2016/07/29/proportional-representation-breaks-the-community-bond
171 Fair Vote Canada, *A Look at the Evidence*. https://www.fairvote.ca/a-look-at-the-evidence/
172 John M. Carey, Simon Hix, "The Electoral Sweet Spot: Low-Magnitude Proportional Electoral Systems," *American Journal of Political Science*, February 1, 2011. https://onlinelibrary.wiley.com/doi/10.1111/j.1540-5907.2010.00495.x
173 VisualCapitalist.com, *Mapped: The World's Oldest Democracies*, July 26, 2019. https://www.visualcapitalist.com/mapped-the-worlds-oldest-democracies/

Notes

174 Fair Vote Canada, *A Look at the Evidence*.
175 Wikipedia, *List of British Columbia general elections*. https://en.wikipedia.org/wiki/List_of_British_Columbia_general_elections
176 Wikipedia, *2018 New Brunswick general election*. https://en.wikipedia.org/wiki/2018_New_Brunswick_general_election
177 Kristy Kirkup, "Trudeau defends electoral reform decision, citing fear of political discord," *The Globe and Mail*, February 10, 2017. https://www.theglobeandmail.com/news/politics/trudeau-cites-leitch-electoral-reform/article33978880/
178 Elections Canada, *Official* Reports, https://www.elections.ca/content.aspx?section=res&dir=rep/off&document=index&lang=e#44GE.
179 Liberal Party of Canada, *A New Plan For a Strong Middle Class*.
180 Elections Canada, *Voter Turnout at Federal Elections and Referendums*. https://www.elections.ca/content.aspx?section=ele&dir=turn&document=index&lang=e. Turnout figures are all expressed as a percentage of registered voters. As a share of the voting-age population, turnout is even lower.
181 Sean Marshall, "Election: Voter Turnout in 2022," Spacing.ca, March 7, 2023. https://spacing.ca/toronto/2023/03/07/election-voter-turnout-in-2022/
182 Institute for Democracy and Electoral Assistance (IDEA), *Voter Turnout Trends Around the World*, 2016. https://www.idea.int/sites/default/files/publications/voter-turnout-trends-around-the-world.pdf
183 IDEA, *Compulsory Voting*. https://www.idea.int/data-tools/data/voter-turnout-database/compulsory-voting
184 IDEA, *Voter Turnout Trends*. https://www.idea.int/sites/default/files/publications/voter-turnout-trends-around-the-world.pdf
185 Australian Electoral Commission. https://www.aec.gov.au/elections/federal_elections/voter-turnout.htm
186 Australian Electoral Commission. https://www.aec.gov.au/Elections/non-voters.htm
187 Law Commission of Canada, *Voting Counts: Electoral Reform for Canada*, 2004. https://publications.gc.ca/collections/Collection/J31-61-2004E.pdf

Acknowledgements

THIS BOOK BEGAN OVER lunch with my editor and publisher, longtime friend and former employer, Ken Whyte. It was he who suggested pulling together all the separate strands of dysfunction in Canada's government into one, unholy mess. Which if nothing else appealed to my collector's impulse.

So let me thank him, first of all, for the inspiration, second for taking a chance on a first-time author, third for his patience, and fourth for his judicious editing. Thanks, also, to all the good people at Sutherland House who helped shepherd it along, including copy editor Chandra Wohleber, editorial assistant Leah Ciani and graphics artist Imran Hossain.

Thanks as well to my editor at the *Globe and Mail* Opinion section, Natasha Hassan, and to David Walmsley, *redattore di tutti redattori* at the *Globe*, for giving me a regular platform (this book draws in part on material I've written over the years for the *Globe*, as well as *The National Post*, *Maclean's*, *The Walrus* and other publications) and for cutting me some slack as I laboured to finish this.

Finally, I want to thank my lovely partner, the journalist Shannon Gormley, not only for her unfailing support and encouragement, her wise counsel, and her own incisive edits, but for putting up with my obsession these many months. She fills every day with joy and laughter, makes everything she touches beautiful, stands up for me when even I wouldn't. I would not have written this book without her, that goes without saying: but I'd be a sadder and poorer man in every other way.

Index

A
Abbott, John, 18
Afghanistan, 29, 43, 99, 100
Alberta, 7, 135, 185–188, 195, 213, 243
Allan, Hugh, 73
Argentina, 74, 233
Aucoin, Peter, 47
Australia, 25, 27, 28, 35, 37, 41, 51, 56, 61, 72, 76, 80, 85, 103, 118, 183, 185, 191, 216, 217, 233, 234
Austria, 220, 221

B
Bagehot, Walter, 83
Belgium, 86, 216, 217, 220, 233
Bolivia, 233
Borden, Robert, 35, 94
Bourassa, Robert, 135
Bowell, Mackenzie, 18, 71
Brazil, 74
Britain, 22, 25, 27, 28, 35, 41, 59, 60, 72, 74, 76, 80, 82, 92, 96, 103, 111, 121, 126, 186
British Columbia, 34, 114, 147, 153, 156, 185–188, 195, 204, 211, 213, 221, 226, 227
Brown, George, 139, 186
Burundi, 86

C
Campbell, Gordon, 153
Campbell, Kim, 113
Cartier, George-Étienne, 94
Cartwright, Richard, 94
Chamberlain, Neville, 242
China, 43, 176, 177, 242
Chong, Michael, 48, 70
Chrétien, Jean, 28, 39, 42, 71, 73–74, 93, 94, 97–100, 115, 152, 258n139
Churchill, Winston, 3, 58, 59
Clark, Joe, 27, 51, 71, 221
Coke, Edward, 127
Cross, William, 181

D
De Montfort, Simon, 8
Denmark, 86, 216, 217, 219
Desmond, Norma, 95
Dexter, Darrell, 153
Diefenbaker, John, 71, 96, 125
Dion, Stéphane, 99
Dixon, John, 141
Dong, Han, 177, 182
Duffy, Mike, 42, 74, 113

E
Europe, 11, 192, 242

F

Fielding, William, 94
Finland, 86, 216, 219
Fortier, Michael, 152
Foster, George, 94
France, 37, 41, 74, 80, 81, 85, 86, 96, 183, 185, 191, 216, 217, 220
Fraser, Sean, 95
Freeland, Chrystia, 95, 99, 102, 239

G

Gallagher, Michael, 193–194, 213, 260n164
Galt, Alexander, 94
Garneau, Marc, 101
Germany, 25, 41, 81, 85, 86, 96, 103, 104, 192, 210, 214, 215, 217, 220, 221
Goldenberg, Eddie, 93
Gordon, Walter, 94
Graham, Shawn, 153
Gwyn, Richard, 24

H

Harder, Peter, 138
Harper, Stephen, 10, 28, 29, 31, 33, 36, 37, 39, 40, 42–44, 72, 74, 87, 93, 97, 99, 100, 103, 113–115, 120, 138, 152, 159, 167, 188, 221, 255n96, 257n117
Heard, Andrew, 121
Howe, C. D., 94

I

India, 81, 101, 176, 192
Ireland, 80, 82, 192, 211, 216
Italy, 41, 74, 80–82, 85, 96, 185, 216, 228

J

Japan, 25, 41, 72, 81, 82, 85, 96, 183, 214, 217, 219, 227
Jarvis, Mark D., 47
Javid, Sajid, 105
Johnson, Boris, 30, 98, 105
Johnston, David, 168
Joly, Mélanie, 95

K

King George V, 32
Kinsley, Michael, 174, 181
Kirby, Michael, 121

L

Labrador, 7, 184
Langevin, Hector-Louis, 94
Lapointe, Ernest, 94
Laurier, Wilfrid, 73, 94, 112
LeBlanc, Dominic, 95
Legault, François, 226
Lepore, Jill, 143
Loat, Alison, 62, 63
Lord Byng, 31
Lord Dufferin, 33
Luxembourg, 216, 233

M

Macdonald, John A., 21, 22, 33, 53, 73–75, 86, 94, 112, 139
MacEachen, Allan, 94
Mackenzie, Alexander, 33, 112
Mackenzie King, William Lyon, 18, 21, 31, 64, 73, 86, 112
MacMillan, Michael, 62, 63
Manitoba, 153, 188, 213
Marland, Alex, 52, 56
Martin, Paul, 10, 30, 94, 99
May, Theresa, 30

Index

McGuinty, Dalton, 154–156
McKenna, Frank, 99
Meighen, Arthur, 22, 31–33, 94
Montreal, 7, 21
Moore, Christopher, 6, 22
More, Thomas, 93
Morneau, Bill, 101
Mulcair, Thomas, 71
Mulock, William, 94
Mulroney, Brian, 37, 73, 86, 97, 99, 113, 152, 188

N
Netherlands, 2, 80, 216, 217, 220, 233
New Brunswick, 34, 99, 153, 187, 195, 204, 221
Newfoundland, 186, 188, 204
New Zealand, 27, 28, 37, 41, 47, 51, 72, 76, 80, 85, 103, 183, 185, 192, 210, 216, 219
Nicholson, Rob, 28
Nixon, Richard, 74
Northern Ireland, 82
Nova Scotia, 153, 187, 204, 221, 228

O
Ontario, 33, 135, 152, 185, 186, 188, 196, 200–202, 204, 210, 221, 227, 228, 244
O'Toole, Erin, 71, 72
Ottawa, 14, 21, 52, 63, 98

P
Pakistan, 74, 176
Payette, Julie, 82
Pearson, Lester, 30, 86, 93, 94
Peru, 74, 233
Pettigrew, Pierre, 99

Philpott, Jane, 55
Poilievre, Pierre, 72, 116, 247
Prince Edward Island, 185, 204, 210, 226

Q
Quebec, 7, 40, 42, 119, 124, 125, 134–135, 137–139, 152, 167, 171, 181, 186, 188, 195, 199–201, 204, 221, 225, 226, 242, 244, 258n140

R
Rae, Bob, 202
Rajapaksa, Mahinda, 86
Redford, Alison, 181
Rich, Richard, 93
Russell, Peter, 249n5
Rwanda, 86

S
St. Laurent, 21, 94, 96
Saskatchewan, 135, 188
Savoie, Donald, 77, 78, 93, 97
Scheer, Andrew, 181
Schmidt, Helmut, 99
Schreiber, Karlheinz, 73
Scotland, 82
Segal, Hugh, 121
Selinger, Greg, 153
Sharp, Mitchell, 94
Shawinigan, 42
Sifton, Clifford, 94
Simpson, Jeffrey, 75, 93
Singapore, 233
Smith, John, 150
Somalia, 42
South Africa, 74
South Korea, 74
Spain, 86

Sri Lanka, 86
Stanfield, Robert, 30
Starmer, Keir, 96
Stronach, Belinda, 31
Sweden, 103, 216, 220, 221
Switzerland, 86, 216

T
Tanzania, 85
Toronto, 7, 21, 177, 196, 228
Trudeau, Justin, 10, 12, 29, 36, 40, 55, 64, 71, 74, 82, 87, 93, 97, 99–101, 103, 114, 182, 226, 238, 247
Trudeau, Pierre, 35, 86, 93, 97, 99–100, 105, 115, 152
Trump, Donald, 88, 99, 155, 237, 238, 243
Tullius Cicero, Quintus, 143
Tupper, Charles, 18, 94
Turnbull, Lori, 47
Turner, John, 18, 94, 152

U
Ukraine, 74

United Kingdom, 20, 44, 81, 92, 184, 192, 216, 217, 240
United States, 1, 23, 74, 75, 79, 80, 85, 120, 163, 192, 217, 223, 237, 242, 243
Uruguay, 2, 233

V
Vancouver, 7

W
WE Charity organization, 29
Westminster, 6, 11, 25, 41, 58, 63, 64, 67, 72, 75, 76, 82
White, Thomas, 94
Wilson-Raybould, Jody, 40, 55, 101
Winters, Robert, 94
Wright, Nigel, 42

Y
Young, Lisa, 181

Z
Zolf, Larry, 115